D1398755

A Teachers' Guide to the Special Educational Needs of Blind and Visually Handicapped Children

Sally S. Mangold, Editor

**Published by
American Foundation for the Blind
11 Penn Plaza, Suite 300
New York, NY 10001**

1995 reprinting of an AFB classic

**Note: For additional information about the AFB
publications and other resources mentioned in this
book, readers may contact the American Foundation
for the Blind, 11 Penn Plaza, Suite 300, New York,
NY 10001, (212) 502-7600 or 1-800-502-7657.**

Design by Sandy Blough

Library of Congress Cataloging in Publication Data
Main entry under title:

A teachers' guide to the special educational needs of
    blind and visually handicapped children.

    Bibliography: p.
    1. Blind—Education—Curricula-Addresses, essays,
lectures.   2. Visually handicapped children—Education—
Curricula—Addresses, essays, lectures.   I. Mangold,
Sally S.   II. American Foundation for the Blind.
HV1638.T4   371.91'1   82-4025
ISBN 9-89128-108-8   AACR2

Contents

Preface

Questionnaires were sent to 349 experienced teachers of visually handicapped students during the spring of 1979. This was an attempt to determine the need for a teachers' guide which would address the unique curriculum essential to the education of visually handicapped students. A total of 271 questionnaires were returned; others were not returned because of inadequate addresses. The impressive percentage of returns was interpreted to mean that practicing teachers feel the need for a manuscript of this type. The responses of the teachers determined the priority areas for inclusion in this book.

Introduction

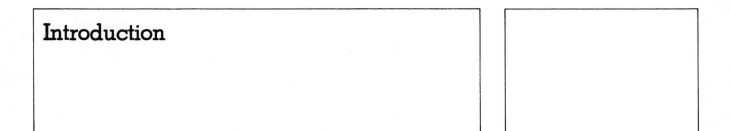

I am certain of nothing but the holiness of the heart's affections and the truth of imagination—what the imagination seizes as beauty must be truth whether it existed before or not.
Letter to Benjamin Bailey from John Keats
November 22, 1817

It is the wise and the persistent who regularly discard the complexities and the abstractions of life in order to occasionally capture the essence of life through direct experience. Only when coming face to face with nature, face to face with our fellow man, or face to face with a simple lump of clay, is man called upon to use his own thoughts, feelings, or actions in order to effect change. It is easy for adults to forget that growth is a series of struggles that go on within every individual. Growth implies change, and change can be frightening if it is not seen by the learner to be important and safe.

This book presents a multidisciplinary approach to the education of visually handicapped students. The wise teacher analyzes each student's abilities and disabilities, designs a curriculum which promotes optimum learning in each student, and respects the right of each student to develop according to his or her strengths, interests, and values.

The regular classroom can provide instruction in basic academic skills and, at the same time, can encourage social and emotional growth as handicapped and nonhandicapped students interact. There are, however, many special skills which must be taught outside the regular classroom. The curriculum presented in this book addresses those special needs.

Years ago, I began to collect curriculum and teaching techniques which seemed to foster positive growth in visually handicapped students. It became obvious that in order to achieve the full potential of every student there needed to be an ongoing program of instruction with appropriate materials and equipment in comfortable surroundings. The most important element in effective teaching was clearly a feeling of excitement in both teachers and students—the excitement of discovery, the excitement of success, and the excitement of fulfillment.

The contributors to this book are teachers who care deeply about teaching and regard it as a great human adventure. They recognize that what is "right" is an elusive something that each teacher must seek and find for each student.

Each chapter in this book will focus on a unique educational need of visually handicapped students. The ideas presented here are not intended to be a complete program of instruction. Many students will need less than is suggested, and others will need more.

S.S.M.

Teaching Reading via Braille

Sally S. Mangold, Ph.D.

CHAPTER 1

Sharon was eight years old. She was an outstanding student who had been total-ly blind since birth and was about to enter the hospital for her sixth corneal trans-plant. The previous five operations had been unsuccessful.

Ten minutes of the reading period had gone by when Sharon began to cry. The quiet whimpers soon were loud sobs and it was obvious that something was ter-ribly wrong.

"Are you worried about the operation, and that it might not work?" asked the teacher in a desperate attempt to console the child.

"No!" shouted the child, "I'm afraid it will work and I'll have to give up my braille!"

Sharon had a wonderful life from an eight-year-old point of view. Her family took a deep interest in her, and invited Sharon's friends to join them on picnics. She loved to read because the school she attended had all kinds of braille books with different textures pasted in them. Her teacher shared something new and in-teresting with the class every day. Sharon had even taught her younger sister the print alphabet by using a braille book that had the print above the braille.

Adults always assume that a student would have a better and happier life if that student were not handicapped. They forget that an individual can only do so many things at one time, and there are so many wonderful things to do that being sighted sometimes only makes the choice more difficult. Being sighted certainly requires much less organization, fewer support services, and fewer family ad-justments, but it does not imply a better quality of life.

A teacher telling a parent, "I am afraid that your child is going to have to read braille," has not learned what Sharon knew at age eight. Braille is a viable medi-um of instruction. It can provide enjoyment and a source of independence as great as that afforded by print. This only happens when the student is given the opportunity to master the medium thoroughly. Exposure to a vast quantity of brailled materials that are presented in a variety of formats is crucial to eventual high levels of reading performance.

The most effective teachers introduce braille symbols with a controlled vocab-ulary approach which utilizes methods of teaching reading. Presenting lists of braille contractions does not afford enough practice with individual contractions and short form words to promote pleasurable and fluent comprehension of braille symbols for most beginning readers. Therefore, the methods by which most teachers learned the braille code when they were adults are not appropriate for teaching visually handicapped students of school age. Grade two braille signs should be introduced as they occur in new reading vocabulary. Using signs in context will enhance learning more than trying to memorize isolated signs presented in a list. The repetition of word usage afforded by basal readers allows the student to practice one sign at a time in a variety of uses. This diminishes the probability of confusions of signs having similar configurations.

Dr. Mangold is Associate Professor in Special Education at San Francisco State University. Prior to this she was a resource teacher for visually handicapped students in a public school setting for 15 years.

First-grade students usually have already become very adept at understanding language by the time they enter school. The sounds they hear have become associated with real objects and events in their day-to-day experiences. Throughout our lives we continue to have more experience in listening than in reading.

It is imperative that students being taught to read via braille be equipped with an understanding of the spoken language. In order to bring meaning to reading, the students must be able to associate the abstract symbol on the page with the familiar sounds that they would have heard, had the words been spoken.

A thorough understanding of spoken language requires that adults in the students' environment provide numerous opportunities for them to examine real objects in their environment. Adjectives are the keys to unlocking understanding within the students. Compile lists of adjectives found in the beginning reader, and use them frequently to reinforce meanings. Categorized adjectives may be lots of fun, like these examples:

The way things feel: rough, smooth, hard, soft, bumpy, spongy.*
The size of things; small, little, tiny, big, fat, huge, gigantic, long, narrow, thick, thin, fat, wide.
The way things smell: sweet, sour, good, icky, awful, wonderful, terrible, delightful.
The categories of adjectives are endless. Students should be aware that adjectives sometimes fall into different categories, depending upon usage; for example,
The way things feel: hard.
The manner in which we work: hard.

Care should be taken not to misrepresent reality by using untrue and romantic adjectives. "The clouds are fluffy and soft like cotton." How fortunate visually handicapped students are in San Francisco. They can climb a hill and walk through a cloud. In doing so, they can discover that clouds are "air full of moisture, which make you feel cold and wet."

Teachers and parents should preview the books that will be used in the first grade in order to be certain that the visually handicapped student has experienced the events that characters in the books experience. Train rides in the zoo, a trip to a farm, opening an umbrella to keep dry, riding a bicycle are all actions typically described in books. Make a list of adjectives that will be used in the first books so that the parents can help in developing an appropriate vocabulary. Nothing helps more to build confidence in students and social interaction among them than the realization that they have had similar experiences to those around them. Sharing common experiences is a pleasant way to meet new friends.

There are a number of programs that present instructional alternatives for teaching braille reading. It is important to have options so that we may provide appropriate instruction to meet the needs of students with different learning styles and abilities. Some students may respond immediately to the introduction of experience stories, which represent real life experiences and bring concrete meanings to abstract symbols on the page. To create a simple example, glue down an uninflated balloon on the page (see Figure 1.1).

Other students may need to use the same abstract words over and over in different contexts—reading them on flash cards, labeling objects with them—before they can comprehend a relationship between the written word and the object or idea it represents.

*I once heard a teacher tell a blind student that the shell she was holding had an edge that was smooth and rough. Not having seen the shell myself, I could not imagine to what she was referring. The term "smooth and rough" was incomprehensible to me because these terms are mutually exclusive. After examining the shell and discussing adjectives with the teacher, it was decided that a more appropriate term might have been "smooth and bumpy."

Students being taught braille must have an understanding of the spoken language.

Teachers and parents should preview books to be certain that the visually handicapped student has experienced the events that characters in the book experience.

Figure 1.1

BALLOONS
I like balloons.
Balloons are fun.
Balloons go pop.

A number of approaches to the teaching of braille reading may be found in Caton and Bradley (1978/79), Harley et al. (1979), Mangold (1977), Mangold (1978), and Olson & Mangold (1978).

HELPFUL HINTS ABOUT TEACHING BRAILLE READING*
The majority of good braille readers use two hands. A skilled two-handed reader usually begins reading a line of braille by placing both hands at the beginning of a line. When the middle of a line is reached, the right hand continues across the line, while the left hand moves in the opposite direction and locates the beginning of the next line. After the entire first line has been read by the right hand, the left hand reads the first several words on the next line, while the right hand moves quickly back to meet the left hand.

Good two-handed readers need to acquire a light touch. If your student has a heavy touch, try the following: place a piece of paper on the table and ask the student to pass his or her hands over the paper so lightly as not to move the paper; place plastic discs or checkers on raised line graph paper and ask the student to pass his or her hands over the objects so lightly as not to move the objects across the lines on the graph paper. Create your own games that would encourage a light touch.

Encourage your students to touch the dots lightly ("tickle the dots"). Try to help him or her develop a smooth movement of the hands from left to right. Avoid having the student stop as his or her hands move across the page. Suggest that your student keep all fingers in contact with the paper. It should be remembered, however, that some braille readers have been known to use unorthodox hand positions efficiently. If your student displays dominant one-handed reading, it may take a long time to develop the coordination and motivation required for two-handed reading. Continue to instruct your student in the two-handed reading method, but respect his or her right to experiment with other methods when working independently.

It is important that the school furniture fit the student. The student's elbows should be on the same plane as, or perhaps a little higher than, the top of the desk or table being used. If the furniture cannot be adjusted, let the student sit on several books (not braille, of course).

Some beginning readers have little strength in their hands or arms. As a result, they may tire quickly. If this is a problem, you might try the following activities.

1. Have the student punch holes all the way around a heavy piece of construction paper using a single-hole punch. Then have the student lace from one hole to another all the way around the border, using medium-weight yarn. The resulting product may be used as a placemat during snack time, or folded in the middle and used as a cover for completed work.

*Adapted from Mangold (1977).

2. As a reinforcer for work completed satisfactorily, let the student use a nut-cracker to crack nuts, after which he or she may eat them. Start with peanuts first.

3. Cut strips of heavy construction paper (about ½" wide). Have the student cut across the strips with scissors to make small pieces of paper. The small pieces may be pasted down to decorate folders.

4. A box containing several dozen nuts and bolts of the same size may be given to the student to put together.

Clean, warm hands are important for rapid and correct braille reading. Be certain that your student washes his or her hands, rinses them thoroughly, and uses a little hand lotion before beginning to read. An old hair dryer is useful on cold days to warm hands before reading. Place the student's worksheets one at a time on top of a rubber pad. This prevents the paper from slipping around the desk and thereby promotes a light reading touch.

Many adults think of braille letters as reversible pairs, for example *w* and *r*. Never, never tell a child that there are reversible pairs of letters in braille. This requires that the student perform a double mental process when he or she applies knowledge of letters to academic assignments. Remember that one of your greatest strengths is your ability to reinforce correct reading techniques. Reinforcing incorrect techniques only shows the student what is "bad," but offers no example of the desired behavior and thereby provides no substitute for the "bad" techniques. Reinforcing correct techniques provides an example of the goal behavior and increases the probability that the desired behavior will recur more frequently. Good reading skills are only mastered after years of practice. Praise your student for correct hand positions when they occur. Remember that no program can effect maximum progress in a student without the support and enthusiasm of the teacher.

CONSUMABLE BRAILLE READING MATERIALS

The opportunity to read new vocabulary in a variety of contexts increases speed, accuracy, and comprehension. Sighted children in the primary grades are given many consumable workbooks and programmed reading materials. Publishers and leaders in the area of education for young children tell us that children seem to learn more easily when they work right on the pages and when they get immediate knowledge of results. Self-correcting programs in reading help strengthen weaknesses and allow for individual differences.

Changes in education for sighted children present new challenges to the educators of visually impaired children and the transcribers who provide basic texts. The special educators must thoroughly understand the concepts being presented in the print material and work with the transcriber in adapting the materials. Many of the basic texts adopted by state departments of education are available through state instructional materials centers for the visually handicapped. Volunteers and paid school transcribers help provide the remainder of the needed materials. State instructional materials centers report that more and more consumable workbooks are requested every year.

We cannot expect the braille user to keep up with sighted peers in the upper grades if he or she has not had the years of practice reading and writing experienced by sighted students. By the time the first-grade student has completed a consumable braille reading book series, he or she has inserted into the braille writer and has read as many as 900 pages. Typical classroom supplemental reading activities that provide valuable practice are such things as calendars, cafeteria menus, rules for games, lists of birthdays, school newspapers, experience stories, and library books.

Print books were designed to be used with children of differing abilities. Most classroom teachers do not use all of the pages with all of the children. Regular teachers need to evaluate books to see which pages are appropriate for a particular child, and they should indicate to the special teacher the pages which should

Clean, warm hands are important for rapid and correct braille reading.

Never, never tell a child that there are reversible pairs of letters in braille.

be adapted. The special teacher should direct the transcriber in preparing meaningful adapted worksheets. The primary grade consumable materials often challenge the imagination and creativity, and demand a multimedia approach to reading by combining braille, tape recordings, and three-dimensional objects in order to present a concept accurately.

The vast majority of beginning reading papers ask students either to circle or to underline the right answer. A pushpin board can be used by the braille users. Use press board, cut to 9″ × 12″ or 12″ × 12″. Cover with contact paper. Place a row of pushpins at the top. The braille users can mark the right answer with a pushpin. This allows the students to go back and see where they stopped, check to see whether they have skipped any lines, and develop finger, hand, and arm muscles needed to operate the brailler. Although blind students *can* use pencils or crayons for marking choices, they cannot afterwards check their work or correct it. The pushpin board affords them this opportunity.

A consumable worksheet contains blank spaces in which the student may write the appropriate answer. Leave two or more blank spaces to the right of the braille dash to indicate where the answer should be written. The answer is written within the blank space. Leave at least two more cells than the students will need to write the appropriate answer. The long dash is shown in braille by dots 3–6 written four times. It always precedes the empty space into which the answer will be placed. The student puts his or her answer directly after, *not above*, the line.

Pictures of different objects are used in print books to help students understand beginning reading concepts. Do not attempt to make raised pictures for the braille user. Real objects, when possible, or a tape recording that gives a brief description of the pictures (e.g., "Page 13. Number 1, sun; number 2, gun; number 3, ball.") may be used efficiently.

Cassette tape recorders and consumable workbooks may be used together to allow the student to work independently in phonetic workbooks and beginning spellers, which employ many pictures in order to convey a concept. The student listens to the tape to gain knowledge of the picture (e.g., "Page 14. Number 1, game.") and then turns off the machine. The corresponding item on the worksheet is read by the student. "Page 14. Number 1, g–t–s." The student indicates with a pushpin the letter that represents the first sound of the item in the picture (game).

The standards for writing braille must be different for students than for transcribers. All children make mistakes and need years of practice to become truly skilled at brailling. A child may be off a great deal in judging spacing and amounts of needed room for a word. Do not be discouraged by a few failures. Through repeated practice with consumable materials, the student will easily obtain the skills he or she needs to read and write accurately.

Real objects, or a tape recording that describes the pictures, can substitute for illustrations to help students understand beginning reading concepts.

It takes years of practice to become truly skilled at brailling.

References

Burns, P. C., & Schell, L. M. *Elementary school language arts: Selected readings.* Chicago: Rand McNally, 1969.

Carter, H. L. J., & McGinnis, D. J. *Diagnosis and treatment of the disabled reader.* New York: Macmillan, 1970.

Caton, H., & Bradley, J. A new approach to beginning braille reading. *Education of the Visually Handicapped,* 1978, **10.**

Forte, I., MacKenzie, J., & Frank, M. *Kids' stuff: Reading and language experiences, intermediate–junior high.* Nashville, Tenn.: Incentive Publications, 1972.

Forte, I., & Mackenzie, J. *Nooks, crannies, and corners: Learning centers for creative classrooms.* Nashville, Tenn.: Incentive Publications, 1972.

Harley, R. K., Henderson, F. M. & Truan, M. B. *The teaching of braille reading.* Springfield, Ill.: Charles C Thomas.

Heilman, A. W., & Holmes, E. A. *Smuggling language into the teaching of reading.* Columbus, Ohio: Charles E. Merrill, 1968.

Huck, C. & Kuhn, D. Y. *Children's literature in the elementary school.* New York: Holt, Rinehard, & Winston, 1968.

Mangold, S. *The Mangold developmental program of tactile perception and braille letter recognition.* Castro Valley, Calif.: Exceptional Teaching Aids, 1977.

Mangold, S. Tactile perception and braille letter recognition: Effects of developmental teaching. *Visual Impairment and Blindness,* 1978, 72, 259-266.

Myers, R. E., & Torance, E. P. *Can you imagine?* Boston: Ginn and Company, 1965.

Olson, M., & Mangold, S. *Guide lines and games for braille reading.* New York: American Foundation for the Blind, 1978.

Petty, W. T., & Bowen, M. *Slithery snakes and other aids to children's writing.* New York: Appleton-Century-Crofts, 1967.

Platts, M. *Spice: Suggested activities to motivate the teaching of the primary language arts.* Stevensville: Michigan, 1973.

<table>
<tr><td>

Faster Braille Reading: Preparation at the Reading Readiness Level

Myrna R. Olson, Ed.D.

</td><td>

CHAPTER 2

</td></tr>
</table>

Teachers of visually impaired persons have long battled with the relative ineffi- ciency of braille reading. Lowenfeld (1973) has indicated that braille readers lag progressively farther and farther behind their print reading peers (in terms of reading rate) as they pass through school. A recent study by the author (1975) re- vealed a negative correlation between age and rate increases made by braille readers after training in rapid reading. It seems important, therefore, to imple- ment techniques for improving reading rate as early as possible in the teaching of braille reading.

This article suggests several activities at the reading readiness level which should later enhance the efficiency of braille reading. These activities might be carried out by a vision teacher in a residential, a resource, or an itinerant pro- gram. In an integrated setting, the regular classroom teacher might also imple- ment several of these activities with the assistance of a vision consultant.

The readiness activities set forth in this article do not represent an exhaustive treatment of what can be done at this level. It is hoped that they will call attention to the specific skills related to reading efficiency. Individual teachers should use the ideas presented here as "springboards" to designing their own activities.

READINESS LEVEL SKILLS

There are basically six skills at the reading readiness level directly related to reading rate. Initially, one would want the child to develop good *tactual discrim- ination.* It is important that *finger dexterity* is developed simultaneously. Once the child is learning to combine these two skills, he or she should be practicing rapid, coordinated *hand and finger movements.* At this stage, he or she needs to refine his or her tactual skills and to develop *light finger touch.* The final skills belonging to the readiness level involve experimentation with book positions and learning efficient page turning. Each of these skills will be analyzed in- dividually, and activities will be suggested for dealing with each one.

Tactual Discrimination

The teacher should begin with large three-dimensional objects that are grossly different from one another (blocks, balls, toys). The child can be asked to sort these into pairs. To reinforce basic concepts, this activity might involve finding objects of the same shape but different in size.

The American Printing House for the Blind puts out a "Touch and Tell" read- ing readiness series that could be used at this time to introduce tactual discrimi- nation of two-dimensional figures (e.g., line drawings, thermoformed replicas). Another option is for the teacher to make materials. A deck of playing cards can be used to make a game of "Touch Old Maid." Pieces of fabric are glued to the cards in matching pairs. The pairs that are grossly different should be intro- duced initially (e.g., rabbit fur, silk, corduroy, velvet). The deck may be utilized as an individual sorting task or used by a group of youngsters applying the card rules for the regular game of Old Maid. The only unpaired card would be the old

Dr. Olson is an assistant professor of special education at the University of North Dakota, Grand Forks. This chapter originally appeared in *The New Outlook*, 1976, **70**(8).

maid, which might consist of the braille symbols for those words. As children become proficient at identifying fabrics that differ little in texture (e.g., two widths of corduroy, two kinds of polyester), additional decks might be made. Pieces of felt, different only in shape or size, might be glued to cards. A sewing tracing wheel could also be used to make lines of varying lengths on these cards. The final step in developing tactual discrimination would be to introduce a deck of cards with braille characters. Again, one would start by introducing the braille characters that differ the most from one another tactually (e.g., full cell, dot 1, dots 1 and 3). This game can be modified to teach all the braille characters once the regular reading program is begun.

Finger Dexterity

A good starting point might be to encourage fine finger manipulations along with various categorizing tasks being used through the general readiness program. This might include putting beads or blocks into boxes. The teacher should attempt to introduce smaller and smaller objects to manipulate (paper clips, small nails). Bead stringing is another task which will serve to increase finger dexterity. The child could also be given a pegboard in which the teacher has made a pattern; the child is instructed to copy the teacher's pattern. Still another activity is to have the child put pinch clothespins on a hanger, as a counting activity or again as a copying task.

Several years ago the cuberithm board was a popular calculating device for the blind. Though the braille writer and abacus have somewhat replaced this device, it has an excellent function at the reading readiness level. The teacher might give instructions to the child on tape for placing the cubes on the board. One instruction, for example, might be "Fill all the spaces on the left; another might be "Start at the top of the board, pick a row, and fill in every other space with a cube until you reach the bottom of the board." This activity not only provides practice in finger dexterity, but also tests basic verbal concepts (left–right, top–bottom). It may be used as a reinforcement for counting skills as well. By taping instructions, the child can work independently and be checked periodically. Two children might do this task together and check to see if their boards feel alike.

In order to develop dexterity in the fingers of both hands, the child should be encouraged to try all the foregoing activities with each hand in turn and both hands together.

Hand and Finger Movements

From the beginning of this phase, the teacher needs to stress the use of both hands and all four fingers on each hand. Eventually children should develop their own styles of hand movement and may favor certain fingers on each hand. Nonetheless, teachers can explain to children that some are "lead fingers" and others "detectives" or "assistants." The assistants can take over for the lead fingers when there is injury or soreness. Using both hands enables them to act together at times (one picking up what the other has missed) and separately at other times (skimming two different pages simultaneously). When two hands are employed, one hand can continue the reading while the other turns pages or shifts the position of the book.

At the readiness level, hand movements are applied to "simulated reading material." For example, children may practice following the edge of a ruler or book to see how the fingers travel when following a line of braille. In this practice situation, some fingers are curved more than others; this will be true in the actual reading situation as well.

At this point, a number of teacher-made materials will come in handy. Strings of yarn may be glued to sheets of braille paper and placed in straight lines of varied lengths as well as in curving and swirling lines. The child is told to pass both hands (using all eight fingers) over the yarn lines without "falling off the line" and to stop when the line stops. Eventually the yarn should attempt to simu-

Stress use of both hands and all four fingers on each hand. Children eventually develop their own styles of hand movement.

Fingers lead, detect, or assist.

late lines of braille reading material in two respects. First, practice should be given with lines initially farther apart (more than an inch) and finally with lines spaced the same distance as single-spaced braille in literary books. Secondly, paragraphing should be illustrated by the yarn lines being periodically indented horizontally and spaced vertically.

Other materials that can provide the same kind of practice would be stick books (popsicle sticks glued in straight lines of varying length), tracing wheel lines on paper, or thread lines made on paper by a sewing machine. A culminating activity, for perfecting this skill might be brailling lines of full braille cells, lines of 1's, or lines of single dots in the braille cell.

All of these exercises will give the child a chance to experiment with varied hand movements, to practice rapid and coordinated hand movement, and to learn rapid "searching" with all eight fingers.

Children can use yarn, stick, and thread books to practice finger movements for braille reading.

Light Finger Touch
The teacher should verbally reinforce the child for applying less pressure in the fingertips as he or she examines materials tactually. Demonstrating on the yarn, stick, or thread books, the teacher can hold the child's hands in such a way as to give him or her the "feel" of lightly touching a surface.

Once braille cells are used for practicing tactual discrimination or hand and finger movements, the teacher can give a child extra incentive for practicing light finger touch. By rubbing the child's fingers with colored chalk, progress in using less pressure can be measured. The lighter the fingers are touched to the page, the longer the chalk will stay on the fingers and the more braille characters will be covered by the rubbed-off chalk. Though the child will not be able to see the result, the teacher can give him or her verbal feedback. The child may even want to chart how many lines he or she can cover in a minute and how many of those lines are colored by chalk.

A braille tachistoscope would be ideal for practicing rapid, light finger movement, although a rough replica can be made by the teacher more cheaply. Braille cells are put on strips of braille paper and pulled beneath the child's fingers. It will help if the child places his or her hands on a book with his fingers curved over the edge for this activity. The child should be able to discern when the braille character used changes to a different one, or when one line of cells ends and another begins.

Page Turning
In the beginning, page turning should be practiced on heavy cardboard pages. Linen books are probably the next easiest to manipulate. The yarn, stick, and thread books, if they are made on braille paper, might provide another set of practice materials. The child should practice finishing the last line on a page with the left hand while turning the page with the right hand.

Measure progress in using less finger pressure by rubbing the child's fingers with colored chalk.

Old braille magazines and books will aid the child in picking up speed and skill in turning pages without worry of tearing the pages of good books.

Starting during the reading readiness phase and continuing into the primary readers, the child should be allowed to experiment with comfortable book positions. These positions might include placing the book on tables of varying heights, using book props at the bottom or top of a book, laying the book on the lap, and slanting the book at various angles. Teacher and child should determine together which book position seems best. Using the simulated reading material, the position which allows for the most rapid rate in combination with the five skills previously discussed should be the one employed.

References

Lowenfeld, B. *The visually handicapped child in school.* New York: John Day, 1973.
Olson, M. The effects of rapid reading training on the reading rates and comprehension of braille and large print readers. Unpublished doctoral dissertation. University of North Dakota, 1973.

CHAPTER 3

Teaching Specific Concepts to Visually Handicapped Students

Amanda Hall, Ph.D.

Students without detailed vision often lack basic concepts and fail to unify integral components in their environment. These concepts must be taught to visually handicapped students so that they can increase their knowledge base and participate equally with sighted peers whenever possible.

It is important to develop systematic methods for teaching concepts in order to determine which concepts to consider for instruction; how to assess these crucial concepts with individual students; what verbal and manipulative procedures best clarify specific concepts for a particular student; and how to reinforce and generalize conceptual understanding once a concept is learned in a specific instructional setting.

The purpose of this chapter is to describe one approach to the systematic teaching of specific concepts. This approach considers logical ways of thinking about concepts that provide direction for the instructional process. Flexibility is the key to the application of the instructional methods described here, since the design of actual lessons will vary with the needs of particular students, the time available for lesson preparation and instruction, and the specific situations in which a concept must be taught.

SELECTING SPECIFIC CONCEPTS FOR INSTRUCTION

In order to begin the teaching of conceptual skills, it is necessary to identify crucial concepts that a visually handicapped student must understand for full participation in activities and daily life in and out of school. A list of these concepts was developed as a class project in a concept development course for teachers and orientation and mobility instructors of the visually handicapped at San Francisco State University. This list is not exhaustive of all the critical concepts that a visually handicapped student should know, but represents an initial step in the identification of crucial concepts. Additions to this list are encouraged.

List of crucial concepts*
1. **Body Awareness** (concepts pertaining to the body)

top, bottom	middle	relationship of body parts
back, front	wholeness of body	lower part of body
left, right	names of major body parts	upper part of body
	waist-high	

Dr. Hall is Director of Assessment, Center for the Visually Impaired Unit at the California School for the Blind in Fremont, California. She has spent the past few years developing a prereading concept program for visually handicapped students as a senior research associate at the American Institutes for Research in Palo Alto, California.

Kinesthetic Awareness
turning
direction of motion
moving, still
gravity in relation to body

Proprioceptive Awareness
bending parts
head up
closed fingers
feet together
posture

Sensations
feelings
smell
taste
touch
hearing
sight

Facial Expressions
smile
frown

Gestures
nod yes
shake no
shrug
point to object
shake hands

Measure progress in using less finger pressure by rubbing the child's fingers with colored chalk.

2. **Environmental Awareness** (crucial objects in the environment and specific relationships among elements in the environment)

divided highway
median strip
crosswalk
intersection
street
sidewalk
driveway
block
pedestrian

traffic light
street signs
fire hydrant
lamp post
mail box
trash can
curb
gutter
corner

truck, car, bus, wagon
tricycle, bicycle
train
airplane
store
house
porch
tree, grass

yard, back yard
stairs
doorbell

landmark
shoreline boundaries
traffic patterns
weather—rain, snow

crib, bed
table, chair
doorway
stove
sink
refrigerator
bathtub

toilet
hallway
desk
closet
dresser

3. **Awareness of Object Characteristics** (general properties of objects)

Size
dry, wet
big, little, small, large, medium
fat, thin, narrow, wide
long, short, medium length
deep, shallow

Color
clear, opaque
dark, light
specific colors
hue, tint

Shape
square, rectangle
round, oval
triangle
diamond
straight, curved, crooked
shapes of specific objects
configuration of words

Texture
smooth, rough, flat, hard, soft, sticky,
    coarse, fine, bumpy, fuzzy, etc.

Sound
high, low pitch
loud, soft intensity
long, short duration
rhythm

Comparative Characteristics
larger, smaller
fatter, warmer, deeper, etc.
same, different

*This list was prepared by class members enrolled in Special Education 757 at San Francisco State University, Spring 1978: Rosemary Appel, Pat Davis, Carolyn Brien-Eddins, Jennifer Fitzgerald, Joanne Fong, Scott Johnson, Debbie Kooyer, Joanne Lowe, Sandy Rosen, Debi Ruth, Charles Ryon, Jim Schaer, Margo Simmons, Peggy Williams, Joan Winter. Instructor: Amanda Hall.

4. **Time Awareness** (concepts pertaining to time)

begin, end
before, after
first, next, last
during
always, never
old, new, young
time-distance relationships

today, yesterday, tomorrow
morning, noon, night, afternoon, evening
sunrise, sunset
day, week, month, year
second, minute, hour
future, past, present, now
clock concepts

5. **Spatial Awareness** (concepts related to position in space)

parallel
perpendicular
round
arc
plane
middle, center, between
diagonal
opposite

degrees of circle or turn
half turn, whole turn
about face
grid pattern
up, down
inside, outside
on, off

next, to, beside
around
in, out
first, last
toward, away from
behind
in order
closed, open

straight, crooked, curved
to, from
high, low
top, bottom
front, back
left, right
forward, backward

separated, together
far, rear, distant, close
wide, narrow
clockwise, counterclockwise
maintaining direction
maintaining distance

Directions
north, south
east, west
northeast
northwest
southeast
southwest

veering
reference point
incline, decline
orientation, disorientation
sound localization

under, over
underneath, beneath
overhead
above, below
upside down, right side up

across, across from
past, beyond
through
here, there

6. **Actions** (concepts pertaining to movement)

writing, typing
buttoning, zipping, snapping
eating, drinking

skip, run
jump, hop
climb, crawl
stand, sit
step
throw, catch
push, pull

swing
duck, bend
kick
slide
roll

stop, start
lock, unlock
circle
follow
on, off

veer
turn
imitate

forward, reverse,
backward
sideways
slow, fast

7. **Quantity** (concepts associated with numbers and number combinations)

specific whole numbers
half, third, quarter
fractions
least, less (than)
most, more (than)
enough, only
several, few, many
equal

pair
zero
increase, decrease
with, without
place, value
all, some, none
infinity

Operations
addition
subtraction
multiplication
division

Measurement
inch, foot, yard, mile
square inch, etc.
cubic inches, etc.
pound, ounce, ton
cup, pint, quart, gallon
teaspoon, tablespoon
miles per hour
metric measurements
  for distance,
   volume, weight

8. **Symbol Awareness** (crucial symbolic concepts)

		Pronouns
compass directions	numbers, zero	I, me, mine
map reading	signs—shape and design	you, yours
letters—print, cursive, braille	pictures	he, she, his, hers
punctuation signs	colors (red = stop; green = go)	we, they, theirs, ours
		it, its

9. **Emotional and Social Awareness** (concepts associated with psychosocial adjustment)

distinguish *I* from *You*	asking assistance, accepting help
discriminate parent from stranger	initiating questioning
self-concept	acceptance and rejection of others and
human sexuality concepts	by others
manners	values
grooming	
body language	sad, happy, angry
nonverbal communication	scared, fear, afraid
voice pitch and intensity	worried, excited

10. **Reasoning** (thought processes in which concepts are used)

traffic patterns	orientation, disorientation
right of way	estimation
detour	time-distance relationships
pedestrian traffic	functioning of objects and parts of objects
one-way street	objects with similar parts
lanes of traffic	
route	all, some, none
route reversal	any, every
patterns in the environment	only, either, or
	sorting
	sequencing (patterns, numbers, sounds)
	categorizing, classification
decision-making	comparing, same, different
real and make-believe	conservation (volume, mass, weight,
realistic expectations for self	quantity)
making judgments—right, wrong,	use of visual memory
good, bad, fair, unfair	common visual terminology

ASSESSING CONCEPTUAL UNDERSTANDING

After determining the concepts to be examined with a particular student by examining the list of concepts, determining curricular needs, and observing the student, it is necessary to assess a student's understanding of these concepts systematically. Both verbal and performance responses should be elicited from the student in the assessment of concrete concepts whenever possible. This serves to clarify the relationship between a student's language ability and performance skills. Students with little or no language ability must be assessed through the use of their available skills, though this makes the assessment process more difficult.

The assessment of concepts requires an examination of the breadth and depth of a student's conceptual understanding. The levels at which concepts are assessed varies with the functioning of the student and the type of concept under consideration. With any concept, the teacher must use his or her judgment to determine which conceptual levels a student can be expected to master, taking into account such factors as past experience and instruction, language ability, visual functioning, and general developmental level. Examples of concept assessment shown in Tables 3.1–3.6 demonstrate different levels at which some basic concepts can be assessed. Since concepts are so varied, these examples cannot cover all types of concepts that must be taught. They can, however, be used as models for developing assessment protocols for other types of concepts.

Table 3.1
Concepts of Concrete Objects

	Familiar Object Exemplifying Concept	Unfamiliar Object Exemplifying Concept
1. Identification: Indicate an object named by teacher Name an object indicated by teacher	_____	_____
2. Describe function of named/ indicated object	_____	_____
3. Describe relationship of named/ indicated object to other objects	_____	_____

Students must be able to identify concrete objects represented by concepts before they can be expected to describe functions or relationships (see Table 3.1). Thus the identification of familiar objects represented by a concept is the first level of assessment for concepts of concrete objects. This is followed by the identification of unfamiliar objects represented by a concept. Important for gaining insight into the understanding of very young or low-functioning students, the latter procedure clarifies, for example, whether a student understands the word "table" to signify only one table in a corner of the classroom or whether it signifies all objects with legs and horizontally positioned, flat tops.

A description of the function of objects represented by a concept should be the next step in the assessment of concepts of concrete objects. A table, for example, is used as a place to put things.

It is then necessary to assess the environmental contexts in which the objects represented by a concept are found. This level of assessment is important because it clarifies the conceptual relationships that a student understands. For example, tables are commonly found in homes, schools, restaurants; they are often located in kitchens or dining rooms; chairs are often associated with tables.

Methods for assessing other types of concepts have been summarized in Tables 3.2–3.6.

Table 3.2
Concepts of Body Parts that can be Touched

	Self		Other Person
1. Identification Indicate part named by teacher Name part indicated by teacher			
2. Describe function of named/ indicated part			
3. Describe relationship of named/ indicated part to other body parts.			

Table 3.3
Concepts of Object Characteristics

	Clear-Cut Examples		Finer Discrimination
1. Identification Indicate characteristic of an object or indicate object with a specific characteristic named by teacher. Name an object characteristic indicated by teacher.			

Table 3.4
Concepts of Actions

	Self		Other Person or Object
1. Identification Imitate movement performed by teacher			
Perform movement named by teacher			
Name an indicated movement			
2. Describe function of an action, if appropriate			

Table 3.5
Concepts of Positions

	Own Body Parts Only		Other Person or Object and Own Body Parts		Other Persons or Objects Only
1. Identification Move to position named by teacher					
Name a position indicated by teacher					

Table 3.6
Abstract Concepts

1. Describe function	_____
2. Name class category, if appropriate	_____
3. Describe similarity or analogy to other known concepts	_____

CLARIFYING SPECIFIC CONCEPTS FOR THE TEACHING PROCESS

Many concepts appear obvious, but this cannot be taken for granted. Take, for example, the concept "front." Imagine yourself facing a table with a chair in between your body and the table. The chair is pushed under the table. You are facing the "back" of the chair, but you are facing the "front" of the table. This is so because the chair has a front and a back which are inherent in the definition of chair. Your position in relation to the chair does not determine its front and back, which never change. On the other hand, the front or back of the table is determined by the position of an observer in relation to the table. The front or back of the table changes as the observer changes position. These distinctions could be quite confusing to a student and must be clarified in the instructional process.

To be certain that a concept is presented in a precise manner to a student, a conceptual analysis is performed. This involves two steps. First, a definition of the concept *as it will be used in the teaching process* is developed. This definition may be different from a dictionary definition since its purpose is to simplify or break down a concept for instruction. The definition helps formulate the conceptual goal of the lesson. For some students, "front" would be defined as part of an object directly facing the front of a person's body, when that object does not have a front or a back. This precision in the definition makes it easier to teach, and as a consequence, makes it easier for a student to learn.

The second step in the conceptual analysis process is to identify all the concepts that must be understood in order to achieve the conceptual goal of the lesson. The conceptual goal is determined by the definition of the concept adopted for instruction. Here is an example for the concept "front."

Conceptual Goal: "Front"
The student will be able to indicate (verbally or by pointing or touching) the front of objects that have no designated front or back, either when the student changes position by moving around the objects while facing them, or when the objects are turned while they are in front of the student (Figure 3.1).

Strategies should be devised that teach concepts from the bottom of the conceptual analysis, working upward in the hierarchy. It is not necessary to teach those concepts in the hierarchy that the student already understands. Thus it is important to determine the student's entry level for each conceptual analysis. A student may have more than one entry level in an analysis, depending on the complexity of the analysis. Concepts should be broken down at least one step below a student's entry level.

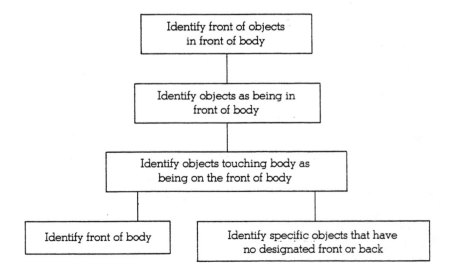

Figure 3.1. Conceptual Goal: "Front"

16

REINFORCING AND GENERALIZING CONCEPTUAL UNDERSTANDING

Concepts must be carefully taught to students using both manipulative materials and verbal explanations whenever possible. In addition, it is important to devise methods that help the student transfer his or her understanding of a concept from the specific teaching situation to other situations in the course of a normal day. Cooperation is needed at this point from parents and other professionals. They can be informed of a specific concept that has just been learned by a student and can, in turn, emphasize that concept with the student as relevant situations arise. This procedure reinforces specific concepts and also makes them more meaningful to the student since he or she becomes increasingly aware that certain concepts represent different aspects of daily life.

EXAMPLES OF TEACHING SPECIFIC CONCEPTS

Two examples of conceptual analysis follow. One example deals with the deceptively simple concept "first," the other deals with the concept "neighborhood." There are other ways to teach these concepts, but the methods used here worked well for the particular students for whom they were devised.

"First"*

The subject in this case was a six-year-old student whose visual impairment, due to retrolental fibroplasia, left her with minimal light perception. Upon initial observation, the child appeared to lack three important concepts—first, middle, and last. The need to locate things or persons in one's environment necessitates an understanding of order and positioning. Because of the student's age, attention span, and the complexity of each of the three concepts, it was decided to begin with one concept—"first."

Conceptual Analysis

Definition of "first": The position or order of an object or person, such that it is preceding all others in space.

Conceptual Goal

Given the directional arrangement of a set (front to back, left to right, top to bottom), the student will demonstrate an understanding of the spatial concept "first" by tactually or verbally identifying the first object or person in the set. (See Figure 3.2.)

Figure 3.2 Conceptual Goal: "First."

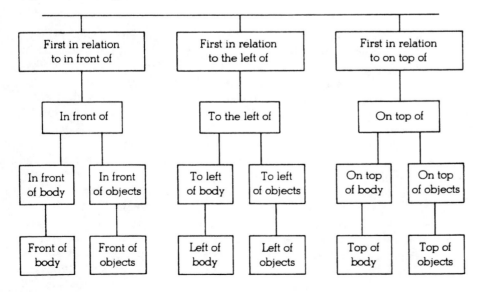

*Prepared by Toni Provost.

In order to determine the entry level of this six-year-old student, the game "Simon Says" was played. The student knew the left and the top of her body, but did not know the front of her body. She did not know left, top, or front of objects. To understand the concept "first," it was necessary to clarify the concepts "left," "top," and "front" for this particular student.

Figure 3.3 Conceptual Goal: "Neighborhood."

```
                    ┌──────────────────────────────────┐
                    │  Combination of many city blocks │
                    └──────────────────────────────────┘

                 ┌────────────────────────────────────────┐
                 │  Relationship of one city block to another │
                 └────────────────────────────────────────┘

        ┌──────────────┐              ┌──────────────────┐
        │  Cardinal    │              │  Cross street to get │
        │  directions  │              │  from block to block │
        └──────────────┘              └──────────────────┘

        ┌──────────────┐              ┌──────────────────┐
        │  *Opposite   │              │  *Parallel and    │
        │              │              │  perpendicular    │
        └──────────────┘              └──────────────────┘

   ┌──────────────────────────────────────────────────────────┐
   │               Components of city block                    │
   └──────────────────────────────────────────────────────────┘

 ┌────────┐ ┌──────┐ ┌───────┐ ┌─────────┐ ┌──────────┐ ┌─────────┐ ┌───────┐
 │Sidewalk│ │Trees │ │ Grass │ │  Four   │ │Rectangular│ │ Parallel │ │ Curbs │
 └────────┘ └──────┘ └───────┘ │ streets │ │  shape   │ │rows of  │ └───────┘
                               │parallel │ └──────────┘ │ houses  │
                               │to four  │              └─────────┘
                               │sides of │
                               │ block   │
                               └─────────┘
                                      ┌────────┐ ┌────────┐
                                      │  Four  │ │  Four  │
                                      │  sides │ │ corners│
                                      └────────┘ └────────┘
```

*"Parallel," "perpendicular," and "opposite" are mentioned only once in the analysis to reduce duplication of concepts, although they are prerequisite to the understanding of several other concepts in the analysis.

"Neighborhood"*

In this case a 16-year-old blind student was to be taught the concept of "city block." This later grew into the concept of "neighborhood," which is essentially only one step further: it is an area of many city blocks. From observations of this student, it appeared that she was not familiar with the concept, as she came from a rural environment. This concept is extremely useful in connection with orientation and mobility, and is a challenge which this student was capable of understanding.

Conceptual Analysis

Two definitions are needed for this analysis, since "neighborhood" is closely related to "city block."

Definition of "city block": A rectangular unit immediately bounded by four streets or the length of one side of such a rectangle. Definition of "neighborhood": A district or section of a number of city blocks with people of similar condition and type of habitation living near one another.

Two definitions of "city block" based upon rectangular units were used in this analysis and taught to the student. Some city blocks are not rectangular in shape, but are irregular. This type of city block was not covered in the analysis. Ideally,

*Prepared by Kathryn Weidenfeld-Smith.

18

it should be taught after a student has mastered the more simple (and common) definitions associated with rectangular city blocks.

The original definition of "neighborhood" did not include commercial districts, but the definition was expanded to include commercial districts during the course of the lesson because this particular student was able to make this transition easily.

Conceptual Goal

The student will demonstrate understanding of "neighborhood" in relation to the "city block" concept. (See Figure 3.3.)

From a discussion with the student, it was determined that she was not familiar with the components of a city block, so the lessons began with that point in the analysis.

CHAPTER 4

A Communication Curriculum for Blind Multiply Handicapped Children

Sally M. Rogow, Ed.D.

It seemed to us that in the use the children made of language we saw the reflection of all their problems. The motor problems, the lack of experience, the disordered perception, the inability to organize what they had experienced, hostility, withdrawal from reality, insecurity, anxiety, immaturity, compulsive drives, and egocentricity were revealed in the use they made of language. (Framption, Kerney, & Schattner, 1969, p. 173)

Teachers who work with blind multiply handicapped children are aware of the range of abilities and variation in language behavior of their children. Some of the children do not speak at all; others speak in words or phrases, and still others speak in perfectly formed sentences, but their speech seems meaningless and unrelated to what they are doing. Emotional disturbance and behavior problems are common; many children seem inattentive, preoccupied and withdrawn, while others appear continuously frustrated and vent the intensity of their feelings in tantrums or other forms of aggressive behavior. Such behavior is often so dramatic that it commands the teacher's full attention and diverts attention from the educational needs of the children. Underlying the emotional intensity of the children's behavior is their need to be able to communicate with and form personal relationships with adults and other children. Most learning and satisfaction of need comes from interaction with other human beings, and children bereft of a well-developed language system are bereft of a means of adequately communicating with their world.

The goal of a communication curriculum is to develop communicative competence, which is best defined as the use of language as a well-developed tool of social interaction.

THE NOTION OF COMMUNICATIVE COMPETENCE

Achieving communicative competence entails not only encoding and decoding of messages in isolation, but also learning how to use these messages to perform communicative functions. These functions are based to a great extent upon the environmental context of the utterance. (Yoder & Reichle, 1977, p. 201)

A functional definition of language states that language is a socially shared means for expressing ideas (Miller, 1971). Communication can be said to occur when both the speaker and the listener understand the same meaning. How children learn to discern meaning from the speech of adults is the subject of much current research. The processes are not yet understood, but it seems clear that language is deeply embedded in the personal interaction of the child with the important people in his or her life.

The purpose of our curriculum is to develop functional communication in blind multiply handicapped children. This means that the content of instruction is focused on the functions of communication. According to Yoder and Reichle (1977), the functions of communication include the following:

1. Getting listeners to do, believe, or feel something.
2. Giving and getting information.

Dr. Rogow is a member of the Department of Special Education at the University of British Columbia.

3. Expressing one's own intentions, beliefs, or feelings.
4. Indicating desire for interaction.
5. Describing and interpreting events.
6. Sharing experiences.
7. Learning new behavior.

Because of the severe restrictions blindness in combination with other sensory, motor, and/or mental handicaps places on the ease of access to information and personal interaction, it is important that children be taught how to learn as well as what to learn. The teacher performs an important role in teaching children learning strategies. This is accomplished by having a clear goal, modelling the desired behavior, and responding to children's efforts to communicate.

The majority of language training programs designed for language-delayed children are based on the idea that language is learned by imitation. The clinician or teacher acts as the initiator and says, "Show me _____" or "You say _____" or "Where's the _____?". In this training model, the child is taught vocabulary, syntactic rules, and sometimes a few semantic relations. But it is misleading to believe that this model teaches communication (Yoder & Reichle, 1977).

Communicative competence combines knowledge of both language form and function and is clearly illustrated by the child who can ask and answer questions, declare, command, make requests, and participate in conversation.

BEGINNING STEPS IN ESTABLISHING COMMUNICATION
The general consensus among investigators is that, over time, signals emitted in a consistent context and interpreted in a consistent fashion during early life come to influence phonological, semantic, and syntactic acquisition. (Yoder & Reichle, 1977, p. 202).

Many multiply handicapped blind children are unresponsive and unaware that they can influence the behavior of others with their use of language or other forms of social signal. A social signal indicates need or desire. Such a social signal is demonstrated when the young child points at something or holds out his or her arms to be picked up. It is behavior which the child has learned "signals" a consistent response from an adult. The young child who holds out his or her arms and is consistently picked up by a responsive adult has learned that holding out arms is a signal meaning "pick me up."

A Social Signal System
The first step in teaching communicative competence is to establish a consistent mode of response. At this stage the child needs to learn a mode of social interaction which employs a signal (motor action, word, or sound) to indicate need or want; to experience having an effect on the environment; to initiate interaction; and to respond to the signals (words or motor actions) of others.

Barry is ten years old and congenitally blind. He speaks in full sentences and is flawless in his imitation of the speech of others, capturing tone, pitch and intensity as well as articulation of words. He sings well and knows the words of more than 20 popular songs and commercial jingles. Barry does not ask questions or use his language to express his own needs or wants. Nor does he initiate conversation or use language to do more than repeat the words of others: "I wish Barry would be a good boy." "Barry, do not tear your clothes," he mutters while walking outdoors with his teacher. Barry's speech seems to lack purpose or relation to the context in which it occurs.

Joey is eight years old, is congenitally blind, and has a history of psychomotor convulsions. He has frequent tantrums at home and at school and appears to have few interests. He has a vocabulary of food words such as "apple," "orange," "milk," "juice," "bread," and "butter," but he does not use them to request those items. He simply cries when he doesn't get the food he wants.

Many multiply handicapped children are unaware that they can influence the behavior of others through language or other social signals.

Young children who hold out their arms and are consistently picked up by an adult learn that holding out arms is a signal meaning "pick me up."

Children who do not seem to have interests or preferences are the most difficult to teach.

Neither Joey nor Barry has established language as a signal system. Both present serious problems in the classroom because of their inability to respond appropriately to the social demands of an educational program. Neither child has established genuine interaction initiative or purposivenss of activity. Nor do they seem to have some activities that they prefer over others.

In order to learn to express preference, children need to have preferences. Beginning programs need to include the following:

1. Teach the child that interaction can be a source of pleasure.
2. Broaden and develop the child's interests.
3. Interpret the child behavior as if it were intentional communication.
4. Provide the child with opportunities to make choices and express preferences.
5. Establish a system of hand signals for nonspeaking children.

Joey threw down the toy truck his teacher had given him. The teacher patted Joey and said "Oh, I guess you don't want the toy truck." She took his hand and led him to a toy box. "Let's find something you do like." By responding to Joey in this manner, the teacher is demonstrating to Joey that she interprets his negative behavior as a signal for "I don't want," and is thereby showing him a communicative response.

The more handicapped the child, the stronger the reward needs to be.

Children who do not seem to have any interests or preferences are the most difficult to teach. Many hours need to be devoted to introducing them do a variety of activities and objects in order to develop their interests. For some children this may involve very basic physical movement and acceptance and use of toys and objects. This is particularly true for very passive blind children who have become accustomed to the lack of demand and expectation and its resulting lack of personal interaction. Any consistent behavior such as a reach, a grasp, or a tug on the sleeve is interpreted as a signal to which the teacher demonstrates a consistent response.

Developing Gestures in Nonverbal Children

It is easier for a child to give a signal and obtain pleasure from the teacher's response than to respond to the teacher's signal. The more handicapped the child, the stronger the reward needs to be (Southwell, 1971, p. 74). Choose an activity that you know the child enjoys. If you show the child that a hand-clap or a sound can elicit a pleasurable response—for example, being picked up or swung around—you need only wait for the weaker attempt at the signal before giving the pleasurable movement as a reward (Southwell, 1971). The signal will be stronger the next time.

After the child has mastered one signal, he or she can be taught a different signal for each activity. Sharp, clearly defined gestures, such as clapping or patting the body, are easier for the child to copy (Southwell, 1971).

Van Dyjk developed gestures for objects by noting the actions used with them and then emphasizing them to the children (Southwell, 1971). Speech should be used in conjunction with gestures so that children can build strong associations between gesture signals and words.

Children like Barry who have acquired a language system should be encouraged to use their language in a social context. These children will develop a meaningful use of their language as their understanding of the communicative functions of the language develops. To use language effectively, children must have something to say and someone to say it to. Children like Barry need to learn that their language will bring them a personal response.

To use language effectively, children must have something to say and someone to say it to.

At the earliest levels of building communicative competence, emotional well-being cannot be separated from cognitive processes. The increase in both the quality and quantity of self-initiated movement toward people and objects demonstrates progress. Changes take the form of positive changes in the child's ability to communicate and an increased amount of communication. These changes nurture each other and are independent.

SPEECH AND LANGUAGE DEVELOPMENT

Speech Development

A child's ability to use language is dependent upon the ability to comprehend and formulate language. (Weiss & Lilywhite, 1976, p. 53)

Blind multiply handicapped children who do not speak require a careful, thorough, and comprehensive program, beginning with a thorough examination by a physician, an audiologist, and a speech pathologist. Even a relatively minor hearing handicap can account for the failure of blind multiply handicapped children to develop speech. Speech is learned behavior, and the neural mechanisms that organize and activate the speech/motor system are not clearly understood. (The speech motor system refers to the coordination of respiratory, phonatory, resonatory, and articulatory mechanisms involved in the production of speech [Mysack, 1976].) Mental handicap, unless it is severe, does not explain failure to develop speech. It is important that teachers do not ascribe failure to learn speech to mental handicap. Sighted mentally handicapped children do develop speech, and several studies in recent years have demonstrated that even severely retarded children can be taught to speak.

The services of a speech pathologist are valuable in the assessment of speech development. They are trained to use standardized formal and informal measures of speech development; they provide age norms for vocabulary and grammatic development. Most valuable for the "difficult to assess" blind multiply handicapped child is a thorough analysis of sequence and types of articulatory difficulties a child may have. Ease of articulation of sounds is essential to speech development, and it is important to know what types of sounds the child is already able to produce. The speech pathologist is also able to examine the breathing mechanism in relation to speech and to offer the teacher valuable information and insight into the child's capabilities for speech. This is particularly important for those children who present motor disabilities in addition to blindness.

Communicative competence can be built on an alternate method of communication for those children who do not speak. Because the ability to communicate is so essential to psychological development, a visual mode of signs (hand signs, Blisssymbolics, simple pictures) or a tactual mode of hand signs may need to be used to establish communication in some children. Even when it is believed that speech development is unlikely, the teacher should continue speaking to the child in conjunction with other modes of communication. There is some evidence that visual modes of communication are more easily acquired by multiply handicapped children than auditory modes. This is particularly true of those children with good near vision.

Janice was 9 years old and extremely frustrated and anxious. Her behavior was disturbing in the classroom and at home. Her mother remarked to the teacher that one thing Janice did enjoy doing was tearing supermarket advertisements out of the newspaper. Janice was tested on a series of visual perceptual tasks and was able to discriminate, recognize, and match simple pictures with some ease, despite her congenital cataracts. Simple signs were made for Janice by pasting clear pictures on plastic chips. Janice was taught to give her teacher a plastic chip to express her choice of activity (or a need like going to the bathroom). Not only did Janice's behavior swiftly improve, but she began to participate actively in classroom activities.

Marie has a well-established response. She is always eager to participate in school activities. She is both severely physically disabled and congenitally blind. Marie responds appropriately to questions and commands, but is unable to articulate words. She tries to speak, but her speech is not intelligible. An

Mental handicap does not explain failure to develop speech.

The ability to communicate is essential to psychological development.

adapted form of Blisssymbolics is being tried to enable Marie to express herself and avoid the frustration that not being able to make herself understood must cause. Since Marie has been using these Bliss symbols, her speech has become more clear. It is not unusual to find improvement in clarity of speech after the pressure on speech has been relieved.

Vocabulary Acquisition

In order to communicate effectively in society, a child must acquire both a vocabulary and a grammar (the system by which words are organized in order to convey meaning). The sequence of language acquisition observed in young children is an excellent guide to the development of a language system in the handicapped child.

Language begins with the child's ability to listen and to extract meaning from the sounds he or she hears. Listening involves hearing, attending, discriminating, understanding, and remembering. Before a child is ready to talk, he or she must know how to listen. Music and musical toys, simple rhymes, action games, dance, and many other activities will help to develop listening skills. *Listening is learned behavior.*

Variety of experience in the social and physical world underlies learning vocabulary. Words are not learned in isolation. They are acquired in association with experience. Words derive meaning from context and experience. The very first words children express are comments derived from social context and experience. "Bye-bye," "Daddy," and "car" are meaningful statements which refer to the actions of people and/or objects as well as to the people and/or objects themselves.

Sensory experiences which lead to the child's ability to utilize sensory information (auditory, visual, tactile, and kinesthetic) are an important part of a communication curriculum because they build the perceptual basis of word meaning. If sensory information is not interpreted, the child is not able to build a sensible interpretation of a sensory event. Blind multiply handicapped children need a variety of sensory experiences to develop a recognition and understanding of sensory information. These are the building blocks of concept development.

Exploratory and manipulative play has an important role in helping children to learn about objects and events. Children must have experience in handling, manipulating and exploring objects to develop skills with which to explore the environment. Reach and grasp, finger and hand development must all be considered. Children who lack movement may need the help of mechanical and electronic means whereby they can learn by their own efforts. If the services of physical and occupational therapists are available, they will offer valuable assistance in developing hand skills, as well as body coordination and other physical skills. It is important that the child be physically comfortable in the teaching situation. Physically disabled blind children often have difficulty in posture control.

Eddy speaks in sentences; he can ask for what he wants, and he enjoys talking to people. He is congenitally blind and has a severe form of cerebral palsy. Confined to a wheelchair, Eddy is only able to hold the objects that are placed in his hands, and he isn't able to retrieve the objects that fall so easily from his grasp. In order for Eddy to learn about the world of objects, his hands need to be guided. Eddy is learning about such concepts as "up," "down," "in," and "out" by working with his teacher, who is demonstrating these concepts to Eddy with a wide variety of toys and objects.

A variety of objects and situations is important so that children can learn to transfer their knowledge of one situation to another. Substantive words like nouns and verbs need to be taught before attributive words such as adjectives and pronouns.

A child may be considered to have acquired a functional vocabulary if he can

Language begins with the ability to listen and to extract meaning from the sounds.

Children must have experience in handling, manipulating, and exploring objects to develop skills with which to explore the environment.

24

consistently associate names with their referents, consistently name familiar persons and objects, and understand 20 to 40 words.

Acquisition of Grammar

Whereas the two-year-old child uses very simple sentences consisting of single nouns and verbs, the slightly older child explands these constitutents. The single noun gives way to noun phrases serving the same grammatical roles but expressing much richer meanings. (deVilliers & deVilliers,1978, p. 95)

The sequence of grammar acquisition described by researchers in the child language acquisition field begins with the use of one-word comments. These single-word comments are sentences. They derive much of their meaning from the context in which they are used, and therefore they are meaningful only to those who are sensitive to those contextual clues. Progress in communication competence is highly dependent on the learning of the grammatical relationships between words. The specific grammatical forms of all human languages are based upon the underlying meaning they convey. The way in which children begin to combine words into phrases and then into complete, well-developed sentences is both orderly and systematic.

The meaning (semantics) of utterances is conveyed both by the words of the utterance and the order in which the words are arranged. Meaning is the essence of language. According to deVilliers & deVilliers (1978) the earliest semantic relations expressed are these:

1. Agent and action: boy cries, Mommy goes.
2. Action and object: see sock, want more.
3. Agent and object: Mommy sandwich (Mommy is eating a sandwich).
4. Negation: no wash (I will not wash).
5. Action and locative: sit chair (Sit in the chair).
6. Entity and locative: cup shelf (The cup is on the shelf).
7. Possessor and possessed: Mommy hat (Mommy's hat).
8. Entity and attribute: ball red (The ball is red).
9. Demonstrative and entity: "there" car, "here" ball, "this" cat, "that" man.

Grammar acquisition involves learning how to order words within an utterance and to use parts of speech. The use of words such as articles, adjectives, adverbs, pronouns, prepositions, and auxiliary verbs is developed during the early stages of phrase development. [This description of grammar acquisition is necessarily sketchy. The reader is referred to Bloom (1970), Brown (1973), Dale (1973), and deVilliers and deVilliers (1978).]

The movement toward fully developed adult speech may be slow in some children, and perhaps never fully attained. Ample time must be allowed for each stage of the acquisition process, and many opportunities must be provided for children to talk. Certainly if speech is to be generalized, children must be encouraged to use speech in every situation where speech is normally required.

Suggestions for Helping Children Learn to Talk

1. Children need to hear language and have their attention drawn to speech. Teachers need to be good speech models, speaking slowly and animatedly.
2. Speech and language learning should be fun and rewarding for the child.
3. Communication activities should be meaningful.
4. Children need a variety of listening experiences.
5. Others should be discouraged from talking for the child.
6. Activities that require a need to talk are important.
7. Games of all types and descriptions should be used. Games can be made of most language activities such as naming and asking questions.
8. Story telling, which includes reading aloud, is important.
9. Teachers should accompany their activities with talk: For example, "Now I will put the spoon on the table."

Grammar acquisition begins with one-word comments.

Children must be encouraged to use speech in every situation in which it is normally required.

Be consistent. Use the same words for the same objects and actions.

10. Teachers should be consistent, using the same words for the same objects and actions.
11. Teachers should establish realistic short term goals.
12. Teachers should chart progress daily.

DIALOGUE AND CONVERSATIONS

At the origin of dialogue as such there is the need to associate the partner with something, to make him participate in his own mental state, if only through the transmission of information (Slama-Cazacu, 1977, p. 90)

The child learns most of what he knows about the rules of conversing not from explicit instruction but through first-hand experience of interacting with others in a variety of situations. (Garvey, 1977, p. 72)

Dialogue is the act of conversing; it is social behavior and requires that children learn to recognize the need for response and take their turns in speaking. To be conversationalists, children must recognize the needs of listeners. They must possess social awareness as well as a mastery of grammar and vocabulary. They need to know that different listeners have different needs for information (e.g., strangers need more explicit information than family members). They must finally recognize the appropriateness of speech in different situations (deVilliers & deVilliers, 1978).

Dialogue is important to the development of the ability to adapt to a social situation; it is the connection and cooperation that occurs between speakers. Shared experiences, games, and symbolic (make-believe) play are excellent means of developing dialogue.

Because of the intricate relationship between language and social behavior, play is a powerful tool of childhood and develops children's capacities to communicate with the world. In the course of play, children learn to abstract from their experience and to comprehend events in relation to the important people in their lives.

The Role of Play

Make-believe helps to develop self-confidence, motivation, and curiosity.

Feitelson and Ross (1973) contend that make-believe play helps to develop attitudes such as self-confidence, motivation and curiosity. Make-believe play is by nature social, even when there is only one actor. Children, when simply imitating the actions of adults, imitate those who are significant to them and thereby validate themselves in relation to these people.

Play, like language, follows a systematic sequence in its development. Symbolic play is the acting out of an idea. As the ideas become more social, so does the play. Make-believe emerges from familiar activities and expresses children's understanding of what they know.

It is important to understand the stages children go through in learning to pretend, because these stages provide a guide for assessing the level of play. This is especially necessary with multiply handicapped children when their age is not a reliable guide to their abilities.

At first children "pretend" an action, such as drinking from a pretend cup. The main feature of this stage is that a single child is the main actor of his or her play and plays with one object at a time. In the next stage, the child endows an object, such as a doll, with the ability to act and react. They may pretend to feed the doll or put it to sleep. In the next stage, children begin to link pretend actions into a sequence, such as putting a pillow on a bed, placing the doll on the bed, and covering it with a blanket.

As children develop speech, they regulate their play with conversation; they use language to establish the theme of make-believe.

As children develop speech, they regulate their play more and more with conversation: "You be the daddy, and I'll be the mommy." They also use language to establish the theme of their make-believe: "Let's pretend the clown is sleeping and you want to wake him up." Even children whose speech is limited to one- and two-word phrases are able to engage in dialogue and assume a drama-

26

tic role in the play sequence. Speech manages the complex activities of make-believe and is a component in the expressive behavior of pretending (Garvey, 1977, p. 76).

Children assume roles in play and express their role in their speech. They assume the role of "mommy," "daddy," or "baby" and learn to characterize these roles. The baby may speak in a high, whiny voice. The daddy may be gruff or bossy. As children assume their roles, they are learning a great deal about role-play and dialogue. The seemingly unrelated and purposeless speech of many blind multiply handicapped children can be brought under control in relation to planned sequences of social interaction.

In addition to developing communicative competence, thematic or symbolic play develops imagination, intensifies interest and curiosity, increases a child's repertoire of behavior, and provides a source of mutual enjoyment between the child and another child or adult.

It should be emphasized here that play is learned behavior. The observation that blind multiply handicapped children do not play spontaneously should not lead to the conclusion that they cannot play. Teachers model play behavior by playing with the children, establishing play themes, and engaging the child in play.

When the child is directed toward others and understands that he is getting a positive response, communication begins and the child begins to feel able to interact.

The blind multiply handicapped child who can ask and answer questions, express feelings, be interested in the feelings of others, and use language to describe and interpret the events of his or her life is truly ready to cope in real and meaningful ways with the demands of society. This is communicative competence.

AN AFTERWORD

This chapter is primarily concerned with the elements of a communication curriculum, but it must be noted that language is the product of all aspects of development, social, physical, sensory, and neurological. Social activities and experiences have been stressed because of their immediate relation to communicative behavior,. There is, however, an important cognitive underlay to language development.

An educational program for blind multiply handicapped children should appeal to the entire child, and no aspect of his development should be ignored.

The teacher of blind multiply handicapped children is a maestro—a keen observer and a creative artist who can fashion learning out of every bit of experience. For many children, learning comes slowly and then speeds up; for others, it takes many repetitions before change is noted. Each child is different, but each can learn if the educational experience is meaningful and motivating.

Parents are the teacher's natural partners, and have a central role in implementing a communication curriculum. Not only can newly acquired communicative behavior be generalized in the home, where the child's most important personal interactions are taking place; but, by communicating in the home, the child is truly able to experience the effectiveness of his or her efforts.

Play is learned behavior. The observation that blind multiply handicapped children do not play spontaneously should not lead to the conclusion that they cannot play.

Parents are the teacher's natural partners. The home is where the child's most important personal interactions take place.

References

Bloom, L. M. *Language development: Form and function in emerging grammars.* Cambridge, Mass.: MIT Press, 1970.

Brown, R. *A first language: The early stages.* Cambridge, Mass.: Harvard University Press, 1973.

Dale, P. *Language development: Structure and function.* New York: Holt, Rinehart, & Winston, 1973.

de Villiers, P. A., & deVilliers, J. G. *Language acquisition.* Cambridge, Mass.: Harvard University Press, 1978.

Frampton, M. E., Kerney, E., & Schattner, R. *Forgotten children: A program for the multihandicapped.* Boston: Porter Sargent, 1969.

Feitelson, D., & Ross, G. S. The neglected factor—Play. *Human Development,* 1973, 16: 202–223.

Garvey, C. *Play.* Cambridge, Mass.: Harvard University Press, 1977.

Miller, G. A. Psychology and communication. In Miller, G. A. (Ed.) *Communication, language, and meaning: Psychological perspectives.* New York: Basic Books, 1971.

Mysack, E. D. *Pathologies of speech systems.* Baltimore, Md.: Williams and Wikins, 1976.

Slama-Cazacu, T. *Dialogue in children.* The Hague: Mouton Publishers, 1977.

Southwell, F. J. The education of young deaf-blind rubella children. In *Deaf-blind children and their education: Proceedings of the International Conference on Education of Deaf-blind children*, St. Michielsgestel, The Netherlands, August 25-29, 1968. The Netherlands: Rotterdam University Press, 1971.

Weiss, C. E., and Lillywhite, H. S. *Communicative disorders: A handbook for prevention and early intervention.* St. Louis, Mo.: C. V. Mosby, 1976.

Yoder, D. E., & Reichle, J. E. Some current perspectives on teaching communication functions to mentally retarded children. In Mittler, P. (Ed.) *Research to practice in mental retardation* (Vol. 2), *Education and training.* Baltimore: University Park Press, 1977.

Instructional Needs of Students with Low Vision

Sally S. Mangold, Ph.D.
Linda Joseph Roessing, M.A.

CHAPTER 5

CLASSROOM ADAPTATIONS FOR THE STUDENT WITH LOW VISION

The student with low vision must master a complex array of skills in order to adapt adequately to visual demands in the educational environment. Eventual mastery of basic skills may require years of practice. Parents and teachers must continue to provide creative and meaningful visual stimulation in order to foster the most important skill—persistence.

In normally sighted students, vision is not static. Fatigue, medications, or stress can alter visual abilities. Students with low vision may have additional visual fluctuations, such as floaters in the visual field, light sensitivities, eye fatigue, degenerative conditions, and so forth.

Given this visual complexity, it is essential that the student understand his or her functional vision and the best techniques for sight utilization. From this understanding will spring a myriad of educational decisions:

1. Classroom modifications for distance—For example, making use of the black board easier.
2. Optimum conditions for near point work—For example, controlling lighting and height of work surfaces.
3. Efficacy and use of prescribed aids most appropriate for reading.
4. Orientation and mobility techniques in familiar and unfamiliar surroundings.

Assessment of the student's functional vision is the initial step in teaching the student how, when, and under what conditions such vision can be used efficiently. The Functional Vision Checklists compiled by Linda Roessing (see Chapter 7) are one such tool for appraisal.

Use of the Functional Vision Checklists is predicated on several assumptions. First, it is assumed that the assessor will have analyzed all physical data on the eye report obtained from the eye care specialist. A low vision eye examination is crucial to any evaluation. Secondly, the information collected on the Summary Sheet should be presented to each student in a vocabulary appropriate for his or her level of understanding. From this data, information in the area of low vision is formulated for the student. For example, some students with a central field defect benefit from eccentric viewing techniques; students with nystagmus need to discover their best posture for reading. Youngsters with tunnel vision will learn head-turning rather than eye movement techniques for reading to maximize the field of vision.

Teachers and parents can never know what children *see*—only how they function. Collecting functional data over a period of years serves two important purposes. It helps students reach maturity with objective knowledge about their visual abilities and disabilities. In addition, it provides a continuous record of changes in their visual status.

Always evaluate vision in familiar and unfamiliar surroundings. It is much easier to move smoothly through a familiar environment where you can antici-

Dr. Mangold is Associate Professor in Special Education at San Francisco State University. Prior to this, she was a resource teacher for visually handicapped students in a public school setting for 15 years. Ms. Roessing is the principal at the California School for the Blind, Fremont, California and Assistant Professor, San Francisco State University.

pate the location of permanent objects. Students with low vision often appear to see more than they do when they are observed in areas which are familiar to them. For example, a six-year-old was observed lifting her foot as though she were ascending stairs whenever she encountered dark shadows in an unfamiliar zoo. She was never observed making this kind of error on the playground or in other familiar areas.

It is essential to indicate on the Functional Vision Checklists only what you actually know. Do not make assumptions about a student's visual functioning. For example, you may observe a low vision student walking around a sleeping dog on the sidewalk. He or she may not know if it was a hole, a dark box, or anything else which might obstruct a walkway. Ask probing questions such as "What did you think that was when you walked around it?" From the student's answer, you gain clues as to what the student was perceiving. This kind of information is invaluable when trying to help the student understand why he performs more easily and accurately in some situations than in others. Teaching each student to anticipate visual inaccuracies that may affect functioning strengthens a student's confidence when entering new situations.

Functional assessments of reading skills is of prime importance. The Functional Vision Checklist for Academics evaluates tracking and directional abilities, such as the skill to read from the end of one line to the beginning of the next. Yet, in the classroom, when a new skill is being introduced and a student is making errors, it is sometimes difficult to know if it is a learning error or a lack of accurate visual information. The best analysis is to isolate those variables that involve only vision. For instance, the ability to obtain information from pictures is extremely important. First- and second-grade phonetic books include both pictures and words. The teacher must know if the student can *interpret* the pictures correctly before applying any academic skill.

Ask the student about a number of different pictures. If there is a picture of a sun, and underneath the choices are "sun, fun, bun," the student is asked to circle the word that tells what is in the picture. If the student calls the picture "cookie" because he interprets the picture incorrectly, he cannot perform that kind of visual academic task correctly. If the same student seems to be able to read the words easily but unable to interpret the pictures accurately, you may want to combine tape recordings and written text in order to provide the information needed in the picture.

An important variable which drastically affects a student's performance is size of print. If a reading error is continually a result of print that is too small or too poorly printed, then the errors will most often be consistent with letters and numerals having similar configurations. This would include confusing the letters *a, e,* and *o* and *f,* and *t,* as well as numerals which are similar, like *3* and *8.*

In order to evaluate the effects of various print sizes, exaggerate the print size. Begin with an exaggerated one inch print size. Use single letters in exercises requiring identification of isolated letter sounds. Can the student read correctly when the letter is very large, but not able to find the same letter when it is written in a line of six letters? Errors of this type may indicate that the print in the books is too small.

A consistent misreading of a word regardless of size of print indicates that the student has not yet learned that word. No determination as to proper type size can be made unless the student has learned the vocabulary being used for visual assessment.

Fatigue is another visual variable that may indicate a need for large print materials. The student's performance must be evaluated throughout the day to see if any fatigue pattern emerges. A bookstand, dark pencil, buff-colored paper, or additional illumination may all be of use to some students who tire easily. Providing large type materials for afternoon classes is a possible solution for those students who become tired when asked to use regular print all day. Maybe

Students with low vision often appear to see more than they do when they are observed in areas familiar to them.

It is sometimes difficult to distinguish between a learning error and lack of accurate visual information.

such students tire during Social Studies when they are asked to change focus constantly from maps, to texts, to glossaries, to film strips.

Just as students may need adapted materials for specific times of day, due to fatigue, they may need special materials for specific subject matter. This requires careful evaluation. For example, students with a field loss may be able to read regular print but may have difficulty reading charts, graphs, and maps. As such students grow and master reading skills, many will select smaller print in the upper grades than they did in the primary grades. Good students will be able to generalize word configuration and patterns of words as they become more sophisticated learners. Beware of generalizing this changing ability to other subjects. A successful reduction in the size of print required may not indicate that pictoral or mathematical presentations should also be reduced in size.

As a footnote to the student's growing ability to use word shapes as reading cues, teachers should always avoid printing words all in capital letters; they are difficult to read. Flash cards and charts which are produced with felt-tipped pens and the large type materials should always present words in standard configuration by using lower-case and upper-case letters.

Functional Vision Checklists and Reading Assessment should report only *observed* student behavior. It is easy to be misled by a student's size and age. We sometimes assume that basic learning has taken place when indeed it has not.

A case in point was a bright 12-year-old boy who was suddenly found to have subnormal vision and was recommended for help from a special teacher. He would not read, write, or attempt any skill other than speaking. After several weeks of building a trusting relationship, the special teacher was able to have the student read a first-grade book. He was unable to read 12 of the 15 vocabulary words. The teacher then asked the boy to say the first letter in each word in the sentence "The cat can run fast." The boy responded, "*E, t, n, n, t.*" He probably didn't see the chalkboard well enough in the first grade to learn where the first letter of a word may be found. Never assume that students have mastered the basics of reading and writing.

A critical educational issue that stems from the Functional Vision Checklists is selection of the appropriate reading media. The criteria for selecting a primary reading medium are simple: Is the student keeping up with the class both in quantity and quality? Is the student's performance at a level commensurate with his or her ability and interests?

There are four considerations in choosing the primary reading medium: working distance from the page, reading speed, visual fatigue, and the amount of effort that must go into task completion.

Selecting the optimum working distance includes evaluation of both reading and writing. Some students require a high degree of magnification in order to read a text. The more magnification required, the closer to the reading material the magnifier must be held. Does the amount of magnification required for a particular student allow him or her enough distance between the lens and the working surface to write easily with a pen or pencil? A distance of at least four inches from the writing surface to the lens is desirable if the student is going to maintain visual focus while writing for an extended period. Students who learn to write with a pen or pencil, but always have a sighted person read back their notes because they cannot read them themselves, will never be independent.

The student with low vision must continually show growth in vocabulary recognition, speed, and comprehension skills if inkprint is to be the primary reading medium. Students who can only read 30 or 40 words a minute with extremely powerful magnification devices will have a difficult time going on to higher levels of academic achievement or entering the job market. Errors that are typical of first- and second-graders, such as confusing small letters, should disappear in the upper grades. Errors in reading made at different grade levels should be typical of all students at that level. If students are spending too much energy just

Students may need adapted materials, such as large print, when they are experiencing visual fatigue.

It is easy to be misled by a child's size and age: We may assume that basic learning has taken place when it has not.

to see, they will probably find it difficult to maintain a satisfactory level of academic achievement.

Frequent visual fatigue may signal a need for larger print materials or a re-evaluation of the efficacy of low vision aids. The length of time a student can use special aids or equipment can only be determined in an educational setting. Some students who perform very well during a low vision examination may tire in the classroom after several hours. Accounts of academic performance in an educational setting will be very helpful in determining the eventual primary reading medium.

Braille is just as viable a reading medium as print is. Educators and parents must believe this in order to avoid negative feelings about braille on the part of the student. It is totally impossible to predict how easy or difficult it may be for a given student to learn braille. Success in reading via braille, when no success in reading via inkprint has been experienced previously, is great motivation and a source of pleasure for the student.

The final selection of an appropriate primary reading medium rests with the student. Educators and parents must afford each student a multitude of opportunities to explore various media in a variety of settings.

Whatever the student's reading medium, care must be taken to provide all reading practice materials in whatever size print or adapted form is suitable for a particular student. Basal readers are only a portion of the reading practice provided in modern classrooms. Reading workbooks, dittos in all subject areas, bulletin board charts, experience stories, school rules, cafeteria menus, and lists of classroom monitors are only a skeleton list. Special students cannot be expected to keep up with sighted peers if special educators do not provide quantities of appropriate materials.

Low vision aids, prescribed by the eye care specialist, afford the student new and sophisticated techniques for utilizing print and exploring the environment. Chapter 8, "Orientation to Low Vision Aids," by Dennis Kelleher, outlines technical considerations and prognostic factors in using low vision aids. In the home and school, responsibility for stimulating interest in using the prescribed aids rests with teachers and parents. Materials used to stimulate this interest should be easily read and should need only short periods of attention. The most useful materials and techniques will involve high-interest recreational reading.

A carefully selected collection of menus offers practice with different sizes of print on a variety of different-colored backgrounds. Vertical columns of numbers or categories of food provides skimming practice.

Many fast-food chains post their menus at some distance from the order counter. This is a great opportunity to practice using a monocular device. Printed menus can be obtained, and perusing them will give great pleasure to students who may be getting their first opportunity to study food selection and price. Students can also compare prices of identical items found on menus from several different restaurants.

Reading fortune cookies can be lots of fun. It sometimes surprises students to discover that written matter that has been creased (often true of the slips in fortune cookies) requires a more powerful magnifier for reading, because the print that has been folded may be harder to keep in focus. The print is usually in black on white and standard configuration.

Crossword puzzle books are now available in vocabulary appropriate for grades two and up. This is a great opportunity for students to practice writing while using a low vision aid. Be certain that the light is adjusted so that students are not working in their own shadows.

Scavenger hunts require that a student who moves from one area to another will need to read the same material in different lighting situations. The folding pocket magnifiers that contain more than one lens and offer several strengths of magnification are sometimes helpful when illumination changes.

It is impossible to predict how easy or difficult it may be for a given child to learn braille.

The final selection of a primary reading medium rests with the student.

Reading fortune cookies is lots of fun.

One mother and father have reported that their child was delighted to discover the value of a monocular device when he first started his paper route. The embarrassment of using the device disappeared when he discovered that by using the monocular he could avoid getting off his bicycle and walking clear to the door of each house in order to read the number. The filling out of receipts was only done independently when he started to use his new reading glasses.

Selecting greeting cards, collecting stamps, checking bus schedules, and balancing a new bank account may bring a new dimension of independence to students who have relied upon others for so much reading during their lives. The mastery of these skills will only be accomplished over a long period of time through persistence, positive motivation, and encouragement from adults in the environment. Encouragement from adults, particularly teachers, should steadily propel students toward independence.

In the classroom, well-meaning teachers often create an environment that they feel is most likely to promote optimum performance in the student. This controlled environment should not always be available. The student must learn to manipulate his own environment. For example, occasionally turn off several lights before the student enters the room. Let him analyze what has changed and why he is having difficulty completing his work. The student should be able to manipulate such variables as lighting, reflection of working surfaces, height of work areas, color of paper, darkness of pencils, and appropriateness of various optical aids.

In order to facilitate choices, materials must be available for student experimentation, such as writing paper from the American Printing House for the Blind, different pencils and pens, visors to reduce glare, a rheostat for controlling the level of illumination, and so forth.

The teacher must respect the student's right to select what he wants to use. If the items he has selected are correct, then he will be able to keep up in quantity and quality. If he begins to fall behind, provide honest evaluation of his performance so that the need for material change is a result of an objective measure and not parent or teacher speculation.

The need for honest evaluation requires maintaining the same standards for students with low vision as for their sighted peers. This provides them with the opportunity to explore their abilities and disabilities in a realistic setting. They will have a much better chance of succeeding in the adult world if their output in school has been evaluated realistically.

Objective performance assessment should be easy because low vision students are being educated in regular classes with sighted peers. Yet many students who appear to be participating fully in regular classes are graduating from school with less than adequate literacy skills. This illustrates that the performance of young students with low vision can be deceptive, and that it is crucial for the special teacher to stay in close touch with regular classroom activities.

For example, a student may correctly complete assignments done at his desk involving picture and single-letter choices with 100% accuracy. The same student may have difficulty completing chalkboard assignments even when he sits near the board or gets up to look at the board. The understanding classroom teacher often excuses that student from those assignments because she knows she will cover that skill in seat work anyway. The demonstrations that the teacher does at the chalkboard may always be unclear to that student unless the special teacher intervenes to teach those missing concepts. The student could have reading and writing problems that may not surface for years. This was the situation with the 12-year-old boy mentioned previously who never learned where to locate the first letter of a word.

A subtle issue in evaluation involves visual ability. Always commend a student for effort, not performance, if that performance is highly dependent on visual ability. Students often know how delighted parents and teacher become when

Maintain the same standards for students with low vision as you do for their sighted peers. They will have a much better chance of succeeding in the adult world if they are evaluated realistically in school.

Commend a student for effort, not performance, if performance is highly dependent on visual ability.

33

Provide information on what the child does visually with a minimum of emotional overtones.

they can see something correctly. This also means that they know parents and teachers become disappointed when they cannot see something correctly. Students should be given factual information about what they do visually with a minimum of emotional overtones. It is all right not to be able to *see* something. Some students may lose vision at a later date, and we do not want those students to equate the quality of life with visual ability.

Assessment, optical aids, teaching curriculum, and mobility training of low vision students are becoming more sophisticated year by year. New assessment tools are being developed. A new set of guide lines for asssessing and instructing students with low vision has been developed by Dr. Natalie Barraga, Professor in Special Education at the University of Texas, Austin. Her materials may be ordered from the American Printing House for the Blind (APH) in Louisville, Kentucky.

We do not want students to equate quality of life with visual ability.

As new techniques are applied in the educational environment, students with low vision have a greater probability of mastering basic skills. It is hoped that such students may grow to be contributing members of society who achieve a quality of life commensurate with their abilities and interests.

Bibliography

Apple, L. E., & Blasch, B. B. (Eds.) *Workshop on low vision mobility: Proceedings of Veterans's Administration, Department of Medicine and Surgery.* Washington, D.C. 1975.

Barraga, N. *Visual handicaps and learning.* Belmont, Calif.: Wadsworth Publishing Co., 1976.

Benton, C. D., & Welsh, R. C. *Spectacles for aphakia.* Springfield, Ill.: Charles C Thomas, 1974.

Braley, W., Konicki, G. & Leedy, C. *Daily sensorimotor training activities.* Freeport, N.Y.: Educational Activities, 1961.

Cowen, E. L. *Adjustment to visual disability in adolescence.* New York: American Foundation for the Blind, 1961.

Faye, E. E. *The low vision patient.* New York: Grune & Stratton, 1970.

Faye, E. E., & Hood, C. *Low vision.* Springfield, Ill.: Charles C Thomas, 1975.

Friedman, G. R. Distance low vision aids for primary level school children. *The New Outlook*, 1976, 70(11), 376-379.

Gregg, J. R., & Heath, G. G. *The eye and sight.* Boston: D. C. Heath, 1964.

Jose, R., & Watson, G. Increasing reading efficiency with an optical aid/training curriculum. *Review of Optometry*, 1978.

Kennedy, W. L. R., Young, C., & Levin, M. A field expander for patients with retinitis pigmentosa: A clinical study. *American Journal of Optometry & Physiological Optics*, 1977, *54*, 744-755.

Krill, A. E. Retinis pigmentosa: A review. *Sight Saving Review*, Spring, 1972.

Kroth, R. L. *Communicating with parents of exceptional children.* Denver, Col.: Love Publishing Co. 1975.

Levin, M. *Low vision update: Proceeds of low vision seminar*, San Francisco, Calif.: San Francisco State University,1979.

Mehr, E. B., & Freid, A. N. *Low vision care.* Chicago, Il.: Professional Press, 1975.

Newman, J. D. & Duke, D. Closed-circuit television and teaching the partially sighted to read. *Optometric Journal and Review of Optometry*, 1974, *111*, pp. 36–37.

Roessing, L. J. Identification of visually impaired students in a California school district. *Journal of Visual Impairment and Blindness,* 73(12), 369-372.

Sloan, L. L. *Recommended aids for the partially sighted.* National Society for the Prevention of Blindness Inc., 1971.

Watson, G., & Jose, R. A training sequence for low vision patients. *Journal of the American Optometric Association*, 1976,*47*, 1407-1415.

| Functional Vision: Criterion-Referenced Checklists

Linda Joseph Roessing, M.A. | CHAPTER 6 |

WHAT IS FUNCTIONAL VISION

A child has two levels of vision. One is physical, and consists of measures of acuity and field and the influence of specific disease, injury, heredity, or prenatal factors on the ocular condition. The other level is functional: the degree to which the child utilizes residual vision to operate within the environment.

The extent to which vision is utilized is as individual as a fingerprint and cannot be predicted as a function of the degree of physical vision. That is, some children with very low vision have learned to use every shred of physical vision to maximize their visual efficiency. Other children, who have good acuities and intact fields, have never mastered the learned behavior of using the eyes to maximum effectiveness and are thus visually inefficient.

The evaluation of functional vision is not related to physical measures of vision. Any degree of vision can be assessed. Children who have the acuity to see hand movements, for example, would be assessed functionally in terms of their use of shapes, colors, contrast, and light cues. This information will have a number of educational implications—for indoor and outdoor mobility, social interactions, living skills, and so forth.

Functional vision is a complex array of factors, the most important of which is the child's motivation. The efficient child is one who knows those conditions that enhance visual functioning. This knowledge will involve field considerations: the best place to sit in the classroom for monocular viewing, the preferred field of view, the best gaze posture for nystagmus, the best compensation for field loss in mobility, and the appropriate use of eccentric viewing techniques. For near vision, the child will know his or her optimum print size for specific materials, best lighting, particular format requirements, tracking skills in reading, necessary time adjustments, best use of optical aids, and so forth. For far vision, the child will utilize information on best seating for a clear view of the blackboard or other materials used at a distance, best use of projection devices such as overhead projectors or films, best use of telescopic aids, and so on.

This kind of visual efficiency is not innate—it is learned. And it is relearned as physical factors change because of progressive or degenerative conditions or because of individual fluctuations at any time.

What can be learned can be taught. Before the teacher of the visually handicapped can intervene to help children utilize techniques and materials that will enhance efficiency, he or she must be able to analyze how such children use their functional vision.

DEVELOPMENT AND TESTING OF CHECKLISTS

A project to formalize criterion-referenced checklists in functional vision grew out of a series of meetings at San Francisco State University by a group of interested professionals that dubbed itself the "Northern California Ad Hoc Committee on Assessment."

Ms. Roessing is the principal at the California School for the Blind, Fremont, California and Assistant Professor, San Francisco State University.

Out of these meetings, in October and December 1977 and February 1978, came a document that was a compilation of checklists submitted by teachers and other workers in the field of the visually handicapped.

This first draft incorporated extensive information on visual functioning in the five IEP (Individualized Education Plan) areas—Academic, Psychomotor, Social, Vocational, and Living Skills—from programs in California, Texas, Illinois, Massachusetts, and other states. A Functional Vision Checklist was prepared in each IEP area—that is, a Functional Vision Checklist in Academics, Functional Vision Checklist in Living Skills, and so on.

It was at once obvious that the document, which ran to 40 pages, needed a summary sheet. This condensation of information gathered from checklists defines the child's visual functioning in terms of the school setting (educational implications of the eye condition, classroom modifications, necessary aids, necessary equipment adaptations, and travel skills).

The checklists needed to be field-tested with visually handicapped students. From field testing, a logical priority and sequence of items emerged; redundancies and extraneous details were removed.

Field testing began in September 1978 with one class of visually handicapped students in the Fremont Unified School District, Fremont, California. The nine students ranged in age from 14 to 18 years. Their visual abilities varied widely. One child used braille and closed-circuit television for short periods of time, and was most efficient in her use of residual vision. Another child had excellent acuities at near and far vision (20/60 OU) but was so visually inefficient that he had difficulty utilizing regular print. Other students fell between these extremes, and three were multiply handicapped due to perceptual or orthopedic conditions.

From December 1978 through April 1980, the Functional Vision Assessment was used with an additional 33 children, bringing the field test group to 42 students. This group ranged in age from four to 20 years old with visual abilities on a continuum from light perception to high partially sighted. Of this group, 20 percent had other handicapping conditions in addition to visual deficit.

Priorities indicated by the testing were revision of the Functional Vision Checklist in Academics and development of a summary sheet. The Academics section was substantially rewritten and condensed.

Checklist items were grouped, prioritized, and sequenced on the basis of two considerations. First, we identified the most important items from the standpoint of functional vision, based on the needs and performances of students. Then we determined how to sequence the items so that areas of evaluation would fall naturally within the teaching setting.

The Functional Vision Checklist in Academics and the Functional Vision Summary Sheet are included in this chapter. Checklists in the areas of Vocational Skills and Social Skills have not been field-tested. Portions of other checklists have been tested, or newly developed, in the following areas:

Psychomotor Skills
The Low Vision Evaluation for Mobility Referral, newly developed by Joanne Low (Orientation and Mobility Instructor, Fremont), enables the teacher of the visually handicapped to determine whether a low vision person should be referred for training in orientation and mobility.

The Physical Education Information Sheet establishes criteria for evaluating the efficacy of a child's participation in a regular physical education program.

Living Skills
The Orientation to Cooking Class and Equipment Adaptations allows the teacher to examine location of equipment and saftey factors in the cooking class, equipment adaptations, and media for testing as well as to make recommendations to regular classroom teachers.

The Orientation to the Cafeteria or Restaurant provides checklist criteria for determining if the child can operate independently at lunchtime.

Much research and testing need to be completed in the area of Functional Vision, in order to develop evaluative materials that are child-based and usable by the teacher of the visually handicapped.

Visual efficiency is learned, not innate; what can be learned can be taught. Once we have evaluative tools that will sketch a profile of the child's functional vision, the next step must be development of curiculum in this essential area.

Figure 6.1. The Functional Vision Checklist Summary Sheet.

Date _____

Student _____ Age _____ Grade _____ School _____

Vision Teacher _____ Contact Phone _____ Room _____

PHYSICAL INFORMATION

Nature of eye condition (describe in simple terms) _____

_____

Educational implications of eye condition _____

_____

Glasses prescribed _____ To be worn _____

Describe prescription (bifocal, aphakic, contact lens)_____

_____

Acuity (Near Vision) _____ Field _____

Acuity (Far Vision) _____ Color vision _____

Preferred eye_____ Child is/is not binocular _____

Preferred field of view _____ Best gaze posture, if any _____

_____

Photophobia _____ Sunshade prescribed _____

CLASSROOM MODIFICATIONS: DISTANCE VISION

Child can use

Overhead projectors _____ Flipcharts _____

Filmstrips _____ Flashcards _____

Television _____ Wall clock _____

Blackboard: Child should be seated

In front row _____ Right front _____ Left front _____ Other _____

Distance aids used _____

Time adjustments (such as extra time to copy from blackboard) _____

_____

_____

_____

CLASSROOM MODIFICATIONS: NEAR TASKS

1. Reading

Optimum reading time _____

Child prefers to improve visual functioning by (finger pointing, marker, etc.) _____

_____

Child's grade level when reading print _____

Print size   Reading _____ Mathematics _____

                 Activity books _____ Ditto papers _____

                 Dictionary _____ Other _____

Adaptations of reading materials _____

_____

2. Near Vision Aids

Use of optical aids_____

Reading stand_____ Marking pen_____ Writing paper_____

Typoscope/marker _____ Ditto filters _____

Closed-circuit television (CCTV):

_____ Best magnification _____ Polarity _____ Reading distance

Special lighting required _____

Auditory (listening) program _____

Child's grade level for auditory reading _____

Type of classwork to be read by ear_____

_____

EQUIPMENT ADAPTATIONS FOR CLASSES

Will the student need special adaptations in

Cooking _____ Sewing _____ Shop _____

Physical education _____ Laboratory _____

Testing situations: Modifications required (time and materials) _____

_____

TRAVEL SKILLS

Student is oriented to _____ School _____ Bus _____ Community

Can travel independently _____

Adaptations for independent travel _____

Time adjustments for travel _____

Additional notes _____

_____

Figure 6.2. The Functional Vision Checklist—Academics.

NEAR VISION TASKS: MEDIA	Date	Yes	No	Comment
1. The child can read print:				
a. Primer or large type				
Reading Distance: Speed (wpm)				
b. Regular or 14 pt. type (fourth grade)				
Distance: Speed:				
c. Paperback books				
Distance: Speed:				
d. Newsprint				
Distance: Speed:				
e. Phone book				
Distance: Speed:				
Optical aids needed for above:				
2. The child can utilize				
a. Standard math text				
b. Standard dictionary				
c. Encyclopedia/atlas				
d. Classroom dittos				
Filters? Preferred color:				
e. Outline maps				
f. Political maps				
g. Standard music notation				

   h. Standard graph paper _____

   i. Standardized tests _____

   j. Card index in library _____

3. The child's format requirements:

   a. Preference in column size _____

   b. Spacing _____

   c. Contrast/color of paper _____

   d. Can utilize pictures _____

4. Using CCTV

   a. Optimum print size _____

   b. Optimum magnification _____

   c. Best polarity _____

   d. Reading distance _____

   e. Reading speed _____

NEAR VISION: READING

1. Physical Factors

   When reading, does the child   Date   Yes   No   Comment

   a. Exhibit unusual posture? _____

   b. Squint, close or cover one eye? _____

   c. Use a head tilt favoring one eye? _____

   d. Have a best field of view? _____

   e. Move eye(s) to objects to focus? _____

   f. Move objects to eye(s) to focus? _____

   g. Have improved functioning using reading stand? _____

   h. Rub eyes frequently? _____

   i. Report eye fatigue? _____

   j. Complain of blurred or double vision? _____

   k. Evidence unusual restlessness, nervousness, or irritability? _____

   l. Report headache, nausea, or dizziness? _____

2. Tracking Skills

   When reading orally, does the child

   a. Hold book appropriately to maximize field? _____

   b. Know how to turn pages? _____

   c. Understand page numbering? _____

   d. Know where to begin reading on a page? _____

   e. Track from word to word? _____

   f. Track with:

      i. head? _____

      ii. finger? _____

      iii. one eye? _____

      iv. both eyes? _____

   g. Frequently lose his place within a line of print? _____

   h. Have difficulties reading from the end of one line to the beginning of the next? _____

   i. Frequently omit small words ("a," "to," "for") —omit in the same general gaze? _____

   j. Skip lines of print? _____

   k. Misalign digits in number columns? _____

l. Mispronounce similar words?

_____

m. Evidence reduced comprehension as
   reading continues?

_____

n. Read at average speed for grade level?

_____

o. Use typoscopes or other book markers?

_____

3. Lighting

Does the child

a. Need extra illumination for near tasks?

_____

b. Find a reading lamp useful?

_____

c. Prefer illumination:

   i. high?

_____

   ii. medium?

_____

   iii. low?

_____

d. Squint or shade eyes to avoid light?

_____

e. Evidence difficulty with glare on work surfaces?

_____

f. Evidence photophobia?

_____

g. Need special classroom seating for glare/
   illumination factors?

_____

NEAR VISION: HANDWRITING

Does the child

a. Exhibit unusual posture for writing?

_____

b. Need a special writing tool (pen or marker)?

_____

c. Need special writing paper (APH) to see the lines?

_____

d. Read handwriting:

   i. manuscript?

_____

   ii. cursive?

_____

e. Exhibit difficulty copying from a text?

_____

f. Skip letters, words when copying?

_____

g. Need extra time to copy or complete work books?

_____

DISTANCE VISION: CLASSROOM TASKS

Does the child

a. Use a telescopic aid?

_____

b. Need special seating for refractive reasons
   (nearsightedness, etc.)

_____

c. Need special seating for field considerations
   (eccentric viewing, scotoma, etc.)

_____

d. Read a chalkboard from:

   i. 5 feet?

_____

   ii. over 5 feet? Distance:

_____

e. See projected images:

   i. overhead projector?

_____

   ii. motion pictures?

_____

   iii. filmstrips?

_____

f. Watch television? Distance:

_____

g. Utilize:

   i. flashcards? Distance:

_____

   ii. flipcharts? Distance:

_____

h. Need extra time for copying from a blackboard?

_____

Figure 6.3 The Low Vision Evaluation for Mobility Referral

Attach information such as eye report or summary sheet with pertinent data on acuity, field, scotopic vision.

	Date	Yes	No	Unknown

Does the student

1. Know right and left? _____
2. Have balance problems (unsteady gait)? _____
3. Have coordination problems? _____
4. Do any moving of head or eyes to aid in scanning? _____
5. Use his or her vision efficiently at night? _____
6. Move around comfortably indoors? _____
7. Display difficulty when traveling either to or from
   classes, office, restroom, library, etc. _____
8. Have occasion to confront stairs frequently? _____
   Use stairs going both up and down safely? _____
9. Play outdoors? _____
10. Ride a bike? _____
11. Get on and off school bus alone? _____
12. See and use crosswalk lines? _____
13. Distinguish real objects from shadows cast on sidewalk? _____
14. See street signs? _____
15. Use his or her vision sufficiently to tell the color
    and position of a traffic signal? _____
16. Know of traffic signs? _____
17. Cross streets alone? _____
18. Watch for cars before crossing? _____
19. Listen for cars before crossing? _____
20. Find his or her own way home from four blocks away? _____
21. Go to the store alone? _____
22. Remain oriented by using large landmarks while in
    moving vehicle? _____
23. Appear to be comfortable moving around in
    unfamiliar place? _____
24. Know of options for mobility (i.e., cab, bus, car,
    dial-a-ride, subway)? _____
25. Use public transportation alone? _____
26. Know how to use a map? _____
27. Visit friends or neighbors alone? _____
28. Know his or her own address and phone number? _____
29. Know how to use a telephone independently
    (both dial and push-button) _____
30. Have any regular responsibilities at home
    (cooking, laundry, washing dishes, etc.)? _____
31. Have any limiting factors at home that would deny
    the student any chances for independent travel? _____

Additional comments: _____

_____

_____

_____

*Prepared by Joanne Low, Orientation and Mobility Consultant, Fremont Unified School District, Fremont, California.

Figure 6.4 The Functional Vision Checklist—Physical Education Information Sheet.

	Date	Yes	No	Comment

1. Distance Vision (For items a–e, specify size of object)

   The child can

   a. Locate and describe *stationary* objects at
      a distance of _____

   b. Locate and describe *moving* objects at
      a distance of _____

   c. Detect a ball in the air at a distance of _____

   d. Visually follow the path of a moving object
      on the floor at a distance of _____

   e. Imitate the pose or gesture of a teacher
      at a distance of _____

   f. Utilize a telescopic aid _____

2. Other Visual Factors

   The child

   a. Has some degree of photophobia _____

   b. Should utilize some type of sunshade, visor,
      or sunglasses _____

   c. Should use a safety strap for glasses _____

   d. Must wear glasses for athletics _____

3. Basic Abilities

   The child can

   a. Walk with certainty _____

   b. Run with certainty _____

   c. Run on lined boundaries _____

   d. See obstructions before coming to them
      (size of obstruction?) _____

   e. Throw _____

   f. Catch _____

   g. Bounce _____

   h. Dribble _____

   i. Kick _____

   j. Climb _____

   k. Swing _____

   l. Jump rope _____

   m. Swim _____

4. Adaptations

   The child

   a. Can participate in regular physical
      education activities _____

   b. Can participate in regular physical
      education activities with the exception of
      certain games _____

   c. Can participate in contact sports _____

   d. Can participate in adapted physical education _____

   e. Has health problems other than vision that might
      affect participation in certain activities _____

Figure 6.5. The Function of Vision Checklist—Living Skills (Cooking Class and Equipment Adaptation).

	Date	Yes	No	Comment

1. Location of oven (Type of oven: gas? electric?) _____
2. Oven dial braille marked? _____
3. Location of stove. (Type of stove: gas? electric?) _____
4. Stove control (heat):
  a. Push button _____
  b. Continuous low-to-high (gas) _____
  c. Control braille marked? _____
5. Burner location _____
  a. Back burners easily reached? _____
6. Location of mixing bowls and other utensils _____
7. Measuring cups for liquids _____
  a. Appropriate? _____
  b. Can pupil see print measures? _____
8. Measuring cups for dry foodstuffs _____
  a. Nested? _____
9. Type of timer used _____
  a. Can pupil see numbers on timer? _____
10. Other adaptations needed:
  a. Label foods _____
  b. Identify ingredients _____
  c. Pour hot liquids _____
  d. Pour cold liquids _____
  e. Devise method for turning foods _____
  f. Establish system for storing foods _____
  g. Locate electrical outlets _____
  h. Protect against oven burns:
    i. supply mitts _____
    ii. pull out racks _____
11. Recommendations to teacher:
  a. Recipes
    i. Braille needed
    ii. Large print needed _____
    iii. Classroom dittos acceptable _____
    iv. Blackboard may be used; child should sit _____
  b. Extra time needed to complete assignment _____
    Description _____
    _____
  c. "Partner" needed in class _____
  d. Summary of equipment adaptations _____

_____
_____
_____
_____
_____

  e. Tests to be taken:
    i. In braille _____
    ii. In large print _____
    iii. In regular print _____
    iv. On tape _____

Figure 6.6.   The Functional Vision Checklist—Living Skills (Cafeteria or Restaurant)

The child can   Date   Yes   No   Comment

1. Find cafeteria from classroom _____
2. Find entrance; find where to line up _____
3. See menu prices, foods offered _____
4. Find tray and utensils _____
5. Go through cafeteria line _____
6. Find where to pay for lunch _____
7. Open and close own lunch box _____
8. Use thermos and replace it in lunch box _____
9. Open milk carton, unwrap straw, place straw in milk _____
10. Find a seat easily _____
11. Carry full tray to chair _____
12. Visually identify utensils placed at random _____
13. Locate food on plate _____
14. Use:
    a. napkin _____
    b. fork _____
    c. knife _____
    d. spoon _____
15. Locate objects on table _____
16. Pass food (family-style) _____
17. Serve self from bowls _____
18. Pour liquids into cups:
    a. hot _____
    b. cold _____
19. Direct order to cafeteria helper or waiter
    independently _____
20. Know where to leave tip _____

44

<table>
<tr><td>

Orientation to Low Vision Aids
Dennis K. Kelleher, Ed.D., F.A.A.O.

</td><td>

CHAPTER 7

</td></tr>
</table>

With the passage of Public Law 94-142, the 504 regulations, and numerous state mandates, many professionals are faced with a new dilemma in attempting to help visually impaired persons achieve their maximum potential. Though "mainstreaming" is a very complex issue that will not be addressed here, the legal mandate for such a concept carries with it inherent problems for integrating visually handicapped persons. As a result, many professionals working in the field have turned to low vision aids as one means of helping to integrate visually impaired individuals into society.

It has been well documented in directories of low vision services published by the American Foundation for the Blind (AFB) and the National Society for the Prevention of Blindness (NSPB) that there is a tremendous lack of comprehensive low vision services throughout the nation. Teachers, counselors, social workers, and other non-eye-care professionals have begun dispensing low vision aids to visually impaired persons out of frustration at the difficulty of obtaining appropriate low vision services for their clients and students. This is certainly not a practice most of the individuals involved feel comfortable with—and one I personally object to on the grounds that poor low vision service often damages patient motivation and is therefore worse than no low vision service at all. I can certainly understand why this practice exists and will continue until comprehensive low vision services are available to all low vision persons.

WHAT IS LOW VISION?

Low vision may be defined as insufficient vision to be able to do a desired task. Low vision cannot be corrected by ordinary glasses, nor is it just the inconvenience of low central visual acuity. The ramifications of low vision most often include problems of controlling the clarity and size of an image, as well as modifying the illumination and contrast of an enviroment. Persons with low vision, that is, individuals with some usable sight—many of whom are legally blind—far outnumber totally or functionally blind people, who have no usable vision at all. As a result of the diverse problems caused by low vision, it is most desirable to have a multidisciplinary team to help implement a rehabilitation program. The composition of the multidisciplinary team will vary from patient to patient, but the nucleus will most likely include an eye doctor, a counselor or teacher, and, it is hoped, the patient. Many low vision patients need to learn orientation and mobility techniques or to relearn print-reading techniques, and since many patients need to be reassured that using their eyes will not damage their vision or cause it to deteriorate, a teacher, counselor, psychologist, social worker, low vision technician, or other team member(s) should plan on spending substantial time in helping the low vision patient.

The eye doctor should certainly be aware of special examination techniques and have the necessary specialized equipment to asess visual performance and prescribe appropriate low vision aids. In addition to this equipment and the will-

Dr. Kelleher is the area manager of special education in Santa Barbara County, California. This chapter originally appeared in *Visual Impairment and Blindness, 73*(5), 1979.

Figure 7.1.
Non-optical aids take many forms: large print; typoscope; filters; stands; lamps; felt tip pens.

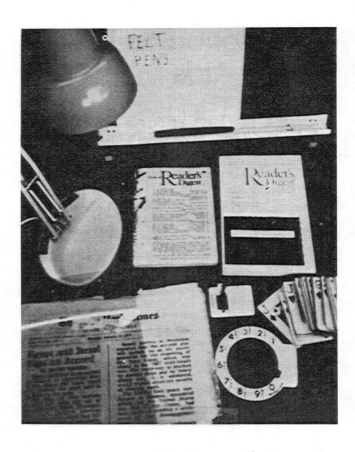

ingness to spend additional time with the patient, the doctor must have a genuine interest in the problems caused by low vision. There are many outstanding doctors who have expertise in other areas of eye care, but are not aware of the state of the art in the field of low vision. It is highly likely, therefore, that a patient would receive the most help from a low vision specialist.

Many low vision patients fear the unknown, so encouragement and explanations are extremely important in order to maintain patient motivation. Further, many patients are afraid to ask the doctor for an explanation of their eye disease in terms they can understand. To help cope with this difficulty, a useful tool has been produced by the New York Association for the Blind: *A Worker's Guide to the Characteristics of Partial Sight* (Faye, 1966), in which functional characteristics and physical needs are related to the most common eye diseases.

Acuity Scores

Patients are often unaware of what the visual acuity figures mean, especially at near point, since there are so many different systems. Visual acuity is expressed as a fraction ($VA = d/D$), the numerator d being the test distance at which a standard-size target could be seen by a normally sighted person. Therefore, 20 over 200 visual acuity means the person is able to identify, at a distance of 20 ft., letters, words, numbers, or other targets that a normally sighted person can identify at a distance of 200 ft. Near point visual acuity uses the same notation system, in that the fraction is expressed as the test distance over the distance at which a normally sighted person would recognize the object. The unit of measurement is not, however, always familiar to all observers. It is therefore recommended that a person obtain a conversion table so that in the event near visual acuity is reported in terms of Jaeger type, printer's type, metric type, or any one of the several other systems, such as newspaper-size print, want-ad-size print, or textbook-size print.

The patient should be made aware of the significance of visual acuity—what it does and does not indicate.

It does *not* indicate the following:
    the diagnosis
    the distribution of eye disease
    the adequacy of visual function
    the refractive error
    the effect of lighting and glare
    the perceptual or mental status
    the physical, social, or intellectual status
It *does* indicate these factors:
    the size of the retinal image that can be appreciated by the diseased eye
    at what distance a person can see objects of a known size
    level of vision for classification of legal blindness
    what range of magnification will be used for prescription of visual aids

THREE CATEGORIES OF LOW VISION AIDS

A low vision aid may be defined as anything that helps people use their vision more efficiently. Many persons erroneously think of low vision aids as solely optical devices. Many aids do indeed involve optics, but many other useful aids have not optics at all (see Figure 7.1). A third type of low vision aid, electronic aids, uses the principles of projection enlargement to create high mangification and allow fine control of contrast.

Optical aids are available in a wide variety of shapes and styles for both distance and near vision (a few are illustrated in Figure 7.2). Some optical aids incorporate illumination as an available feature. Optical aids include the following:

1. Hand-held magnifiers and telescopes.
2. Stand magnifiers:
    a. Fixed focus
    b. Focusable
3. Head-borne aids:
    a. Spectacles
    b. Clip-on loupes and telescopes
    c. Press-on optics
    d. Head-band style aids

A few generalizations can be made about optical aids:

1. The larger the lens, the weaker the magnification, and the further away from the lens the material can be held for image clarity.
2. The stronger the lens magnification, the less the depth of field, and the more

Figure 7.2.
Optical aids come in several forms: hand held and stand magnifiers (fixed focus and focusable); loupes; telescopic glasses (full fields and bioptic).

critical it becomes to hold the lens exactly at a given distance from the material in order to be able to see the material clearly.

3. The stronger the magnifcation, the smaller the area the user can see through the lens at any one time.

4. The closer the lens is held to the eye, the greater the area the user will see through the lens, regardless of the magnification. (Note that the distance between the lens and the material, often referred to as the "working distance," will depend upon the magnification power of the lens, but the distance from the eye to the lens may be varied according to personal preference or need.

5. Cost varies according to the strength, quality, and housing of the lens or lens-system.

6. The shape of the lens is a matter of personal preference, and different magnification ranges are available in different shapes.

7. Plastic lenses are lighter than glass, but they scratch more easily.

Non-optical low vision aids include such things as lamps, reading and typing stands, filters, pinholes, tints, large print, visors, side shields, typoscopes, dimmers, and signature and writing guides, to name some of the more common. The importance of non-optical aids is often overlooked because of their simplicity. However, there are many cases when a low vision patient can be greatly helped with a non-optical aid where an optical aid offers none.

Electronic aids include opaque and transparent projection systems (e.g., slide projectors, microfiche readers) and closed-circuit television systems. This group is usually the most elaborate and most expensive, but it also offers patients the best possibilities for achieving independence.

Which Aid is Appropriate?

One of the major problems in dealing with low vision aids is how to determine the most appropriate aid or aid combination to enable the patient to achieve his or her goal. Numerous factors that enhanced the successful use of low vision aids should be considered. Patients will *generally* respond to low vision aids if they

1. Have had their low vision condition for a long period of time and psychologically they demonstrate an acceptance of it.

2. Have a stable eye disorder which is not deteriorating.

3. Have fair-size visual fields without extensive blind spots.

4. Have some ability to move their eyes and focus on objects.

5. Have some usable central vision (they probably have it if they can recognize some color or distant detail).

6. Have a reasonable amount of manual dexterity and mental ability.

There are, nonetheless, exceptional individuals who respond well despite some of the above characteristics being absent. Conversely, some individuals whose eye disorders seems suitable for low vision aids do not respond well.

Most important of all, however, a low vision patient must have motivation—a desire and need to see better. The stronger the motivation to succeed, the more chance for acceptance and successful use of low vision aids. Obviously there are additional factors that contribute to successful use of low vision aids, and the more of these factors that are present, the better the chances are for a patient to achieve success.

The nonclinician should also be familiar with how low vision aids work so that he or she can explain the function to the patient. Though there are many kinds and styles of low vision aids, they all function in one of several ways. Low vision aids

1. Control focus or image clarity: for example, ordinary glasses which correct a refractive error.

2. Control illumination and contrast: for example, typoscope, filter lamps, dimmer.

The importance of non-optical aids is often overlooked because of their simplicity.

The stronger the motivation to succeed, the more chance for successful use of low vision aids.

48

3. Control magnification of size of the image on the retina. The size of an image on the retina may be enlarged in three different ways:
   a. Relative distance magnification involves moving closer to an object. For example, if you are 10 ft. from an object and you move to 5 ft., you will be getting 2 times magnification since you are doubling the size of the image on your retina.
   b. Relative size magnification involves making the object you want to see physically larger during the preparation stage. Large print is a good example of this type of magnification.
   c. Angular or optical magnification involves enlarging the image of an object on the retina by passing the image of the object through some light bending material such as a lens or lens-system.

Training in Aid Use

One of the primary responsibilities of the nonclinician will probably be training the low vision patient to use the aid effectively. Aids will be more acceptable for use by the patient if

1. The aid enables the patient to do what he or she wants to do.
2. The aid appears as conventional as possible so it does not attract attention.
3. The aid is easily portable so that it is readily usable wherever the patient goes.
4. The patient is motivated and feels success is possible.
5. There is extensive follow-up training to assist the patient's adjustment to using his or her aid. It must be remembered that prescription and dispensing of a low vision aid is only the beginning of the rehabilitative process and not the culmination. There is, however, some debate about how much follow-up training is required, and in England only a few hours' training is found necessary for the majority of cases.

A low vision patient must often relearn visual habits. Prescription of ordinary glasses to a non-visually-impaired patient is not the same as prescription or dispensing of low vision aids because a low vision patient must learn how to use the aid and interpret the visual stimulus which he or she receives as a result of its use. This is a tedious process and the patient must be constantly encouraged and learn to be persistent.

Orientation Phase

During the orientation phase, the characteristics of the individual aids should be discussed with the patient. These include the following:

1. *Working distance*—the distance between the aid and the material. The stronger the magnification, the shorter the working distance, and the more difficult such tasks as writing will become.
2. *Field of view*. Though the area of view through the lens will increase as the aid if held closer to the eye, different distances from the eye should be demonstrated so that the patient can determine the distance that is most comfortable for holding the aid which suits his or her needs best.
3. *Depth of focus*. For any patients with tremors or physical impairments, a strong magnification aid, which consequently has minimal depth of focus, would probably be unsuitable. One technique where an extremely strong magnification aid is prescribed might be to start with an aid of less magnification power so that the patient could become accustomed to holding an aid at a specific distance and gradually work up to a stronger power aid.
4. *Weight of the aid*. This should be discussed with the patient, especially when the aid will be used for long periods of time, such as reading a book, as opposed to short periods of time where the patient might use it merely to read a price tag. If an aid is especially heavy, and is prescribed for long periods of use, the patient may not become aware of the significance of weight during the brief trial period in the doctor's office.

Prescription of a low vision aid is only the beginning: follow-up training is a must.

The individual with low vision must learn how to use the aid and interpret the visual stimulus he or she receives as a result of its use.

5. *Style of the aid.* The patient should be made aware that a particular aid can be made available in spectacle form, hand-held form, stand-form, or clip-on form. The advantages and disadvantages of each form should be discussed with respect to the intended use of the aid by the patient.

6. *Appearance of the aid.* Though many patients may claim that the cosmetic effect of an aid is of little importance, many aids have ended up in a dresser drawer because patients were fearful of sharing their true feelings regarding the unusual appearance of an aid. Many patients do not want to appear ungrateful to the doctor if they are unwilling to accept any help which is available. One effective indication of how a patient feels about an aid is how much the patient wears the aid or uses the aid when not involved in a training or testing session.

Many an aid ends up in a dresser drawer because its owner does not like the cosmetic effect.

The instructional pattern should include the following:

1. *Routine.* The repetition of tasks will help the patient to remember instinctively such things as working distance and depth of focus.

2. *Success-oriented training.* This will develop positive attitudes towards using the low vision aid, and enhance the patient's motivation. Patients already have failed too much and are aware of what they cannot do—they now need to be shown what they can do.

3. *Short periods, gradually increasing to longer periods.* Since the tasks are usually tedious at first, and since the patient may often be using muscles that had not been used in a while, which may result in discomfort, several short practice periods should be attempted rather than one or two longer practice periods. In this way the muscles can be strengthened and a tolerance for fatigue built up.

4. *Relevance of the materials.* Obviously, if a patient cannot link the task to an end product which is valuable, the patient will not be highly motivated. For example, if a patient wants to read the Bible, do not start him or her practicing with reading the newspaper.

In summary, any aid will be rejected by the patient if, from his or her perspective, the advantages of using the aid do not outweigh the disadvantages. In conjunction with the person training them to use the low vision aid, patients will develop appropriate and effective techniques and sequences to help them achieve their personal goals. Training should be supervised activity or else it will more than likely end in failure. Though each training sequence may be slightly different, some successful training sequences are as follows:

1. For learning to use telescopes:
   a. Learn to locate stationary objects while the patient is stationary.
   b. Learn to locate moving objects while the patient is stationary.
   c. Learn to locate moving objects while the patient is moving.
   d. Develop visual discrimination, visual memory, and visual association skills so that the patient can learn to cope with specific problems, such as depth perception and telescopic parallax. One caution should be noted: Patients using full-field telescopic glasses should not attempt to walk or drive vehicles, since their peripheral or side vision is eliminated or greatly reduced, and this will create a mobility hazard for them. They should learn to locate moving objects with their telescope while they are passengers in a car, train, or bus, for example.

Training should be success-oriented: individuals are aware of what they cannot do—they need to be shown what they can do.

2. Magnifiers sequence:
   a. Locate material to be read.
   b. Adjust angle of lighting for comfort.
   c. Hold the magnifier and position the material so that a comfortable posture with minimal fatigue can be assumed.
   d. Look through the center of the lens to minimize distortion.
   e. Learn to read or scan by either moving the head or the material or a combination of both. Keeping one's place on a line may be made easier by using

a typoscope or placing the finger at the beginning of each line, for example.

3. Using closed-circuit TV magnifiers and other electronic projection magnifiers:
   a. Orient the patient to the equipment.
   b. Have the patient demonstrate using the equipment to you after you have completed orienting him to verify his understanding.
   c. Learn how to coordinate movement of the material for reading and writing.
   d. Learn how to adjust magnification, contrast, and polarity.

And then, with all three sequences, practice, practice, practice.

CONCLUSION

The foregoing outline of some of the more important factors of low vision care and use of low vision aids is certainly not exhaustive, and is oversimplified in some aspects for the sake of brevity. The intent of this overview is not to train the non-eye-specialist to dispense low vision aids, but merely to provide an orientation to some of the complexities of low vision aids, and, it is hoped, increase an awareness of some of the activities and considerations involved. Many persons with low vision instinctively find and modify objects to help them cope with the inconvenience of low vision, indicating high motivation. The most important consideration is to enhance motivation, and so increase the chances for successful visual rehabilitation, by using some of the above factors wherever possible. If possible, try to help patients avoid discouraging experiences—such as being told by a doctor, "No more can be done for you"—by attempting to direct patients to low vision clinics and specialists where comprehensive services are available.

As the number of persons with low vision increases, and an awareness of low vision technology increases, it is likely that we will solve at least some of the problems that face low vision patients and providers of low vision care services.

BRIEF LOW VISION RESOURCE LIST

Agencies

American Foundation for the Blind, 15 West 16th St., New York, N.Y. 10011
National clearinghouse for information; publishes books, monographs, bibliographies, films, low vision services directory; sells aids and appliances.

National Association for the Visually Handicapped, 305 East 24th St., 17 C, New York, N.Y. 10010
Agency dedicated to serving only low vision persons. Supplies information and referral regarding low vision services; large print materials, monographs, recreation programs.

National Society for the Prevention of Blindness, 79 Madison Ave., New York, N.Y. 10016
Distributes information on care, safety and prevention of sight loss, produces screening test, professional publications, and a low vision clinic facilities list for the United States.

New York Association for the Blind, 111 East 59th St., New York, N.Y. 10022
Information, referral on low vision services, training programs for low vision personnel, catalog of aids available to eye doctors.

Professional Organizations

American Academy of Optometry, Low Vision Diplomate Program, and Continuing Education Courses
Primarily open to eye care professionals or fellows of the Academy of Optometry who are involved in low vision in clinical settings.

American Association of Workers for the Blind, Low Vision Interest Group

Open to all AAWB members interested in the field of low vision.

Low Vision Clinical Society, recognized by the American Academy of Ophthalmology
Open primarily to eye doctors or persons who have made a significant contribution to the field of low vision.

Books

Barraga, N. *Increased visual behavior in low vision children.* New York: American Foundation for the Blind, 1964.

Faye, E. E. *A worker's guide to the characteristics of partial sight.* New York: N.Y. Association for the Blind, 1965.

Faye, E. E. *The low vision patient.* New York: Grune & Stratton, 1970.

Faye, E. E. *Clinical low vision.* Boston: Little, Brown, 1976.

Faye, E. E., & Hood, C. M. *Low vision.* Springfield, Ill.: Charles C Thomas, 1975.

Fonda, G. *Management of the patient with subnormal vision.* St. Louis: C. V. Mosby, 1970.

Mehr, E. B. & Fried, A. N. *Low vision care.* Chicago: Professional Press, 1975.

Sloan, L. L. *Reading aids for the partially sighted: A systematic classification and procedure for prescribing.* Baltimore: Williams & Wilkins, 1977.

Monographs

Feinbloom, R. E. *Techniques of examination of the partially blind patient.* New York: Designs for Vision, 1958.

Gerensky, S. M. *Advances in closed circuit TV systems for the partially sighted.* Santa Monica, Calif.: The Rand Corp., 1972.

Teaching Nonacademic Skills

Suzi Bogom-Haselkorn, M.A.
Susan Benton, M.A.

How would it be if a high school graduate could not make himself a sandwich? Or tie his own shoes, or buy his groceries, or cut his food? What about an elementary school visually handicapped (VH) child who does not know how to make friends, or spread butter on bread, or tell time? Working on these tasks can and should be part of the VH program. Skills for living independently should be the core of all VH programs. The teaching of the skill concepts can happen in conjunction with academic subjects, or it can be a separate lesson given during a specific time daily or weekly. The most important point is not the length of the lesson, but a consistent approach at concept development in each of the areas. For example, it is not our goal to make a gourmet cook, but we want all students to be familiar with the standard kitchen tools and their uses.

TEACHING NONACADEMIC SKILLS

Some of the skill concepts we teach in our classes are listed below. Accompanying most of them is an activity for the elementary-level student, and one for the junior high student. No attempt has been made to put the concepts in sequence, or to give actual lesson plans for the activities. The list is meant merely to give the teacher ideas with which to plan his or her own living skills program.

LIVING SKILLS CONCEPTS

Social Skills
Problem Solving
    Example: Give student a situation that would create a problem or ask them to choose a card from several "I am in a pickle" cards from N.I.C.E. Love Publishing Co.
    One problem made up by teacher: You have a social studies test on Friday. It is now Thursday P.M. You have left your studying until the last minute and your friend calls and asks you to come over.
    Would you:
1. Go over to your friend's and forget about the test?
2. Stay at home all night and study for an hour and sulk the rest of the night?
3. Study until you know the material and then spend some time with your friend?
4. Study for the test, postpone your time with your friend until the weekend, and relax before going to sleep?
    Ask for student's own solution without choices.
    The students should try to:
1. Define and solve problem with help. Ask student whether the problem is that (a) you should study; (b) you should see your friend; (c) you want to do both.
2. Define and solve problem by self.
3. Choose the most logical of these for his or her own situation with help or by self.
4. Carry out solution with help.
5. Carry out solution independently.

Ms. Bogom-Haselkorn and Ms. Benton are teachers for low vision and blind students in a general education setting for the San Francisco Unified School District.

Obtaining information

If students are able to:

1. Request information from peers, in everyday situations insist that students ask that party directly. Make up little interviews that they can carry out on their own time and have them bring back answers to discuss with you.

2. Request directions from strangers, during a lunch period take the student to a nearby store, and ask them to locate a certain numbered building. Have them ask for directions from people on the street.

3. Call information on the telephone, have them call up a service they may need through telephone information. Prior to this, discuss information they may wish to obtain by taking notes or keeping it in memory. If possible, use a nearby school phone.

Determine whether students are able to:

4. Repeat back information received from memory or written notes.

5. Distinguish which person to speak to regarding problems in such areas as:

    a. at school.

    b. using public transportation (e.g., routing department, bus driver, supervisor in relation to VH pass).

    c. at home. Follow up important message to be given to parent by some form of communication such as a phone call or a tear-off sheet from note sent home for reply.

    d. on the street. Practice sending student on school neighborhood errands.

ORGANIZATION

Students are able to:

1. Keep track of personal belongings related to problem solving. Ask for students' own solutions. If unable to give any, offer suggestions such as having a book bag or check list on the inside of locker or shelf.

2. Bring expected materials to school. Using a point system, give points for bringing everything to school or reward students for continued good response.

3. Know school schedule. Periodically ask them what time they have to be to a certain class; ask what time of day that class is held, what period, and the like; have them keep a schedule inside of binder for first month of school.

4. Write down and complete work assignments. Have them keep a binder with an assignment sheet to be checked and interlined (written in inkprint above the braille—so that parents are aware of assignments) at the end of the day.

5. Be aware of how they are doing (grade-wise and behavior-wise) in each class. Remind students to question regular teacher as to their grade and progress; ask regular teacher to give honest answers; periodically check graded papers in notebook.

6. Plan free time. Teach games, and encourage students to plan free time during the day without adult intervention; introduce them to braille books and how to order them; introduce them to Library of Congress tapes and where to get them.

7. Plan study time wisely. Teach scheduling of some homework time and some free play time; work into a home schedule, modeling it after class schedule.

Dressing

Prepare a checklist of these items, first checking with students and then with parents.

Undressing

Students may use Montessori frames, large dolls, or themselves.

1. Removes garment, pulls down elastic (go on swimming event and make this more realistic and meaningful).

2. Removes pullover garments (i.e., T-shirt).

3. Opens front zipper (pants or jacket).

4. Opens separating front zipper (jacket).

5. Unbuckles belt or shoes.

Students can practice requesting information by carrying out little interviews with their peers.

6. Opens back zipper.
7. Unties back buttons.
8. Opens back buttons.
9. Undresses independently.

Dressing
1. Puts on pullover garments.
2. Puts shoes on correct feet.
3. Inserts belt in loops.
4. Dresses independently.

Fastening Garments
1. Buttons large buttons.
2. Closes front snaps.
3. Buttons series of three buttons.
4. Closes front zipper, locks tab.
5. Buckles belt and shoes.
6. Closes jacket zipper.
7. Closes back zipper.
8. Snaps back snaps.
9. Ties apron sash in front.
10. Buttons back buttons.
11. Ties apron sash in back.
12. Ties tie (for junior high students, have a formal party for which everyone dresses up).
13. Laces shoes.
14. Ties first knot (use Montessori frames, dolls, or real people).
15. Ties shoe-laces in bow-knot.
16. Wraps boxes (make gifts for Mother's Day or some other occasion and wrap them).

Clothes
    Have two checklists of these items to check with parents and students.

Care
1. Hangs on hook (in class, coats can be hung up—reinforce behavior).
2. Puts in accessible place (encourage this in classroom with placement of class materials on student's own shelf).
3. Hangs on hanger.
4. Turns right-side out (teach seams and how to distinguish them).
5. Puts dirty clothes in container.
6. Brushes loose soil from clothes (encourage brushing of crumbs off clothes after eating).
7. Wipes shoes off on doormat when coming in from outdoors.
8. Cleans dirt from shoes with brush.
9. Polishes shoes (activity can be connected to dress-up party for junior high students).

Cleaning
    Plan an activity at a nearby laundromat or in a home economics room equipped with washing machines and dryers (junior high and senior high level).
1. Able to use washing machine.
2. Able to use dryer.
3. Washes own clothes.
4. Dries own clothes.
5. Puts clean clothes in proper places (activity can be connected to clean-up from party at which tablecloth, napkins, or placemats are used).
6. Able to keep track of sock colors (use metal tags or sock sorters).
7. Able to take soiled dry-clean-only clothes to cleaners (can be tied into Obtaining Information activity).

Coordination
1. Chooses clothes to wear by verbal help of sighted individual.
2. Chooses what clothes to wear by color tags.
3. Shops for clothes with the verbal help of another individual who accompanies the student.
4. Shops for clothes with the verbal help of a salesperson.

Grooming
Care of Teeth
1. Uses brushing motion on tooth surface (with finger) with adult supervision.
2. Wets brush, applies toothpaste to finger, and places paste on tongue (with supervision).
3. Combines all operations (prepares, brushes, rinses) with supervision.
4. Does all of item 3 independently.
5. Brushes teeth after meals or at routine times (keep toothbrush available at junior high level, and remind them to brush if they neglect doing so).
Care of Nose
1. Indicates by gesture awareness of runny nose.
2. Wipes nose with tissue, requests a tissue to wipe nose, or attempts to blow nose when requested with adult supervision.
3. Blows nose without assistance.
Care of Hands and Face
1. Dries hands unsupervised.
2. Washes hands unsupervised.
3. Disposes of paper towel into wastebasket.
4. Replaces towel on accessible rack.
5. Washes hands and face at appropriate times (discuss importance of frequency and thoroughness of washing).

Bathing
    Practice bathing with students on dolls. Stress the importance of keeping underarms and genitals very clean.
Care of Nails—Elementary
1. Files and polishes nails for attractiveness (junior high).
Care of Hair
1. Washes hair.
2. Parts hair.
3. Sets and styles own hair (junior high).

Eating and Preparing Food
Utensils (Spoon, Fork, and Knife)
1. Cleans and holds properly.
2. Have a party prepared by students to practice skills.
3. Teach cooking as a once-a-week activity, during lunch period (also include clean-up).
Washing Food
    Stress the importance of scrubbing fresh fruits and vegetables.
Washing Dishes
    Practice washing dishes (can be part of clean-up).
Putting Away Food for Storage
    Demonstrate the use of Tupperware and other containers. Demonstrate the use of tin foil, wax paper, and plastic wrap.
Appliance Knowledge
1. Can opener—(teach how to use it; show different varieties available).
2. Mixer—portable and stationary.
3. Frying pan—on stove and electric.
4. Turn on stove burners (explore cold stove; communicate with parents to allow child some supervised access to stove and oven).

5. Set oven temperature.

6. Open jars (introduce "screwy lewy" rubber lid opener which makes job easier).

7. Measuring cups and spoons.

8. Toaster.

9. Sharp knife.

10. Electric skillet.

Food Preparation

1. Boiled (pot) foods such as soup.

2. Cut foods such as salads.

3. Spread foods such as sandwiches.

4. Baked goods such as cakes.

5. Roasted foods such as chicken.

6. Broiled foods such as steaks.

7. Grilled foods such as pancakes, eggs—skillet foods.

Shopping Skills

1. Prepares list with help.

2. Prepares list independently.

3. Knows location of store.

4. Labels can.

Time

1. Understands spatial time—seasons, calendar, days.

2. Understands clock time.

3. Understands concept of time passing.

System of Money

1. Coins.

2. Bills.

3. Banks (checking and savings).

4. Management of money.

5. Plastic money (buying on credit with interest).

Career Exploration

1. Awareness of jobs, job shadowing.

2. Good use of organization, obtaining information, and problem solving skills. Give a problem to solve such as a possible job interview, having students obtain information on their own. If a real interview is not possible, then role play the interview. In the role play, teacher plays the potential employer. Be sure the student gives home phone number.

3. Seeking employment independently (role play or real). Have students go out for an interview being sure they give after school or in-school information. Use unfamiliar surroundings and have students dress the part.

4. Good use of conversation (interview) skills. Conduct a (role play and/or real) interview.

Use of Public or Other Forms of Transportation

1. Local transportation.
   a. Buses (field trips).
   b. Streetcars (field trips).
   c. Electric buses (field trips).
   d. Cabs (once-a-year excursion, but not too far!).
   e. Subway (junior high—teach use of subways, take downtown).

2. Intercity buses (inform students of usage and location).

3. Out-of-city buses, trains, airplanes (inform students of usage, location, and regulations in regard to VH persons).

Health and Nutrition
1. Basic body needs: vitamins, minerals, proteins, carbohydrates, fats, water, air.
2. Food groups and nutritious foods (instruction in planning well-balanced meals for self and classmates).

Safety
Instruct students in first aid for cuts, burns, sunburn, headache, and stomach ache.

Housecleaning
Instruct students how to clean tables, floors, and other surfaces as well as in towel folding.

Use of Household Tools
Instruct students in the use of leverage tools, push-pull tools, and screw drivers.

General Orientation to Spatial Concepts (Cratty & Sams, 1968)
Spatial concepts are extremely important. Most living skill activities will be much more difficult, if not impossible, to teach without them. Students should:
1. Know where their houses are in relation to school.
2. If lost, be able to tell which part of city their house is in, its street number and name, their parents' first names, correct person to approach for help (i.e., policeman).
3. Know what state they live in and where it is in relation to the rest of the country.
4. Know what country they live in and where other countries are in relation to it.
5. Know what rivers, lakes, oceans, and continents are.

We have found this list of resources helpful in planning our living skills programs.

List of Resources

Cooking

Hey What's Cooking: A Kitchen Curriculum for the Parents of V.H. Children
South Metropolitan Asociation for Low Incidence Handicapped
Robert Van Dyke, Director
250 W. Sibley Boulevard
Dolton P.O.
Harvey, IL 60426

A Child's Cook Book—primary print
656 Terra California Drive, No. 3
Walnut Creek, CA 94595

A Special Picture Cook Book—large print
Freida Reed
M and M Enterprises, Inc.
P.O. Box 3342
Lawrence, KS 66044

Betty Crocker's New Boys and Girls Cookbook—regular print
Western Publishing Co., Inc.
Racine, WI

Preprimer Cooking or Cooking Techniques for the Blind, Vol. 1 and Vol. 2—large type
Sally Jones
American Printing House for the Blind
Louisville, KY

I Think I Can Learn to Cook or *I Can Cook to Think & Learn*—Rebus and regular print recipes
Jane S. Triebel, B.A. and Mary Carol Manning;, M.S.
Academic Therapy Publications
1539 Fourth Street
San Rafael, CA 94901

Easy 'n Thrifty Recipes for 2—large print and braille
Rice Council of America
P.O. Box 22802
Houston, TX 77027

Cooking with Betty Crocker Mixes—
4th large type edition
Betty Crocker Kitchens
General Mills, Inc.
Box 1113
Minneapolis, MN 55440

Cooking and Nutrition (junior high)

*Creative Food Experiences for
Children*
Mary T. Goodwin and Gerry Pollen
Center for the Science in the Public
Interest
1755 S. Street, N.W.
Washington, D.C. 20009

Good for Me, 1978
Burns and Clifford
Little, Brown and Company
Boston, MA

*Beyond T.V. Dinners: 3 Levels of
Recipes for V.H. Cooks*
Prepared by P. Canter, B. Hatlen,
and M. Cole
Living Skills for the Visually Handi-
capped
2444 Road 20, Apt. #C-105
San Pablo, CA 94806

Perceptual Visual Training, Non-
Game

Fairbanks-Robinson 1, Level 1,
Teaching Resources Corporation
100 Boylston Street
Boston, MA 02116

*Perceptual Motor Development
Program*
Jay Lev
Academic Therapy Publications
1539 Fourth Street
San Rafael, CA 94901

Vanguard School Program
Janet I. Robinson, M.S.
Teaching Resources Corporation
100 Boylston Street
Boston, MA 02116

*Frostig Program for the Development
of Visual Perception*
Follett Publishing Company
Chicago, IL

Ann Arbor Tracking Program (1976)
1. Maze Book
2. Symbol Tracking—large print

3. Cursive, Manuscript, Letter
Tracking
4. Cues & Signals in Reading

Games

Trac 4—ages 8 and up (patterns)
Lakeside Games
4400 West 78 Street
Minneapolis, Minnesota 55435

Brainy Blocks—ages 3–6 (can be
used with older children)
Leisure Learning
50 Greenwich Avenue
Greenwich, CT 06830

Erie Program, Part 4—perceptual
card and dominoes games (1969)
Halton with Pizzat and Perikawski
Teaching Resources Corporation
100 Boylston Street
Boston, MA 02116

Perceptual Skills Look Alikes (1974)
Teaching Resources Corporation
100 Boylston Street
Boston, MA 02116

Cricket's Tangrams (1977)
Merle Peek
Random House
New York, NY

Listening

Listen and Learn
American Printing House for the
Blind
Louisville, KY

*Listening—A Curriculum Guide for
Teachers of V.I. Students*
Illinois Office of Education
100 North First Street
Springfield, IL

Listening Skills Program
Dorothy Kendall Bracken
Educational Progress
Division of Educational Development
Corp.

Listen and Think (1968)—levels C–F
Perrone, Carter and Zucker
McGraw-Hill, Inc.
Educational Developmental
Laboratories
New York, NY

Main Idea—Study Skills

Getting the Facts (1976)—Specific
  Skills Series, levels A–G
Richard A. Boning
Barnell Loft, Ltd
958 Church Street
Baldwin, N.Y. 11510

Drawing Conclusions (1976)—
  Specific Skill Series, levels A–G
Richard A. Boning
Barnell Loft, Ltd.
958 Church Street
Baldwin, N.Y. 11510

Getting the Main Idea
Comprehensive Games Corporation
63-10 Woodhaven Boulevard
Rego Park, NY 11374

Creative Writing

Wishes, Lies, and Dreams
Kenneth Koch
Vintage Books/Chelsea House Pub-
  lishers
New York, NY

Finger Play Poems and Stories
Fletcher

Art

Craft Center (1974)
Creative Teaching Press, Inc.
Monterey Park, CA

From Petals to Pinecones
Katherine N. Cutler
Lothrop, Lee and Shepard Co.
105 Madison Avenue
New York, NY 10016

Creative Art Tasks for Children
  Taylor, Artuso, Hewett
Love Publishing Company
Denver, CO 30222

*Making Things, Book 2: A Hand
  Book of Creative Discovery* (1975)
Ann Wiseman
Little, Brown and Company
Boston, MA

Handwriting

Script Raised Letters
Lectro Learn, Inc.
Box 127
Berwyn, PA

*Learn-to-Write Cursive or
  Manuscript Letters*
Milton Bradley
74 Park Street
Springfield, MA 01101

Alphabet Practice Cards
Ideal School Supply Company
Oak Lawn, IL 60453

Longhand Writing for the Blind
Elizabeth Freund
American Printing House for the
  Blind
Louisville, KY

Dubnoff Writing Program
Teaching Resources Corporation
100 Boylston Street
Boston, MA 02116

Typing

Typewriting for Blind Students
  (1975)—good for beginners, with
  tapes
American Printing House for the
  Blind
Louisville, KY

*Typing Keys for Remediation of
  Reading and Spelling*
Maetta Davis
Academic Therapy Publications
San Rafael, CA 94901

20th Century Typewriting—large
  print
South-Western Publishing Co.
Cincinnati, OH

*Braille Drill and Practice Sentences
  for Primary and Intermediate
  Students*
Dorothy Quentin Joseph
1490 44th Avenue
San Francisco, CA 94122

Gregg Typing, New Series—large
  print
National Aid to Visually Handicapped
3201 Balboa Street
San Francisco, CA 94121

*Typing for Partially Seeing and Blind
  Pupils*—tape
CD HS AMS
California Depository for Handi-
  capped Students
State Department of Education

Personal Typewriting for Junior High Schools (1970), 3rd edition—large print
Wanoos and Haggblade
South West Publishing Company
Cincinnati, OH

Motor

Frostig – MGL
Marianne Frostig, Ph.D. in association with Phyllis Maslow, M.A.
Follett Educational Corporation
Chicago, IL

Perceptual Motor Lesson Plans
Jack Capon
Front Row Experience
564 Central Avenue, Suite 213
Alameda, CA 94501

Motoric Aids to Perceptual Training
Chaney-Kephart

Daily Sensorimotor Training
William T. Braley, M.Ed., Geraldine Konicki, and Catherine Leedy
Peek Publications
164 East Dana Street
Mountain View, CA 94040

A Guide to Movement Exploration
Hacket and Jenson
Peek Publications
164 East Dana Street
Mountain View, CA 94040

Movement without Sight
L. E. Kratz
Peek Publications Box 11065
Palo Alto, CA 94306

Yoga for Children (1976)
Eve Diskin
Warner Books
75 Rockefeller Plaza
New York, NY 10019

Keep on Steppin'—record with music by Stevie Wonder (exercises to do)
Jack Mullane
Educational Activities, Inc. (have free catalog)
Box 392
Freeport, NY 11520

Get Fit While You Sit—tape and booklet
Educational Activities, Inc. (have free catalog)
Box 392
Freeport, NY 11520

Hap Palmer Record Library (a must for every early childhood and special education class)
Educational Activities, Inc. (have free catalog)
Box 392
Freeport, NY 11520

Alley Cat and Chicken Fat Plus Other Fun Dances
Golden Records (have free catalog)
250 West 57th Street
New York, NY 10019

Communication

TELESONIA: Communication by Telephone—an elementary grade program on telephone communications
Educational Representative
Bell Telephone Co.

ALIVE...AWAKE...A PERSON: a "developmental model for early childhood services with special definition for visually impaired children and their parents"—chapters on self and social awareness and social education and citizenship
Compiled & edited by Rosemary O'Brien, Ph.D.
Montgomery County Public Schools
Rockville, MD

100 Ways to Enhance Self-Concept in the Classroom—A Handbook for Teachers and Parents (1976)
Jack Canfield and Harold C. Wells
Prentice-Hall, Inc.
Englewood Cliffs, NJ

Checklists

Pupil Developmental Progress Scale
—level II
Monterey County Office of Education
SPED (Special Education Department)
P.O. Box 851
Salinas, CA

Skills Center
P. Canter, M. Cole, C. Fox, B.
  Hatlen, P. Hatlen, and J. LeDuc
Living Skills Center for the Visually
  Handicapped
2444 Road 20, Apt. #C-105
San Pablo, CA 94896

*Informal Assessment of Develop-
  mental Skills for Visually Handi-
  capped Students* (1978)
compiled by Vision Staff of California
  State University, Los Angeles, CA
Edited by Rosemarie Swallow, Ed.D.,
  Sally Mangold, Ph.D., and Philip
  Mangold, M.A.
American Foundation for the Blind
New York, NY

Career Education

Entering the World of Work (1978)—
  text and workbook, regular print
Kimbreil-Vineyard
McKnight Publishing Company
Bloomington, IL 61701

Career Exploration Kit (1977)—sec-
  ondary school students (cards)
Marion H. Sandalls
Career Aids, Inc.
Lakeshore Curriculum Materials
  Center

Finding Work (1977)
Follett Coping Skills Series
Follett Publishing Company
Chicago, IL

Financial Management

*Money Management—Income and
  Expenses* (1977)—duplicating
  masters and teacher's guide
Nesbitt Miliken Publishing Company
St. Louis, MO

Spectrum Mathematics Series
  (1973)—blue and purple level
Laidlaw Brothers, Publishing
River Forest, IL

Useful Arithmetic (1972), Vols. 1 and
  2 workbooks, regular print
John Wool and Raymond J. Bohn
Frank E. Richards Publishing Co.,
  Inc.
Phoenix, NY 13135

*Mathematics for Individual Achieve-
  ment* (1975)
Denholm, Hankins, Herrick and Vojtko
Houghton Mifflin Company
Boston, MA

Budgeting (1977)—print work book
Follett Coping Skills Series
McVey and Associates, Inc.
Follett Publishing Company
Chicago, IL

Everyday Economics (1976)—cards
Beverley Logan
Westinghouse Learning Corporation

References

Cratty, B. J., & Sams, T. A. *The body image of blind children.* New York: American
  Foundation for the Blind, 1968.

Sexuality Education Methodology

Jan Neff, M.A.

CHAPTER 9

SEXUALITY OF THE VISUALLY IMPAIRED: OLD AND NEW ATTITUDES

During the early to mid-1970s, the small amount of available literature regarding the sex education of the visually impaired consisted mainly of justifications for the existence of such programs. Parents, teachers and administrators alike were of basically the same cultural background. A generation of adults who had grown up in a society frightened of sex found it difficult to deal openly with children in regard to sexuality, especially those children with physical, emotional, or mental impairments. As a result, visually impaired youngsters had little or no hope of reaching sexual maturity.

In recent years, attitudes toward sexuality of physically, mentally, and emotionally impaired individuals have been modified considerably, with an increasingly larger portion of our society recognizing that sexuality is unconditionally a part of humanity. Along with this recognition comes the task of fulfilling the impaired individual's human right to be a feeling and informed sexual being to whatever degree is possible. For some such individuals, this may involve only alleviating the fear that accompanies the onset of menses or teaching self-care skills; for others it may involve instruction in more complex areas of awareness, such as conception or ovulation information. This places a great responsibility on all members of our society, but especially on the professionals attending to the educational needs of these sensorially impaired individuals, and on their parents, who are usually the primary role models from birth onward.

The implementation of the right of impaired persons to be feeling and informed sexual beings has been fraught with questions, concerns, and moral issues that continue to obstruct the fulfillment of these rights and educational needs. These factors are multiple and varied, yet ultimately each has an effect on a teacher's or parent's ability either to accept or to deny the responsibility to teach sexuality education—to put it another way, the ability to approach it positively by intentionally imparting information or negatively by avoiding the subject. Therefore, it is imperative to consider some of these issues in a discussion of sexuality education methodology.

It is quite common for those who are sensorially impaired to be considered asexual. This erroneous supposition probably became prevalent for many reasons, but partially at fault is the generally held view of what it means to be a "sexual" being, together with the notion that there are definitive ways in which we must all act out or upon our sexuality. Traditionally, our views of sexuality have been restricted to the context of marriage and procreation. Since an impaired person's physical disabilities often prevent the acting out of his or her sexuality in these traditional, "accepted" ways, it is frequently concluded that

Ms. Neff is a former teacher of sexuality education at the California School for the Blind, Berkeley, where she developed a sexuality education curiculum that was published by the American Foundation for the Blind. Following her work at the Berkeley school, she joined the staff of the Southwestern Region Deaf-Blind Center, Sacramento, California, as a sexuality education program specialist. Currently she is a sex education consultant to the blind and multiply handicapped deaf. As such, she is a regular lecturer for special education classes at campuses throughout the University of California system and offers workshops and consultations for parents and professionals throughout the country.

physically impaired individuals are not sexual beings in need of sexually oriented information. Nothing could be further from the truth. Indeed, the fact that many of these impaired individuals may not marry and raise children, thus learning about sexuality through trial and error, supports the necessity for directed, intentional teaching.

"Sex" is usually considered synonymous with sexual intercourse, thus accounting for phrases such as "having sex." To define sex in such narrow terms negatively affects the education of the visually impaired individual. First, it creates in the minds of parents and teachers the supposition that sexual information is not necessary in the lives of children, thus delaying or aborting their enlightenment and functioning abilities. Secondly, such a definition contributes to the continuation of the educational voids that render these youngsters unsociable.

Consider the first result still further. Between one and one-half and three years of age, sighted toddlers have repeatedly compared and then contemplated, among other things, the anatomical features of their parents' bodies, those of their own bodies, and those of siblings and peers. Usually visually impaired children have not received directed sexuality instruction during the early formative years, and as such children enter school, they are already years behind their sighted peers in sexuality awareness and development. Based on information gained from my human sexuality students, whose ages ranged from seven to 25 years of age, it appears that the older the impaired children get before receiving directed and intentional sexuality education, the more difficult, if not impossible, it becomes for them to comprehend even the most seemingly basic concepts. I am of the opinion that the younger children are more able to form accurate concepts because they have fewer established misconceptions and inaccuracies. Those in their late teens and older do not, apparently, disregard all that they have previously "learned" when given the facts; rather, the facts only add to the complexity of their misconceptions.

It is never too early to begin the purposeful sexuality education of any child, especially that of a visually impaired child. It has been shown that the sex education of human infants begins at birth through involuntary nonverbal communication. Nevertheless, many adults express anxiety about telling children "too much" about sex "too early" and thus harming them. Research has shown that this fear is unfounded. Children absorb what they are intellectually and emotionally ready to absorb. They cannot be harmed by what they are not ready for or interested in. If given lengthy, detailed explanations, they will take in only the simplest aspects, and then become bored and disregard the remainder. However, we do cause harm by withholding sexual information until after an individual has had a particular sexual experience. For example, not preparing a young girl for the onset of menses instills fear and confusion that is not easily overcome.

In regard to the second negative result of defining sex in narrow terms, physically and mentally impaired individuals are kept from viewing, reading, or discussing the various aspects of sexuality in order to prevent the development of "unsatisfiable aspirations." Further, it is often felt that exposing them to such information will lead to "sexual misbehavior" and create "uncontrollable overstimulation" which may be acted upon irresponsibly. Parents and professionals who pursue this line of thought close their eyes to the fact that impaired children will one day be adolescents with all of the biological urges of this age group. Consequently, sexuality education is avoided whenever possible; it is only undertaken as disaster insurance, or as a way of alleviating any "trouble" in the lives of children. Hence, impaired youngsters reach adulthood, not only childlike, naive, and dependent, but also commonly the subject of sexual abuse and molestation. Sadly, the fact that sexuality education is a learning experience that enriches children's lives, making them more understanding of themselves, their families, their peers, and even society, is usually not even a consideration.

In view of the effects that all of these factors have upon the sexual conditioning

Visually impaired children are usually behind their sighted peers in sexuality awareness and development.

The older impaired children are before receiving sexuality education, the more difficult it becomes for them to comprehend even the most basic concepts.

of visually impaired youngsters, it would be advantageous to view "sex" in a more expansive way than is traditional. Many of the fears and anxieties can be eliminated by considering it as something all-encompassing, rather than in the usual narrow terms. I regard it as something we *are*, not something we *do*; as a major aspect of personality rather than merely a physical expression. It encompasses one's emotional, social and cultural growth as well as physical development. Kirkendall points out that "Probably nothing so greatly influences one's life pattern as his sex membership. An individual's sense of identity, his ways of thinking and behaving, social activities, choice of associates, mode of dress, and many other important factors are strongly conditioned by being male or female" (Kirkendall, 1968, p. 40).

SEXUALITY EDUCATION FOR THE VISUALLY IMPAIRED: STRATEGIES

Reassessing and expanding the meaning of sexuality clarifies the educational goals in this regard since they correspond with other developmental areas. The connection between all areas of learning and development has been demonstrated. For example, it is now accepted that coordination and movement therapy will positively affect an impaired person's reading readiness. This connection applies to sexuality development as well. It is practically impossible to develop any sense of identity (the essence of oneself as a unique individual) without identifying onself as either a male or a female. Also, it has been shown that there is a connection between gender identity differentiation (the establishment of one's maleness or femaleness) and language acquisition (Money & Tucker, 1975, p. 88). Where gender identity has not been firmly established within the normal range, underachievement of learning exists.

A methodical approach to the establishment of a firm gender identity is clearly an initial goal of the visually impaired youngster's sexuality education. Ideally, this begins at a very young age; in typical situations remediation is required. Parents and teachers of normally functioning, able-bodied children do not usually follow any prescribed plan or method of making their children or students aware of their sexual identity. Commonly, such awareness depends solely on spontaneous visual input. It works to some degree. Sighted toddlers make comparisons among family members of differing sex and age while in the course of daily living activities. However, even for children who see, hear, and think at appropriate developmental levels, there remain many unanswered questions and concerns: for instance, "Did my sister have her penis cut off?" or "If I'm naughty, will I have my penis cut off?" A child with vision and language is able to voice these concerns; the same option is not available to many impaired children with poor conceptual development.

The gender cues in our society are very difficult for even young normally seeing children to sort out; for the blind child it can be impossible. You can no longer tell a male from a female by the length of the individual's hair; by the absence or presence of bracelets, necklaces, or even earrings; by the fact that the individual is wearing pants; by whether or not the individual carries a shoulder bag; or even by the individual's name. In many cases, these are the only determinants children have available to them in their attempt to form gender concepts.

The most cogent foundations for gender conceptualization are the differences between male and female genitals and the functions of the genitals in the reproduction process. In our culture, this information is guardedly kept from children. As they grow older, they learn about these things at random, often developing gross misconceptions along the way. Many visually impaired individuals never develop accurate gender concepts and thus behave as neuter beings with distorted sense identities.

Parents and teachers can help visually impaired children conceptualize gender similarities and differences and can improve the child's body awareness in a variety of ways. In doing so, encourage the use of as many of the functioning

The establishment of gender identity and the acquisition of language are connected.

Gender cues in our society are very difficult for young sighted children to sort out; for blind children they can be impossible.

senses as possible. In my experience, allowing youngsters to grasp a tangible item, rather than relying on words alone, has always accelerated the conceptualization process. The following suggestions might prove helpful:

Vocabulary Building

Establish a developmentally appropriate vocabulary which includes the anatomically correct names for genitals and reproductive organs, as well as terminology for sexually oriented items and behaviors. The visually impaired toddler can learn "penis," "vagina," "testicle," or "breast" for example, as easily as "wee-wee" or "ding-dong." Substituting these unnecessary, meaningless syllables for the names of body parts and bodily functions eventually retards the youngster's efforts to communicate significantly, and it frequently induces ridicule from peers. A "developmentally appropriate sexual vocabulary" is one that coincides with language content in other areas, not one which deems these terms unnecessary. If a young child is learning about "ears," "nose," "arms," and "legs," at that time "penis," "anus," or "vagina" would be equally appropriate, although "ovaries," "uterus," or "scrotum" would be introduced somewhat later. As a child demonstrates an understanding of and the correct use of terms, the teacher or other role model should introduce additional and increasingly more complex terms.

Teaching Anatomical Differences and Similarities

Acquaint the child on a daily basis, in the normal course of living activities if possible, with the differences and similarities between males and females. This can be accomplished as parents or siblings bathe with the visually impaired child, encouraging body exploration which is accompanied by a constant flow of verbal and tactual information, quizzing, and game-playing. In this manner youngsters can learn about body hair, differences in anatomy, and variations in size and shape. As a child becomes older, this can also be an opportunity to work on sexual vocabulary by taking the child's hand, touching a body part on him or her, and saying the name of that part. If the child and the parent or sibling are of like gender, the parent or sibling can take the child's hand, touch the same part on himself or herself, name it, and point out that all children and adults of like gender have that part. While bathing with a child of the opposite gender, the parent or sibling can say the body part of the child and then say "no," or "different," while taking the child's hand and touching the appropriate part of himself or herself. If the part in question is a body part common to both genders, it can be pointed out that all humans alike have that particular part.

This same type of comparative instruction can take place in the classroom with a variety of dolls. Anatomically accurate rag dolls can be made of cotton or stuffed hosiery (snaps make excellent nipples; the concave portion of the snap closure on an infant doll forms a mouth that can attach to the mother doll's breasts). Commerically manufactured dolls that differentiate the genital area according to the doll's gender, such as Creative Playthings' Little Brother and Little Sister and the Archie Bunker's Grandson doll, are also available.

If a child has functional vision, mirror play can be beneficial in developing body awareness. Sit or stand the child in front of a full-length mirror for daily undressing and dressing. After removing an article of clothing, gleefully "find" the exposed body part, then say its name. Attempt to portray the same positive attitude upon "finding" the penis or vagina as you do toward "finding" the cute little toes after removing a stocking.

The available models that enhance gender conceptualization have improved over the past few years. The Nasco torso models are an excellent addition to those available, but the cost is prohibitive for many schools and certainly for home use. The Nasco fetus model set* is considerably less expensive and should be includ-

*The Human Fetus, available from Nasco West, 1524 Princeton Avenue, P.O. Box 3837, Modesto, California 95352.

Parents and siblings can bathe with the visually impaired child to teach anatomical differences between males and females.

If a child has functional vision, mirror play will help develop body awareness.

ed in the media center for any school serving visually impaired children. The set allows youngsters who have never seen charts and cross-section illustrations of the developing fetus to comprehend how the human fetus grows and becomes increasingly more lifelike. The set includes fetuses from seven to eight weeks to eight to nine months; both male and female specimens are available, and some include the cord and placenta. Young children in my classes delighted in putting the fetus models under their sweaters or shirts and pretending that they were carrying a fetus. This role playing allows children the opportunity to experience the cause of a pregnant woman's increasingly expanding abdomen. Supplementing this type of role playing with large water-filled balloons (each containing a previously inserted marble or plastic object to simulate the fetus) illustrates the protection afforded the developing fetus by the placenta and amniotic fluid. This greatly relieved my youngsters, many of whom had bumped into pregnant women from time to time, for they feared this accidental bumping perhaps damaged the developing fetus.

Another model set, which can be highly recommended for both the reasonable price (models are individually priced and within financial reach of many families so that they can be used in the home) and their versatility, is the set known as the Jim Jackson Models of Human Genital Anatomy.* These models can be used in explaining intercourse, conception, birth, menstruation, and contraception, as well as gender and anatomy.

Department store mannequins are also beneficial in place of, or, ideally, in addition to the genital models; many times they can be obtained free of charge. Use of mannequins enables visually impaired individuals to explore the male and female shape tactually and make comparisons with their own bodies. In so doing, they are able to locate the breasts on the female, to note the difference in the female's waist and hip measurements as compared to the relatively straight line between the male's waist and hip, to note the broader shoulder and chest structure of males as compared to females, to note the generally more shapely thighs and calves of females as compared to males, and to note the female hip and pubic bone structure—to name only a few of the valuable comparisons that can be made while using these teaching materials. Mannequins of male and female children can be used to illustrate the many differences and similarities in children and adults, although often the young child's actual body can be used for these lessons.

The adult mannequins can be made even more realistic by gluing curly hair to the genital and underarm areas. The hair can be collected from beauty salons or can be cut from discarded wigs.

Teaching Sexuality Awareness: Household Projects

Include visually impaired youngsters in household tasks that will enhance the child's understanding of male and female differences and similarities. An enormous amount of information, essential to the child's total development, can be imparted while sorting laundry. If the child has some functional vision, it helps to stand line drawings of nude family members along the table or counter where that person's clothing will be stacked. Rag dolls (anatomically correct) could be substituted for the totally blind child. Many would be surprised to find out how very little blind individuals know about clothing worn by the opposite sex. These lessons were very popular and informative as far as my students were concerned.

Put the visually impaired child on the sorting table or upon a tall stool, as you come to a bra, for example, allow the child to feel the cups and then point to the breasts in the line drawing of the mother (or sister), or touch the breasts on a doll, or touch the breasts of the mother. Say the word "breasts" to familiarize the child with the word. Explain the function of a bra and, pointing to the drawings or dolls

Department store mannequins can be used to explore the male and female shapes tactually.

Household tasks enhance a child's understanding of sexuality: an enormous amount of information can be imparted while sorting laundry.

Many would be surprised to discover how little blind youngsters know about clothing worn by the opposite sex.

*Models of Human Genital Anatomy, available c/o Jim Jackson, 16 Laurel Street, Arlington, Massachusetts 02174.

of a male, indicate that bras are not worn by or necessary for males. Allow the child to feel the fly front opening on the father's or brother's underwear. Point to the penis in the drawing or on the doll, and say its name. Explain the function of the opening and indicate that such an opening is not necessary or present on female underwear. In making these explanations to a little girl, insert a finger through the fly opening to simulate the penis and familiarize her with how it can fit through the opening. Encourage her to pretend her finger is a penis and to try fitting it into the opening.

Among my former students were blind boys nine and 10 years of age, who over the years had been dressed by others and never exposed to the specifics of male-and female-oriented clothing; as a result they did not know what the fly opening on their own underwear was for, and they always opened their trousers at the waist, dropped them to their ankles, and sat on the toilet (another educational void) to urinate. On the other hand, some of my female students, who had not had the opportunity to examine male clothing or models and who inadvertently came upon a male standing and clothed while toileting, either erroneously assumed that the boy was "having an accident" or became totally confused and developed some gross misconception to account for the phenomenon.

In the laundry sorting process, the child can also be exposed to sex-linked differences in size (men's and women's stockings and shirts) and texture (for example, nylons, lace and embroidery on feminine items, compared to men's cotton knits), as well as a variety of gender-determined items (slips, half-slips, sanitary belts, jock straps, etc.).

Teaching Sexuality Awareness: School Projects
Incorporate into the visually impaired child's educational program lessons and activities that will reinforce developing gender concepts. Often, for art projects, a child lies on large paper and is traced around; the figure is then cut out and dressed. This activity can be more beneficial to the visually impaired child if the life-sized figure is left undressed. Add button or felt eyes and mouth and yarn hair. Glue or sew on button nipples and navel. For male children, three cotton-stuffed balloons (two small round ones and one long narrow one wonderfully simulate the genitals). Gently puncture the paper (or better still, the poster board) figure in the genital area, put the open end of the balloon through the tiny hole, tie or knot it, and tape it in place. Broad felt-tip pens can be used to draw some features for those children with some vision, and lines of dried white glue can be used for children with no functional vision. Hang the figures around the room and assist the children in comparing height, length of hair, number of fingers and toes, and so forth, and also the differences of male and female genitals and similarities of male and female chests in children. The similarities of male and female children from the back can also be discussed.

Cutout figures can also be used in the classroom to teach clothing differences. Begin by giving the children their own figures and a box of their own clothing. Show the children how to lay the articles of clothing in place on the cutout figure. When they are able to do this, add figures of the opposite sex. Initially, use only the outer items of clothing that the children wear. Later incorporate the underwear also. Do this with the cutouts of the opposite gender, too.

Later, depending on the children's developmental level, the activity can be expanded still further. If the children use braille or large print, show them a card labeled (with a picture or cutout if necessary) with the name of an article of clothing in the box. Have them find it and place it on the figure. Thus, the children are aided in forming a connection between the name of a piece of clothing, its function and its association to the body. These lessons can be done using a mannequin or doll as well.

Make use of community resources to reinforce these gender concepts, also. Take the children to museums where they can be permitted to explore nude

Cutout figures can be used to teach sexuality awareness. The children lay clothing in place on the figures.

Take children to museums where they can explore nude statues tactually.

68

statues tactually. Take them to department stores where they will be permitted to try on adult shoes and to explore the differences in male and female shoes. Make the same comparisons regarding swimsuits, sleeping apparel, hats, coats, and the variety and different scents of cosmetics and grooming aids.

Teaching About Sexual Intercourse

Inform youngsters about sexual intercourse and the function of the penis and vagina in the reproduction process. Begin by determining the student's current knowledge of conception and birth and dispelling as many myths and misconceptions as possible.

If a family or school system does not have commercially available models it is possible to use some household items and make something that the youngsters can touch that will aid his comprehension of these complex ideas. For example, an empty toilet roll or an eight oz. paper cup that has been compressed substitutes nicely for a vaginal canal. The cup can be made even more helpful by lining its interior with plasticene clay, cutting an opening in the bottom, and modeling the inner and outer folds of the labia over the bottom of the cup. One can put a smaller cup with an opening in the bottom on top of it to simulate the uterus. Puncture an opening on each side of the "uterus" and insert two sections of hollow tubing about six inches long. Fringe the outer end by cutting narrow ¾ inch slits. Glue or insert a small ball for each ovary (such as the little ball that comes with a set of jacks) into the fringe on each side. During explanations, a small bead can be rolled through the tubing, and into the uterus and embedded into the clay lining. This helps the students understand what takes place during ovulation, menstruation or conception, and pregnancy. A penis can be simulated with a rectangular balloon slightly filled with air, a vibrator, a hot dog, or a finger. Also, a penis, a scrotum, and testicles can be modeled from clay. In my sexuality classes boys and girls alike attempted to form, after exploring models, both male and female genitals out of clay. The students offered each other help while attempting to shape the genitals of the opposite sex.

Using models of the penis and vagina (homemade or otherwise), illustrate how the parts fit together. Trace the route of the sperm racing to be first to get to the egg as it comes from the ovary. Explain to the child how the fertilized egg moves down into the uterus and stays there while it grows into a baby. It is important to make the child aware that intercourse takes place most often because it feels nice and is a way of expressing affection, not simply because it is the means of reproduction.

Using a vaginal model with a uterus, explain that a vagina is a narrow tunnel which, during birth, stretches wide to allow a baby to pass through it. Point out that at the upper end of the vaginal "tunnel" there sits a uterus, or "baby nest," where a tiny egg from the ovaries can grow into a baby. Explain that although the nest-uterus is normally small, it can stretch like a water-filled balloon as the baby grows inside it. Explore the ovaries, "where the baby eggs are stored," and the fallopian tubes, "which carry the eggs to the nest."

On a penis model, show the youngsters the testicles, "where the sperm are stored until they are needed to join the egg and make a baby grow." Explain that millions of tiny cells called sperm ("tiny round bodies without legs and with wiggly tails, like fish or tadpoles") come out of the testicles, go through the vas deferens ("tubes") and out the small opening at the end of the penis as a liquid. Trace a route on the model. Explain that all of the sperm wiggle and race to get to the female egg first, since only one can win, thus joining the egg to make a baby start to grow. Elaborate by adding that in order to give the sperm a better start, the penis gets stiff and fits into the vagina, and that this is called sexual intercourse.

Continuing with the female model, tell the child how the fertilized egg moves into the "nest" and stays there while it grows into a baby. Review the fact that

Household items can be used to make models to teach about sexual intercourse and reproduction.

After exploring the models, have the children shape male and female genitals out of clay.

69

when the baby is ready for birth, the cervix ("the opening of the uterus") stretches just as the vagina stretches, and the baby moves through the vaginal tunnel, pushed by the mother's muscles, to be born.

Teaching about the Genitals
Acquaint visually impaired youngsters with the names, locations and functions of their genital body openings. Most girls, even the nondisabled, are confused about their genital body openings and often assume that blood and urine come from the same opening. This makes the concept of tampon usage beyond their comprehension. Males are baffled by the urine and sperm coming from the same opening and frequently put forth questions and concerns (as do females) regarding the likelihood of a male urinating into the vagina during sexual intercourse. Females should be encouraged to explore their own genital areas privately and to become familiar with the various parts. It is very difficult for a girl or woman to communicate with a physician regarding discomfort and medical problems when she does not have a notion of how her own body is constructed and functions. An excellent teaching aid for this purpose, developed specifically for the visually impaired, is the set of cassette tapes called *Your Changing Body—A Guided Self-Exploration*, by Pat Allen and Lee Ann Lipke.*

Teaching about Menstruation
All prepubertal girls should be prepared both emotionally and physically for the onset of menses. This means not only that a young girl should be prepared to deal with the self-care skills necessary during her menstrual periods, but that she must also be assured that the menstrual cycle is a normal, healthy part of being a female. Avoid instilling the notion that she will be burdened with a curse. An entire booklet could be written on the methods of accomplishing this. The limitations on this chapter prohibit this, so only a few suggestions will be made. Girls usually begin menstruating between the ages of 11 and 14, but earlier is not uncommon. A visually impaired girl should be given ample opportunities to observe, tactually or visually, other females dealing with the practical aspects of menstruation. The necessary information should be presented sequentially over a long period of time, initially with the girl observing only, then being encouraged to become involved in the steps (such as getting out a necessary pad or tampon) and finally being encouraged to initiate a step (such as marking the period on a braille or pegboard calendar).

The self-care instruction can be reinforced with the help of a few miniature aids and mannequins or anatomically accurate dolls. Sanitary belts can be cut down for the dolls; pads for the belts or self-sticking pads can be cut from those of the standard size.

Teaching about Sexual Exploration and Masturbation
Make visually impaired boys and girls aware of what constitutes appropriate time and place for private sexual activities. Privacy is a very vague concept for one who does not see. Parents and teachers have little difficulty dealing with toileting and privacy, but when it comes to masturbation or fondling between a male and a female, the adult often panics and avoids any instruction at all.

Parents and professionals alike are often unaware that early masturbation and sex play are evidence of a child's development and growth as a total human being. While able to accept and derive pleasure from the spontaneous hugs and kisses of toddlers and to understand these behaviors as being entirely natural in the developmental process, the adults observe children exploring their own bodies or those of playmates or siblings and assume that such sexual curiosity is wrong and potentially damaging. In fact, it is children's insatiable curiosity at this age which brings about these actions. Children are equally curious about

A visually impaired girl needs ample opportunity to observe, tactually or visually, other females dealing with the practical aspects of menstruation.

Privacy is a vague concept for one who does not see. Help visually impaired children to become aware of the appropriate time and place for private sexual activities.

Your Changing Body—A Guided Self-Exploration, available from the Institute for the Development of Creative Child Care, 927 Bemis, S.E., Grand Rapids, Michigan 49507.

everything in their environment. Visually impaired children, usually less mobile than other children and in many ways isolated from the environment, satisfy their curiosity with the one constant and ever present variable in their world, their own bodies. These children, like all others, appreciate the pleasure their bodies afford them through erotic stimulation.

Those who harbor repressive attitudes toward masturbation, exhibit shock and disgust upon discovering it, and deal sternly with masturbating children leave them with feelings of guilt, shame and anxiety which they do not welcome or understand. Emotional problems can result from such treatment and attitudes but not from masturbation itself.

However, as children grow older, they must be instructed that although certain actions are acceptable and pleasurable in private, it is not appropriate to engage in these same behaviors in public. One must advise the youngster as to what constitutes an appropriate time and place in each individual case. When a bedroom or bed is shared with a sibling, privacy at some times is not available there, and the shower or tub in the bathroom may be the suggested location. If a youngster is sent to a private location, he or she must be aware that this is not a form of punishment if the youngster has in the past been sent to his or her room as a form of discipline.

CONCLUSION

Additional subject areas that need particular attention in a sexuality program are the following: social skills, relationships, life styles, grooming and makeup application, sexual self-protection, and contraception. A willingness to meet these educational needs, declared by parents of visually impaired children and professionals serving the visually impaired population, will bring about the specific methods and materials to meet these needs.

References

Kirkendall, L. Sex education. *Medical Aspects of Human Sexuality*, May 1968, pp. 40.
Money, J., and Tucker, P. *Sexual signatures: On being a man or a woman.* Boston: Little, Brown, 1975, p. 88.

CHAPTER 10

SAVI (Science Activities for the Visually Impaired)

Linda De Lucchi, M.A.
Larry Malone, M.A.

If you surveyed a number of Individualized Educational Plans prepared for visually impaired youngsters, you would probably not find any mention of needs in the area of science. You would undoubtedly find references to needs for the development of auditory discrimination skills and sequential ordering skills, or perhaps needs for the enhancement of self-image and the development of better relationships with instructors and peers. If youngster have needs in any of these areas, then science *must* be included in their educational program. Science is much more than an academic discipline, especially where visually impaired youngsters are concerned. Science can be used as a motivator to stimulate learning in a number of different academic and social areas.

During the last five years, a team at the Lawrence Hall of Science, University of California, Berkeley, has developed science activities for visually impaired youngsters in the upper elementary grades. This chapter describes the following:
1. An overview of science-based materials available for visually impaired students.
2. Our curriculum development process and the product of one federally funded project.
3. Some materials and methods found to be effective for teaching science concepts and the related cognitive and manipulative skills.
4. Our view of science as an integral part of every visually impaired youngster's overall educational plan.

Our expertise is with youngsters ages nine to 13 years; we do offer references for high school- and university-level science materials, but we do not focus on this age level.

THE STATE OF THE ART
What elementary science materials are available to meet the special needs of the visually impaired youngster? Standard textbooks, the most widely utilized "science program" for visually impaired (VI) students, are available in braille

Ms. De Lucchi (B.A. and M.A. in Zoology/Ecology) has worked for eight years in science curriculum development and teacher training in the areas of life science instruction, environmental education, and science education for physically handicapped youngsters. She was a member of the OBIS (Outdoor Biology Instructional Strategies) development staff and is currently an author/developer and the Coordinator of the SAVI (Science Activities for the Visually Impaired) and SELPH (Science Enrichment for Learners with Physical Handicaps) projects at the Lawrence Hall of Science, University of California, Berkeley. She has served as a program consultant to school districts, university departments, and recreational and camping associations.

Mr. Malone (B.A. in Biological Sciences, M.A. in Education) has worked for 16 years as a science curriculum developer and teacher trainer in the areas of elementary science education, environmental education and science education for physically handicapped youngsters. He assisted with materials development for the original SCIS (Science Curriculum Improvement Study) project, and he later served as an author for the OBIS (Outdoor Biology Instructional Strategies) project and as co-director of the OBIS bilingual translation project in Migrant Education. He is currently an author/developer of the SAVI and SELPH projects at the Lawrence Hall of Science, University of California, Berkeley. He has served as a program consultant to school districts, university departments, and recreational and camping associations.

and large print. The American Printing House for the Blind (APH) in Louisville, Kentucky has published the ninth edition of its *Central Catalogue*, which lists these resources. APH also markets a number of educational aids in science for primary grade youngsters. These include a simple pull-apart model of a cell, an insect identification kit, a dial thermometer unit, tactile ruler instructional units, and a simple machines introductory unit. Each state's department of education should have its own depository of APH materials.

Several major equipment-based science programs were developed under federal grants in the 1960s. Of these, only one, the Science Curriculum Improvement Study (SCIS), was adapted for use by the blind in a project called Adapting Science Materials for the Blind (ASMB). ASMB teacher guides, student manuals, and equipment were available through Lawrence Hall of Science from 1969 to 1977. In 1978, the SCIS program was revised, and, unfortunately, monies have not been available to revise ASMB materials. However, the philosophy and approach exemplified by the ASMB project have survived in other projects, both at the Lawrence Hall of Science and elsewhere.

At American University in Washington, D.C., Doris Hadary has spearheaded an effort to adapt several activities from other major elementary science curriculum projects and has used these in concert with ASMB materials to develop a mainstreamed, multidisciplinary program for handicapped children between the ages of five and 11. In a recent book, Dr. Hadary describes this unique program (Hadary and Cohen, 1978).

Other creative educators have developed and adapted science materials for their own use with elementary aged, VI youngsters (see references and bibliography at the end of this chapter), but these are not available to other special educators or mainstreamed classroom teachers. We think most educators will agree that the state of the art, with the exception of isolated individual efforts, is quite primitive.

But those of us who feel that there is a real need for materials-centered discovery science activities that allow visually impaired youngsters to have the extensive concrete experiences that are so important to cognitive development have reason to be optimistic now. When Public Law 94-142 passed in 1975, it was truly the shot heard around the special education world. Opinions concerning the effect the law has had on education are still at odds, but no one can deny that public and professional awareness of special education has increased manyfold. Happily, one question brought to light was that of science education for visually impaired youngsters. Action followed.

Building on seven years of experience in working with VI youngsters, the staff at Lawrence Hall of Science, under a grant from the Office of Education's Bureau of Education for the Handicapped, began a new project—Science Activities for the Visually Impaired (SAVI)—in August 1976. The primary goal of the SAVI project was to produce science activities that give VI youngsters, ages nine to 13 years, structured experiences with real objects and organisms. We knew that the most effective way for youngsters to learn, particularly VI youngsters, was with hands-on activities, designed to encourage the students to exercise all available sensory input to make discoveries. Through such multisensory experiences we hoped to enhance the youngsters' scientific literacy, logical thinking abilities, and manipulative skills. As the project developed, other high-priority goals emerged: development of the students' language skills, general application skills, and self-concept.

We started out to develop a science program that met the needs described by educators of VI students. Soon, however, we found ourselves developing a science-based program that not only conveyed key science concepts, but enhanced growth in a number of academic and social areas. Instead of the SAVI materials fitting only into existing science curricula, we found that the activities had a broad base of application and found a place in a multitude of curricular areas.

The most effective way for visually impaired youngsters to learn is through hands-on activities with real objects and organisms.

Multisensory science experiences enhance not only logical thinking and manipulative skills but language ability and self-concept as well.

73

Curriculum development begins with an exploratory phase: Staff members generate activities and try them out with students. Feedback from local and national trials results in a final product.

THE CURRICULUM DEVELOPMENT MODEL

The development model described here is not unique to the SAVI project, but is one used in many curriculum development projects emanating from the Lawrence Hall of Science. It is a three-phase process:

1. *The exploratory phase.* Staff members generate activity ideas and try them out with youngsters in their normal learning situations. After trials with a number of students, a preliminary draft of the activity and prototype equipment are prepared for local trials.

2. *The local trial phase.* The materials are given to local teachers of visually impaired youngsters after a training session at the Hall of Science, and the teachers use the activities in a variety of teaching situations (itinerant, resource room, residential class). Feedback is gathered by direct staff observations, written and verbal teacher feedback, and written evaluations of the students' progress as indicated on the Follow-Up tasks provided in each activity.

3. *The national trial phase.* Activity write-ups are revised and printed in folio format, revised equipment packages are manufactured, and these materials are shipped to national trial centers. The trial center directors come to the Hall of Science for training so that they can then train teachers in their locality. SAVI had seven centers across the country where a total of 60 teachers and 250 students used the science activities. These centers represent various geographical locations, educational settings, and science programs (if any) for visually impaired youngsters. Feedback results in a final product.

SAVI had two other valuable sources of information and direction: a local and a national advisory board whose members bring to SAVI their expertise in the fields of special education, science education, curriculum development, program evaluation, and staff training.

SAVI activities fall into nine modular areas: structure of life, scientific reasoning, communication, environments, mixtures and solutions, environmental energy, measurement, kitchen interactions, and magnetism and electricity.

THE PRODUCT OF OUR LABORS

The SAVI product is not a science curriculum meant to supplement a program already in operation, but is rather a series of activities that can enrich and supplement an existing science program for visually impaired youngsters. SAVI can, however, form the core around which a science program can develop. It is not geared to dovetail with any one text or program, but is designed to be woven into any of the currently used upper-elementary programs.

SAVI has developed 48 activities that fall into nine modular areas: Structure of Life, Scientific Reasoning, Communication, Environments, Mixtures and Solutions, Environmental Energy, Measurement, Kitchen Interactions, and Magnetism and Electricity. SAVI's modular format gives a great deal of flexibility to the program. Each module of four to seven sequenced activities includes some lower-level and some higher-level activities. Depending on the experience and needs of the youngsters, the suggested sequence of activities can be followed or altered to suit the particular situation. SAVI activities are designed to take from 30 minutes to an hour, including 10 minutes for the Follow-Up evaluation task.

Each activity appears in a SAVI folio which includes the following sections:

1. Overview: a brief synopsis of the activity.
2. Background: information about the science concepts of the activity for the teacher.
3. Purpose: specific objectives of the activity.
4. Materials: a list of equipment needed for the activity. (In our trials we provided standard equipment kits for all activities.)
5. Anticipating: what the teacher must do to prepare for the activity; prerequisite skills or activities needed by youngsters.
6. Doing the activity: the step-by-step lesson plan.
7. Follow-Up: an evaluation activity done immediately after the main activity.
8. Going Further: extensions of the activity.

9. Language Development: suggested communication skills activities related to the science activity.

10. General Application Skills: everyday application of skills and science concepts developed in the activity.

BEYOND SAVI

After the SAVI project goal of developing and testing a series of science enrichment activities for visually impaired students was completed, we wanted to extend the project to include students with other disabilities. With separate support from the Bureau of Education for the Handicapped, we started a new project called Science Enrichment for Learners with Physical Handicaps (SELPH). The two-fold purpose of the SELPH project was to adapt and modify the SAVI materials and procedures to be appropriate for orthopedically handicapped and learning disabled students, and to develop models for science learning centers in mainstreamed classrooms. The SELPH project completed its goals on August 8, 1981.

The result of the two projects is a single product: the SAVI/SELPH Program. The activities are appropriate for use in a wide range of educational situations with students exhibiting a number of disabilities. SAVI/SELPH activities have been used in self-contained L.D., O.H., and V.I. classrooms, non-categorical resource rooms, and in regular education classes where disabled students are mainstreamed. (See sample folio: *The Sugar Test,* pages 76-81.)

EFFECTIVE MATERIALS AND TEACHING STRATEGIES

The Logistics of Learning

Discovery-oriented activities require small groups. Four is about the greatest number of students one instructor can effectively guide when liquids are being poured, seeds planted, angles measured, and electrical circuits built. Currently, SAVI modules are packaged with enough equipment for four students to work together. Even with four students, often we find that they work at radically different rates, making even a lower student/instructor ratio advisable.

Students work at radically different rates: Four is about the greatest number of students an instructor can effectively guide.

The location of instruction is important to the success of the science program. Where a science room exists, there is usually no problem concerning work space, storage space or conflicts with other subject matter. Experiments can be set up and maintained or observed over time with relative ease. But where no science room exists, teachers must often be a bit creative. One alternative is to find a neutral location for science: a corner of the library, the cafeteria, a utility room, a corridor, or the auditorium. Itinerant teachers often find that these unoccupied spaces become their "labs" when they feel it is desirable to work only with their VI student. The problems of storage and the inconvenience of leaving an experiment to develop are obvious.

Learning centers are gaining popularity and offer several advantages for mainstreaming youngsters. A table at the back of the regular classroom becomes the work space, and a nearby cabinet provides secure storage. A VI student can learn science with a subset of his or her peers while the remainder of the class works on other subjects. Science is shared by everyone in the class, providing a common experience, but in a more intimate context.

In the case of the science room, or the classroom learning center, experiments and organism habitats can remain right in the students' learning environment. This is great because the VI student can assume the responsiblity for watering plants, feeding crayfish, monitoring environmental conditions, and recording changes over time. Taking the responsiblity for organisms and experiments is good for enhancing the students' self esteem.

Being responsible for experiments can enhance the visually impaired student's self-esteem.

Use of Equipment

It is our experience that a blind youngster must have his or her own set of materials to manipulate if learning is to be complete and efficient. In some cases

THE SUGAR TEST

OVERVIEW

In *The Sugar Test*, the youngsters have a second encounter with yeast. The youngsters conduct controlled experiments that enable them to compare the relative amounts of sugar in 2 kinds of cereals. They gain more experience recording data on record sheets and using some of the SAVI measuring tools (i.e. the balance, syringe, and volume tube).

BACKGROUND

Many packaged foods contain sugar, but how much — 5%, 10%, 25% or more? Manufacturers list a food's ingredients in order by percentage of weight, but do not indicate the exact percentages. The exact amount of sugar may be obtained from the food companies, but can also be approximated by using the SAVI Sugar Test.

The amount of sugar in one food can be compared with the amount of sugar in a second food. The comparison involves mixing equal weights of each food with yeast and water under identical conditions. By comparing the volume of carbon dioxide released by the yeast after all the sugar in each sample has been consumed, we can determine which sample contained more sugar. All variables in the experiment must be controlled (i.e. kept the same), except the one being tested — the kind of food.

Variables affecting the rate of carbon dioxide production (i.e. yeast metabolism) can be examined — temperature, for example. Yeast produces carbon dioxide fastest at about 45°C. Temperatures much higher than 45°C will destroy the yeast cells and stop metabolic action. At lower temperatures, the yeast metabolizes more slowly. The rate of carbon dioxide production (i.e. metabolic rate) depends in part on the yeast's environmental temperature.

Yeast can utilize only certain simple sugars for food. Starch, such as that in wheat flour, is composed essentially of simple sugars chemically combined in such a way that the sugars are useless to the yeast. But flour contains enzymes, too. These enzymes break the starch down into sugars that the yeast can use; however, the breakdown process takes hours. Thus, the yeast in the bread dough will be fed even if the cook doesn't add sugar when he mixes the dough. It just takes longer. This is actually desirable in making bread — the slower the rising process, the more uniform the texture of the bread.

PURPOSE

In *The Sugar Test*, the students:
1. Conduct controlled experiments using yeast as an *indicator* of the amount of sugar present in different foods.
2. Compare the amount of sugar in 2 cereals by using the results of their yeast experiments.
3. Gain experience with measuring tools:
a. The SAVI syringe (to measure and transfer 50 ml of water).
b. The SAVI balance (to weigh 3 grams of food).
c. The SAVI volume tube (to measure the volume of gas produced by the yeast).

MATERIALS (Supplied for four students)

For each student:
1 SAVI balance
1 syringe with 50-ml stop
4 plastic cups
3 1-gram pieces
3 zip bags
1 water bath (styrofoam container)
3 packages of dry baker's yeast
1 set of labels for the zip bags ("sugar," "Cheerios," "Natural")
1 Sugar Test Record Sheet

For each pair of students:
1 volume tube
1 water jug with lid
1 container of sugar
1 spoon (5 ml)
2 plastic containers (for storing the Cheerios and Natural)

For the group:
1 box of Cheerios
1 box of Natural
adhesive tape (for sticking labels to the bags)
recording dots
1 timer
1 thermometer (for teacher's use)
scissors*
paper towels*
water, 45°C* (See "Anticipating #2.")

For the FOLLOW UP:
1 Granola Bar

*Supplied by the teacher

ANTICIPATING

Prerequisite skills: The students should have completed *The Cookie Monster* before beginning this activity. Be prepared to review *The Cookie Monster* results with the youngsters. You may need to show them the use of the syringe and the volume tube, as well as the technique for removing the air before sealing the zip bags.

1. The activity is designed so that each youngster prepares all 3 experiment bags. However, you may have 2 students work together as a team and conduct 1 set of experiments.

2. If there is no hot water supply in the classroom, arrange to bring some water with you. You will need 1 jug of 45°C water for each pair of students. The water jugs provided can be transported inside 2 styrofoam containers (i.e. the water baths) to insulate the water. The water will cool gradually during the activity. This is OK.

3. Pour some Cheerios and Natural into separate plastic containers for each pair of students.

4. Cut out the labels for the bags.

5. Fill the volume tube bottles 1/2 full of water and secure the lids.

DOING THE ACTIVITY

1. REVIEWING YEAST. Give each youngster a package of yeast. Have the youngsters open the packages and dump the contents into a plastic cup. Ask them to tell you what the package contained:

☐ **"What happens when yeast is mixed with a cookie and warm water?"** [Gas is produced.]

☐ **"Which ingredient in the cookie is food for the yeast?"** [Sugar.]

☐ **"How do you know?"** (Review results from *The Cookie Monster,* if necessary.)

Review the term *indicator.* Tell the youngsters that yeast may be used to indicate the presence of sugar in foods, as well as the amount of sugar in foods (just as baking soda may be used to indicate the presence of acid in foods).

2. BRINGING OUT THE FOOD. Give each pair of youngsters a container of sugar and 2 plastic containers of cereal (Cheerios and Natural). If you feel that tasting these foods is all right at this time, tell the youngsters so. Don't let eating interfere with the activity.

3. FINDING MORE SUGAR. Ask the youngsters, **"Tell me how you would find out which of these cereals has more sugar in it than the other."** The youngsters will probably describe an experiment, but may not control all the variables. Remind them that all conditions must be the same in each experiment (i.e. in each bag), except the kind of cereal used. The students should *control* for:

a. The amount of water (50 ml in each bag).

b. The amount of yeast (1 package in each bag).

c. The amount of cereal (3 g in each bag).

d. The amount of time (15 minutes).

e. The temperature of the water (environmental temperature).

Suggest that the youngsters set up 3 bags: 1 with pure sugar as food for the yeast; 1 with Cheerios as food; and 1 with Natural as food. They should keep everything else in each bag the same. Explain to the students, **"At the end of the experiment we can compare the amounts of gas in the 3 bags. The more gas in a bag, the more sugar in the sample."** Remind them that 1 bag will contain 100% sugar as food.

4. MEASURING UP. Show the youngsters the balance and review its use. Show them how to place one plastic cup at each end of the balance arm and to check for "balance" by feeling the pointers. (When the 2 pointers line up, the weight on the 2 sides is equal.) Give each youngster a balance, 2 cups, and 3 1-gram pieces, and let them practice. Then ask them to explain how they would weigh out 3 grams of sugar.

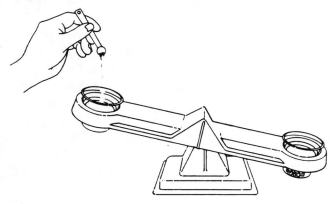

5. SETTING UP THE SUGAR TEST.
Follow this procedure:

a. Give each youngster 3 zip bags, 3 labels, and 2 more packages of yeast. Help the youngsters tape 1 of the 3 labels ("sugar," "Cheerios," "Natural") to each bag. Tell them to be careful not to poke holes in the bags.

b. Have the youngsters weigh out 3 grams of sugar (a spoon is helpful here) and transfer it to the "sugar" bag. Then have them weigh out 3 grams of Cheerios and 3 grams of Natural and transfer each to the proper bag.

c. Have the youngsters add 1 package of yeast to each zip bag.

d. Give each youngster a syringe and a cup of 45°C water. Instruct the students to put 1 syringeful (50 ml) of 45°C water into each bag. Have them bounce and squeeze the bags to mix the contents thoroughly. (Once the water is in the bags, you should encourage the students to work quickly until the bags are in the bath and the timer is set.)

e. Help the youngsters remove the air and seal the bags as soon as all the contents are thoroughly mixed. (Follow the same sealing procedure described in *The Cookie Monster*.)Ask the youngsters to check the seals on all the bags.

f. Have each youngster measure the starting volume of one of the bags with the volume tube.

g. Bring out a water bath for each student and fill the baths to a depth of 4 to 5 cm with 45°C water. Have the youngsters put their bags into the bath.

h. Help the students set the timer for 15 minutes.

6. WAITING 15 MINUTES.
While waiting, the students should clean up their work area and then go over the Sugar Test Record Sheet. Reinforce what is the same (i.e. kept constant) in all 3 experiment bags, and what is different in each of the experiment bags. Emphasize that the kind of food (i.e. pure sugar, Cheerios, and Natural) is the variable being investigated, and that any differences in the results of the experiments can be attributed to the different foods being investigated. (The more gas in the bag, the more sugar was present in the sample.)

Sugar Test Record Sheet		
Amount of yeast		1 Package
Amount of Food		3 Grams
Length of Time (min)		
500 ml	500 ml	500 ml
450	450	450
400	400	400
350	350	350
300	300	300
250	250	250
200	200	200
150	150	150
100	100	100
50	50	50
0	0	0
Cheerios	Natural	Sugar

7. KEEPING IN TOUCH.
Encourage the youngsters to feel the bags in the bath and gently push them down in the water during the experiment.

8. MEASURING THE RESULTS.
At the sound of the timer bell, have the youngsters measure the amount of gas in each of the 3 bags with the volume tube.

Have them record the results on the Record Sheet with the felt dots. Discuss the results with the youngsters and ask them which cereal has more sugar in it. Have them compare the cereal bags with the "sugar" bag.

9. GOING ON. If you have time, allow the experiment to continue. Ask the youngsters to put the bags back into the water bath and to measure the volumes at 30 minutes and at 45 minutes. After 45 minutes, all the sugar in each bag will be used up and it will be possible to estimate the percentage of sugar in each cereal by comparing the volume of gas released in the cereal bags with the volume of gas in the "sugar" bag. (If a cereal bag has about 1/4 as much gas as the "sugar" bag, the cereal sample is about 25% [1/4] sugar.) In order to calculate the percentage of sugar accurately, it will be necessary to prepare a larger volume tube. (See "Going Further #1.")

FOLLOW UP (Work with each student individually.)

Have 1 Granola Bar available.

1. Say to the student:
a. **"My friend Herb is on a diet. He is not supposed to eat much sugar. Would you recommend a breakfast of Cheerios or Natural?"**
b. **"Explain your answer."**

2. Give the student the Granola Bar and say:
a. **"Tell me exactly how you would find out how the sugar content of this Granola Bar compares with pure sugar. Explain exactly how you would conduct the experiment."**
b. **"Yesterday I tested for sugar in a Granola Bar. I used the zip-bag procedure you used today. After leaving the bag in the 45°C water bath for 15 minutes, I measured 100 ml of gas in the bag. Which of the foods you tested today has about the same amount of sugar in it as the Granola Bar?"**

GOING FURTHER

1. Looking for a science fair project? Here's one you might consider. Have the youngsters allow the sugar test experiment to go to completion (45 minutes), and then check the volume of gas in each bag. (See "Doing the Activity #9.") You will need to help the youngsters build a volume tube that is larger than the one provided in the equipment kit. Here's how to do it:
a. Cut the top off a half-gallon bleach container.
b. Cut a vertical slot in the side of the resulting cylinder. (See the illustration.)
c. Use a can with a diameter slightly smaller than the bleach container for the inner cylinder. (A 1-lb. coffee can with a cardboard circle glued to the bottom works well.)
d. Water placed in the can will serve as the weight in the inner cylinder.

The youngsters will have to calibrate the new volume tube. Give them a zip bag, a syringe, and some water. Help them follow this procedure for calibrating the tube:

e. Put 50 ml (1 syringeful) of water in a zip bag, remove the air, seal the bag, and put the bag into the new volume tube.

f. Set the inner cylinder (can) in the tube on top of the bag. Mark the spot where the bottom of the can appears in the slot on the outer cylinder. This is the "O" gas volume mark.

g. Put 100 ml (2 syringefuls) more water in the same zip bag, remove the air, seal the bag, and put the bag into the volume tube. Set the inner cylinder in the tube on top of the bag. Mark the spot where the bottom of the can appears in the slot. This is the "100 ml" gas volume mark.

h. Repeat this procedure with 200 ml, 300 ml, 400 ml . . . 700 ml of water. (You will need 700-ml capacity to measure the volume of the "sugar" bag.)

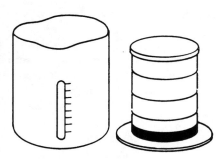

Have the youngsters compare the volume of gas in the "sugar" bag with the volume in the cereal bags, and use this information to calculate the percentage of sugar in the cereals.

2. Have the youngsters design a controlled experiment to investigate the effect of temperature on the sugar/yeast interaction. Try using cold water, room-temperature water, warm water, and very hot water.

3. Have the youngsters experiment with other cereals, and with cookies, crackers, and bread.

4. Have the youngsters use honey, molasses, or fruit juices instead of sugar, and find out what the yeast does with these foods.

LANGUAGE DEVELOPMENT

Vocabulary

Indicator: any substance (or device) used to inform an observer that something is present or occurring.

Yeast: a living organism that requires sugar, moisture, and warmth to grow. Yeast is purchased dry in stores and is used in making bread, beer, and wine.

Communication Skills

1. Have the youngsters make a list of prepared foods that yeast can use for food.

2. Have the students write to a few cookie or cereal companies and ask for literature on the percentage of sugar in their products.

SKILLS FOR EVERYDAY LIFE

1. Every food package contains a list of ingredients. The ingredients are listed in order by percentage weight. Help the youngsters locate and read these labels.

2. Have the youngsters read and discuss different bread recipes. Have them find out how yeast is used in bread and other foods. Then try some of the recipes.

This work was developed under Grant No. G00-76-02944 with the U.S. Office of Education, Department of Health, Education, and Welfare. However, the opinions expressed herein do not necessarily reflect the position or policy of that Agency, and no official endorsement should be inferred.

a piece of equipment can be shared by two, but each student must have the total hands-on experience using the apparatus to gather his or her own data. The balance is such an example. Usually it is not necessary for each student to have a balance, but it is important for each student to do his or her own weighing when such data is needed. Blind students, unlike their sighted peers, simply do not have the ability to make passive observations; learning must be active. Consequently, an active science program demands a definite commitment to materials. The return will more than justify the initial effort.

The Hardware

All student materials in activities must be carefully selected with the blind youngsters' needs in mind. For example, in SAVI, the large size and short germination period of seeds used in planting experiments, the simple habitat requirements and durable structure of crayfish, and the different textures of the powders and salts used in the solutions activities have all been selected after repeated trials with youngsters. We want to ensure that blind students can easily and effectively handle all of the experimental materials.

A great deal of time and effort went into the preparation of the SAVI scientific tools to make certain that the blind students can make measurements and observations equivalent to those made by their sighted peers. When we could not find an appropriate braille and large print Celsius thermometer on the market, we designed one and manufactured it (see Figure 10.1). Similarly, meter tapes, increment volume measurers for gases and liquids, balances, and sorting trays, all appropriate for the needs of blind students, were made in our shop. And, not surprisingly, these same blind-appropriate scientific tools were excellent for sighted students. Consequently, blind and regular students work side by side making equivalent observations with identical tools.

The story of the SAVI balance is a good example of ways to modify existing equipment to provide a versatile tool with many applications.

In order to develop the concept of mass in the SAVI Measurement Module, we needed a measuring tool that was suitable for use by the visually impaired. We finally decided to use a balance instead of a spring scale or other device, and this decision resulted in some unexpected dividends for the project.

We looked at a lot of balances and even built a few of our own before we made the decision. Finally we chose a simple, vacuum-formed model that is commercially available at a reasonable price. Then we went to work on it.

First, we cut out the bottoms of the two balance pans so that a paper or plastic cup could be dropped securely into the hole and then removed easily. Then we added a tactile balance indicator. These modifications made it possible for blind students to determine weight to an accuracy of one gram!

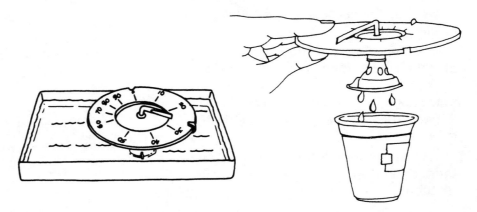

Figure 10.1. At the left, the braille and large print Celsius thermometer designed for the SAVI project. At right, the thermometer in use.

The removable cup was the breakthrough we needed to make accurate weighing easy for visually impaired students. Both the weights (20 g, 10 g, 5 g, 1 g plastic pieces) and the objects or substances to be weighed automatically centered in the cups, thus eliminating discrepancies due to the position of objects in the cups. An object, substance, or liquid can be removed from the balance *cup and all*, a new cup inserted, and a new material weighed. There's no more trouble "getting all the powder out," or "transferring all the beans"; the objects stay in the cups.

The students use the balances to verify that 50 ml of water (measured with a modified SAVI syringe) weighs 50 g, thereby establishing the relationship between volume and mass (see Figure 10.2).

Since its introduction, the SAVI balance has crept into other modules. The Kitchen Interactions Module features an activity that focuses on the concept of density. Density is defined operationally using the SAVI balance: equal volumes of two different liquids are compared on the balance, and the heavier one is identified as the *denser* liquid.

In the Magnetism and Electricity Module, the students investigate the force of attraction between two magnets, using the SAVI balance. The balance is set up on a special stand so that a magnet glued to the bottom of one of the cups is positioned to come into contact with a second magnet that is secured to the stand. The two magnets stick together, but when enough weight is added to the second cup, this weight will break the force of attraction between the two magnets. The students then go on to observe and measure the force of attraction when "spacers" of varying thickness are placed between the two magnets.

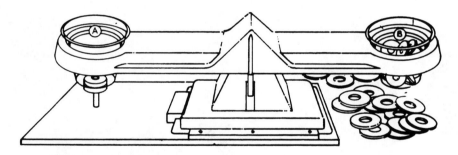

Figure 10.2. The SAVI-modified balance being used to determine the force of attraction between two magnets.

Another versatile tool SAVI uses is the 50 ml plastic syringe. We modified this peice of equipment in two ways:

1. A metal stop was attached in such a way that when the plunger of the syringe is pulled all the way to the stop, exactly 50 ml of liquid has been drawn up into the syringe.

2. In the *Acid Test* activity, the syringe is used to measure 5 ml of liquid and also to measure the amount of CO_2 that evolves during an acid/baking soda reaction. In this case there is no stop. Instead, notches (half circles made with a paper hole punch) at ¼, ½, and ¾ capacity were cut on the plunger. A 5 ml "step" (v-notch) was also cut into the plunger. When the plunger is pulled out so that the step is even with the end of the syringe barrel, 5 ml of liquid has been drawn into the syringe (see Figure 10.3).

Plastic tripour beakers (50 ml, 100 ml, 250 ml) are handy for measuring larger volumes of water when the challenge is to transfer the *same amount* of water to several cups or planter pots. Using the dip method, the student holds the tripour beaker by one flange, dips the beaker into a wide-mouth pitcher of water, and takes a *full* beaker of water—up to the brim. This is then poured into a cup or a

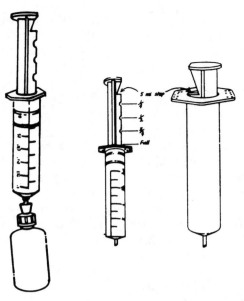

Figure 10.3
The SAVI-modified
50 ml syringe,
with a close-up
of the 5 ml "step"
in the plunger.

solar water heater or used to water plants. Using a 100 ml beaker in this fashion allows for the transfer of about 125 ml of water (see Figure 10.4)). When it is essential that exactly 100 ml be transferred, the beaker is modified with a hole punched at the 100 level. The student places the beaker in a tray and pours water into the beaker until water spills out of the hole. When it stops dribbling, exactly 100 ml is in the beaker.

Figure 10.4.
A plastic tripour
beaker being
used as a dipper
for measuring
and transferring
water.

We modified a graduated cylinder with a tactile floating scale. The cylinder is used (with the 50 ml syringe) to measure small volumes of liquid. To use the modified cylinder, water is poured (or squirted) into the cylinder. The scale is then dropped into the cylinder so that the measuring stick points up. By pinching the scale at the spot where the scale intersects the top rim of the cylinder, pulling the scale out of the cylinder, and counting down from the top notch (0 mark) to the pinch spot, the volume of water can be determined to the nearest 2 ml (see Figure 10.5).

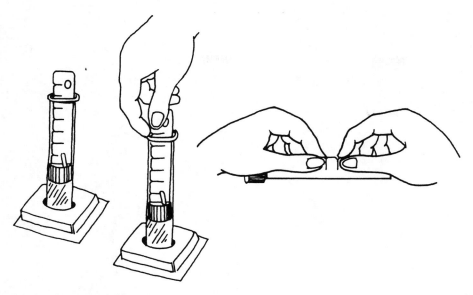

Figure 10.5. A graduated cylinder with a SAVI-designed tactile floating scale.

Organization and Recording

In line with effective materials development, we've learned (the hard way) the need for organization of the work space. The most important organizational aid is some sort of tray with compartments. We surveyed the field and tested many models with youngsters. Ultimately we designed our own, and it has proved to be both effective and versatile.

Figure 10.6. The SAVI sorting tray, here being used as a planter for a seed-growing experiment.

The SAVI sorting tray is 40 × 25 cm, and the six round compartments are about 3 cm deep. Students use it time and again for many purposes. One time it is used to sort a collection of seeds (see Figure 11.6); another time it is a planter tray used to organize a series of seed-growing experiments. The tray is at other times an organizer for cups of liquids to minimize spills, and a tactile 2 × 3 graph in other activities. Using the tray in such ways saves time and reduces frustrations caused by loss of materials and spills (see Figure 10.7).

Figure 10.7. The SAVI tray has many uses; here it serves as an organizer for cups of liquids and other materials.

There are other tricks for helping youngsters keep their work space organized. Providing materials when needed and removing them when they are no longer needed reduces clutter and confusion. When we go outdoors, we take along a large piece of cardboard. This provides a comprehensible surface upon which investigations are organized. A few more general rules that we have tried to adhere to include: keeping experimental set-ups to a size that the student can easily reach out and feel in their entirety; keeping individual pieces of equipment small enough that they can be manipulated and oriented with one hand; and taping pieces of apparatus or electrical connections to a work surface once they are positioned in their proper places.

Closely akin to organizational considerations are the needs for labeling and for specialized recording techniques. In SAVI we provide dual-format labels: sheets of thermoformed labels with large print above each row of braille type. The large print is applied first (by a commercial printer), followed by braille thermoforming. For a small number of copies, use a Sharpie pen to hand-letter large print on labels after the braille has been thermoformed. For "braille-only" labels, the braille dymotape (available from the American Foundation for the Blind) or the self-adhesive plastic Braillable works well. Permanent marking pens on masking tape work fine for print readers. These labels are taped onto cups, a sorting tray, planter pots, or plastic bags. All these labelling techniques provide waterproof labels. Dual-format labels, whether on the back of a crayfish, on a sorting tray, or on plastic cups, are usable by blind, low vision, and regular students working together. Most labelling is best done by the teacher before the activity or as the activity proceeds (see Figure 10.8).

Figure 10.8. Dual-format labels, printed in both large print and braille.

swollen	split open	seed coat off
has a root	has a stem	has leaves
swollen	split open	seed coat off
has a root	has a stem	has leaves
swollen	split open	seed coat off
has a root	has a stem	has leaves
swollen	split open	seed coat off
has a root	has a stem	has leaves

Students need to learn how to record the results of their experiments for later interpretation. In SAVI, record sheets are prepared in either large print or braille, but are identical otherwise. Students use gummed felt or rubber dots to record data on number lines representing heart beats, degrees Celsius, grams, milliliters, and so forth (see Figure 10.9).

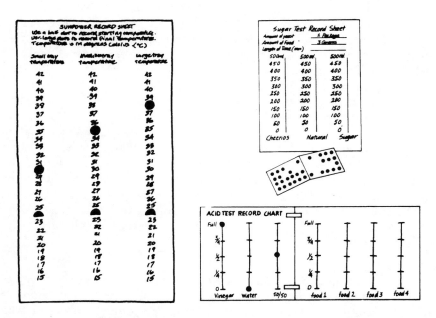

Figure 10.9. A SAVI record sheet in large print (it can also be prepared in braille). Students record data by attaching gummed dots to the numbered lines.

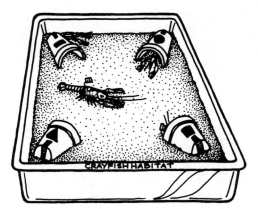

Figure 10.10. The SAVI crayfish habitat and "crayfish graph."

Simple graphs are more complicated for youngsters, but with some instruction they can also be used to record data for later use. In an activity where students study the territorial behavior of crayfish, the student record sheet is a thermoformed three-dimensional graphic representation of the crayfish habitat with crayfish houses in place. Each day the student locates the crayfish in the habitat and records their locations on a record sheet by sticking little plastic crayfish on the sheet. Data recorded in this manner is available for analysis by blind and regular students alike (see Figure 10.10).

Concept Development

The goals of a science program for VI students fall into three major, generalizable areas: the development of manipulative skills, the development of science process skills, and the development of science concepts. The manipulative skills (the student is able to accomplish the mechanical operations required) and the process skills (the student understands how to measure the mass of an object) are closely associated with the selection and appropriateness of the tools and materials the students use. These topics have been covered in the "Hardware" section.

Science concepts, too, need to be delivered with special considerations. Learning situations must be engineered so that the student has an experience, and then a concept is attached to that experience in terms of an appropriate *operational definition*. For example, when salt is mixed with water, the sighted student sees that the salt has disappeared and the mixture is clear. Hence, the visual definition of a solution. However, "clear" has no concrete meaning for a blind student, so we must take the process a step further; filter the resulting salt/water mixture. If no material is reclaimed on the filter paper, that is the blind student's equivalent of "clear." So we now invent a concept. If a solid material and a liquid are mixed, and the two cannot be separated with a filter, the mixture is called a "solution." We must use an operational definition that is tactile, rather than the usual visual definition. Similarly, the concept of "reflection" is based on *feeling* heat from the sun reflecting on the student's face, rather than the more common concept of light or image "reflection" developed with sighted learners. Using these specialized definitions with all students enriches their understanding of the concepts under investigation and encourages a multisensory approach to information collecting.

Motivation

One of the most exciting discoveries that we made during the process of developing the SAVI program was the student enthusiasm for the project. Even students who claimed they "hated science" when interviewed before involvement with any activities became dedicated "scientists" when introduced to hands-on discovery activities. As time progressed we began to realize that science has a great potential for being more than a discipline; science could be the medium—a motivational vehicle—for involving students in active learning in fundamental areas. Living skills, language arts, computation, and self-concept all can be integrated into the flow of a science program. The limited work we have done in this area has been very exciting, and we urge teachers to be sensitive to the interdisciplinary opportunities that appear spontaneously in just about every activity.

SCIENCE AND THE EDUCATIONAL PLAN OF VISUALLY IMPAIRED STUDENTS

As we indicated at the beginning of this chapter, science is rarely if ever indicated as a priority in the individualized educational plan for VI students. The priority areas tend to deal with survival skills, both academic and social. Because we feel so strongly that science is fundamental to every person's perception and understanding of his or her universe, and the mental training ground for the development of a class of thinking skills—logic, analysis, synthesis, proportionality, to name a few—we will always strive to increase the appeal of science programming. In addition to making the activities exciting and enjoyable for the learners, we also must make them versatile and convenient for teachers to incorporate into educational plans. At this time, that translates into "Does it teach the fundamental three R's? Does it contribute to the social growth of my student?" We have attempted to illuminate opportunities in each activity that contribute to growth in these fundamental areas, so that we can say, "Yes, science and fundamentals go together!" Let's consider some examples from the SAVI program.

Science, though fundamental to one's perception of the universe, is rarely a priority in the IEP.

Dropping In is an activity in the Communication Module. Youngsters are introduced to the idea of sound discrimination. They listen to the sounds created by a variety of objects when they are dropped onto a hard surface. Once familiar with the different sounds, two youngsters are challenged to select six objects that are easily discriminated, and they assign letters of the alphabet to them. Of course, both students must work together so that they arrive at identical six-letter alphabets. They send messages back and forth by dropping "letters" (objects) one at a time.

The game atmosphere stimulates the students to apply their developing skills of spelling, phonetics, letter sequencing, writing (brailling), and speaking while tuning up their auditory discrimination skills. As language skills improve, more letters (objects) can be added to the alphabet, blends (*sh, ch,* etc.) inserted for single letters, suffixes and prefixes added, and mystery letters utilized. Language is fun in the context of science.

Seed-grams is an activity in the Structures of Life Module. The students open pea pods, count the number of peas inside, and record this information on a histogram. Math concepts such as "range," "average," and "mean" can be explored in the context of the activity. At a lower level, arithmetic concepts such as "count," "number," "more," "less," and "add" can be exercised. Word problems are suggested, and more can be generated in the context of the activity. Math comes to life in a science activity.

In addition to making activities enjoyable for the learners, we must make them convenient for teachers to incorporate into educational plans.

In order to make it simple for a teacher to identify the opportunities in each activity for developing fundamental skill areas, we are providing a matrix with each SAVI module overview. The matrix has specific information related to the activities in the module, but the matrix language is general enough to be appropriate for direct incorporation into a youngster's IEP.

The Sugar Test

As an example, the following is the matrix information on the activity that appears in this chapter—*The Sugar Test* from the Kitchen Interactions Module.

Activity/Description

After learning that yeast uses sugar as food (in the SAVI Cookie Monster), the students set up experiments to determine the amount of sugar in a selection of breakfast cereals. They mix equal samples of pure sugar and two different cereals with yeast and warm water and allow the mixtures to interact for 15 minutes. The students measure the volume of gas liberated in each case and use this information to compare the sugar content of each cereal.

Science Concepts

Yeast is a living organism that requires sugar, moisture, and warmth to grow. Yeast releases a gas as it metabolizes.

Yeast can be used as an indicator of the presence of sugar in foods.

Process Skills

Conduct controlled experiments to determine the relative amount of sugar in foods.

Compare the amount of sugar in two cereals by using the results of their yeast experiment.

General Application Skills

Organizational skills: Organize work space effectively.

Cooking skills: Use tools effectively (syringe, balance, volume tube); measure accurately; understand food package labels and recipes.

Perceptual motor skills: Develop fine motor skills involved in using measuring tools.

Pre-vocational skills: Learn to follow directions.

Language Development

Vocabulary: "Yeast." "indicator."

Oral language: Receive and respond to instructions; explain and demonstrate a procedure.

Written language: Read scales for gathering data; read record sheets to draw conclusions; write letters to corporations to gather information.

Related Learning Areas

Math: Understand numerical values for weight and volume; calculate percentage of sugar in foods.

Consumer education: read package labels for understanding.

SELF-CONCEPT

We often see growth in self-esteem and social responsibility stimulated by science program materials, but the event, object, or situation that initiates such growth is often hard to anticipate. Generally, however, living organisms, both plant and animal, seem to get students animated. We've seen VI students who were charged with the responsibility for the care and maintenance of crayfish become the school "experts." One youngster visited every class in school and shared her knowledge with everyone. Subsequently, many new friendships were made and the student's self-concept was greatly elevated. The interest generated by science materials can act as a social ice-breaker.

In conclusion, we would like to share with you a comment from a special educator using SAVI with a mainstreamed exceptional youngster in the elementary grades. The boy was involved in the *Sprouting Seed* activity in the Structures of Life Module.

"The (regular) classroom teacher reports that John is very proud of his activity. Each day he hurries to water the sprouts and taps the drain for the entire 10 minutes to make sure they drain properly. This is a student some teachers report to be extremely lacking in motivation! John filled out a chart with times for watering and for noting changes in the seeds daily, and gave it to me the next week. His sprouts looked great. He has explained the activity to teachers and classmates and takes very good care of all the materials. The activity seems to have given him a great deal of status at his school."

SAVI PROGRAM MATERIALS

Of the 48 activities developed in the SAVI program, 40 have been revised and prepared for national distribution. The 40 activities are grouped into nine

Living organisms, both plant and animal, seem to get students animated.

The interest generated by science materials can act as a social ice-breaker.

modules, and a student equipment kit is available for each module. In addition to the printed folios, which are the teacher guides, and the student equipment kits, SAVI/SELPH also offers a guide to student reading called SAVI/SELPH *Reading Further*, and a leadership trainers manual to help local leadership people implement science programs for disabled students.

The nine modules cover a number of content areas in both the physical and biological sciences, and utilize both indoor and outdoor study sites. The following is a list of the module titles, with a brief description of each, and a listing of each activity title within the modules.

Measurement module.
This module contains four activities that introduce your youngsters to standard metric measurement. The students use a variety of specially developed tools that not only permit easy measurements, but help to stimulate the development of manipulative skills. (*The First Straw, Take Me to Your Liter, Weight Watching, The Third Degree*)

Structures of Life module.
The primary goal in this module of seven activities is to provide experiences with both plants and animals and to help the students learn something about the organisms they explore. The two major concepts that students explore in this module are *growth* and *behavior*. (*Origin of Seeds, Seed Grams, The Sprouting Seed, Growing Further, Roots, Meet the Crayfish, Crayfish at Home*)

Concepts of growth and behavior are explored through such activities as "The Sprouting Seed" and "Crayfish at Home."

Scientific Reasoning module.
The five activities in this module are designed to help students develop skill in making observations and processing the information they obtain from those observations. These activities are concerned with the concepts of *variable* and *controlled experimentation*. (*Jump It, Howdy Heart, Swingers, Plane Sense, Rafts*)

Communication module.
This module contains four activities dealing with the physics of sound. The specific goals include: sharpening the students' sound discrimination skills; helping the youngsters become familiar with sound sources, sound receivers, and sound amplification; introducing the concept of *pitch*; and bringing the youngsters to an understanding of the relationship between vibration and sound. (*Dropping In, Small Sounds/Big Ears, What's Your Pitch?, Vibration = Sound*)

Magnetism and Electricity module.
The four activities in this module provide your student with the basic concepts of *magnetic attraction* and *repulsion*, circuit, insulator, conductor, and *electromagnetism*. These concepts are integrated as the students build a telegraph and send coded messages. (*The Force, Making Connections, Current Attractions, Click It*)

Mixtures and Solutions module
This module contains four activities that are designed to introduce your students to the concepts of *mixture, solution, concentration, saturation*, and *evaporation*. These activities also foster growth in manipulative skills (e.g. measuring, transferring, and filtering), organizational ability, and observational skills. (*Separating Mixtures, Concentration, Reaching Saturation, The Fizz Quiz*)

Students learn about magnetism and electricity as they build a telegraph and send coded messages.

Environments module.
The four activities in this module introduce your youngsters to the concept of discovering which factors make an environment a suitable place for an organism to live. During the course of their investigations, the students find that different organisms require different types of environments and that a suitable environment fosters growth and survival. (*Environmental Plantings, Sea What Grows, Isopods, The Wanted Weed*)

Kitchen Interactions module.

The four activities in this module provide experiences with common household substances: baking soda, yeast, lemons, salt, and cookies. These somewhat higher-level activities call upon several techniques and tools introduced in other SAVI modules, e.g, controlled experimentation and metric measurement. (*The Acid Test, How Dense?, The Cookie Monster, The Sugar Test*)

Environmental Energy module.

In this module of four activities, the youngsters construct solar water heaters and pinwheels to collect environmental energy from the sun and wind. (*Solar Water Heater, Sun Power, Blowin' in the Wind, Wind Power*)

The specialized nature of the SAVI/SELPH materials, and the thin market potential created some difficulty when we began to seek a commercial publisher. Ultimately we decided to publish the program at the Center for Multisensory Learning at the Lawrence Hall of Science on a non-profit, cost recovery basis. (See References.)

References

Baughman, J. and Zollman, D. Physics lab for the blind. *The Physics Teacher*, 1977, *15*, 339–342.

Benham, T. A. Science for the blind. *American Journal of Physics*, 1956, *24:* 45.

Boldt, W. The development of scientific training in blind children and adolescents: Results of empirical research regarding the teaching of science in schools of the blind. *Education of the Visually Handicapped*, 1969, March.

Bran, C. A. Secondary school sciences for the blind. *International Journal for the Education of the Blind*, October 1956, pp. 11–18.

Bunner, W. R., and Bunner, R. T. What about your visually defective student? *The American Biology Teacher*, Volume 30 No. 2 (February 1968), 108–09.

Central Catalog (9th ed.). Instructional Materials Reference Center for Visually Handicapped Children, Louisville: American Printing House for the Blind.

Cravats, M. Biology for the Blind. *The Science Teacher*, April 1972, p. 5.

Egbert, M., Glass, R. & Ricker, K. *Science for the handicapped: An annotated bibliography.* Columbus, Ohio: Ohio State University, ERIC/SMEAC Information Reference Center.

Eichenberger, R. J. Teaching Science to the Blind Student. *The Science Teacher,* December 1974, pp. 53–54.

Francouer, P., and Belhah, E. Teaching the mammalian heart to the visually handicapped: A lesson in concrete experience. *The Science Teacher*, December 1975, pp. 8–11.

Franks, F. L. *Institute report on introducing basic science concepts to primary grade visually handicapped students.* Louisville: American Printing House for the Blind (Instructional Materials Reference Center), 1972.

Garvey, J. Touch and see nature trail. *Science and Children*, October 1968, pp. 20–22.

Gottesman, M. Comparative study of Piaget's development schema of sighted children with that to blind children. *Child Development*, 1971, *42*, 537–538.

Gough, E. R. Common sense and sensibility in teaching the blind. *The Science Teacher*, December 1978, pp. 34–35.

Hadary, D. E., and Cohen, S. H. *Laboratory science and art for blind, deaf, and emotionally disturbed children: A mainstreaming approach.* Baltimore: University Park Press, 1978.

Henderson, D. R. Laboratory methods in physics for the blind. Pittsburgh University, ERID ED 011-155, Number 9, September 1967.

Kaschner-Jagoda, S. Viewing the earth with closed eyes. *Science Activities,* Fall 1978.

Kaufman, A. S. Science for the blind in the secondary schools. Paper presented at National Science Teachers Association, Philadelphia, March 1979.

Lennon, E. M., Feirer, J. L., Purdy, W. K. Metrics for visually impaired persons. *New Outlook for the Blind*, 1976, *70*,1–4.

Lewis, M. *Elementary Science Teacher*, Tennessee School for the Blind (Evaluation of Xerox Science Materials).

Linn, C., and Thier, H. Adapting science materials for the blind (ASMB): Expectation for student outcomes. *Science Education*, 1975, *59*, pp. 237–246.

Malone, L.. and De Lucci, L. Life science for visually impaired students. *Science and Children*, Februrary 1979, pp. 29–31.

Pappas, C. Teaching chemistry at Perkins. *Proceedings of the 40th Annual Convention of the American Association of Instructors of the Blind*, 1950, 27–129.

Piltz, A. Gardening for the blind child. *Science and Children*. October 1968, 25.

Ricker, K. S. Extending a learning center to the visually handicapped. Paper presented at the CAUSE Symposium, NSTA National Convention, Atlanta, March 1979.

SAVI/SELPH Program. *Activity modules*. Berkeley, CA.: Center for Multisensory Learning, Lawrence Hall of Sciences, University of California, 1981.

Schwartz, R. Survey of nature trails for the visually impaired. *Journal of Visual Impairment and Blindness*, 1977, *71*, 54–61.

Thier, H. D. Laboratory science for visually handicapped elementary school children. *The New Outlook for the Blind*, 1971, *65*, 190–94.

Tombaugh, E. D. Biology for the blind. 1973, Euclid Public Schools, Euclid, Ohio.

Thompson, B. Science for the Handicapped Association, Bibliography. University of Wisconsin—Eau Clair, April, 1979.

Vermeij, G. J. A blind teacher speaks out on teaching the blind student. *Today's Education*, November-December 1978, pp. 77–78.

Weems, B. A physical science course for the visually impaired. *The Physics Teacher*, 1977, *15*, 333–338.

CHAPTER 11	# Nurturing High Self-Esteem in Visually Handicapped Children
	Sally S. Mangold, Ph.D.

Nurturing high self-esteem in a visually handicapped child requires that his social, emotional, and academic development be well balanced. Realistic goals must be set in the light of the child's individual achievement and capabilities. Establishing a meaningful environment demands identifying any developmental differences that may result from visual deprivation. Educators and parents should provide activities that will help the child fully understand basic concepts, their interrelationship in the environment, and the dynamic role of the individual in determining his own future. The quality of life need not be compromised because of a visual defect. The most important element in a child's eventual appreciation of his existence is the harmony of thought and action that results from promoting strengths rather than deficits. This chapter reviews what is known about the perceptual organization of visually handicapped children, examines the work of Dr. Stanley Coopersmith and other authorities interested in the development of self-esteem, and offers practical suggestions for nurturing high self-esteem in visually handicapped children.

THE PERCEPTION OF VISUALLY HANDICAPPED CHILDREN

The perceptual organization of the visually handicapped child is best understood by recognizing that tactual and visual information differ greatly and cannot be assumed to foster identical concepts. Visual information is rich with a variety of detail. Shape, color, size, and function are perceived simultaneously to form the association that underlies object recognition. The child who is congenitally blind must build concepts about the world around her without benefit of visual information. She must derive her meaning from other data: texture, weight, temperature, and shape. These four impressions merge into the formation of a tactually oriented concept. Objects perceived as a sequence of touch sensations are recognized through discernible touch qualities (Scott, 1969). Because the visually handicapped child forms her ideas about objects and their interrelationships from tactual, not visual, properties, awareness may be altered (Rogow, 1975). Not only is perception of distance, perspective, angles, and relationships between objects different for the visually handicapped child, but also those features that are perceived first and seem most simple to the sighted child may represent more complex relationships to the visually handicapped. On the other hand, the ability to identify objects by touch alone comes later for sighted children.

It is fascinating to examine the contradictions in knowledge related to the perception of the visually handicapped child. There are often developmental delays in auditory discrimination and motor coordination in the young visually handicapped child. The techniques of attending to auditory cues used by older visually handicapped children may be more highly developed than in their sighted peers. Differences may well occur in imagery between visually handicapped

Dr. Sally Mangold, associate professor in special education at San Francisco State University, has for fifteen years been a resource teacher for visually handicapped students in the Castro Valley Unified School District. She has written several publications to aid teachers of the visually impaired and is also much in demand as a lecturer. This chapter originally appeared in *The Self-Concept of the Young Child*, Thomas D. Yawkey, ed. Provo, Utah: Brigham Young University, 1980.

and sighted children when they are presented with identical stimulus. The degree of difference seems to be influenced by the child's visual history (Clark and Warren, 1978). The disparate findings of investigators strongly suggest that many factors other than vision influence the development of each visually handicapped child. Many attempts to study the perceptual strategies used by visually handicapped children have concentrated upon verbal abilities. Tillman and Williams (1968) found visually handicapped children to be superior to normally sighted children on a word usage task. Witkin et al. (1968) found visually handicapped children to be often superior to normally sighted children on verbal ability. Opposite findings were reported by Zweibelson and Barg (1967); they reported that visually handicapped children were inferior to normally sighted children on tests of verbal abstraction ability. Similar findings have been reported by Axelrod (1959); he found visually handicapped children to be deficient in abstraction when they were measured by tactual and auditory tasks. Research data, therefore, is sometimes contradictory. Because many tests are idiosyncratic to the investigator, it is almost impossible to compare the data in a systematic way. Research data is also relatively sparse and is usually produced by limited samples. Extraneous variables that might dramatically alter the results of the studies are frequently overlooked. In some cases subjects are inappropriately matched; in other instances subjects having multiple handicaps, severe deprivation, and emotional disturbance are insufficiently screened.

Research that addresses the perceptual organization of visually handicapped children is desperately needed. Researchers can help us answer the following questions:

- What is the correlation between high tactual discrimination and imagery abstraction ability?
- Do children who have a rich background of experience possess higher self-esteem than those who gain information only through verbal explanations?
- Are the variables that influence self-esteem the same for visually handicapped children and sighted children?
- What quantity and quality of input about life will enhance high self-esteem in the visually handicapped child?

Practical answers to questions such as these will help teachers and parents create an environment for the visually handicapped that will nurture feelings of high self-esteem.

We do know for certain that few identifiable characteristics typify *all* visually handicapped children. A careful analysis of each child's abilities, disabilities, pleasures, and fears will yield the most useful information for designing a program to promote high self-esteem. As we have no indication that the lack of vision has a universal effect upon children, it seems appropriate to study and utilize those techniques that promote high self-esteem in sighted children. Given appropriate adaptations, the majority of visually handicapped children are now educated along with their sighted peers. The resulting achievement levels parallel those reported for "normal" students having equivalent abilities. Therefore, the formation of high self-esteem in visually handicapped children appears to parallel that of their sighted counterparts, and the factors that influence the development of self-esteem seem to be indentical for all children, regardless of prevailing handicaps.

GUIDELINES FOR PARENTS AND PROFESSIONALS
The conditions that influence the formation of self-esteem have been extensively studied by Dr. Stanley Coopersmith. His findings provide increased understanding of how and why identifiable circumstances in a child's life affect his growth as they do. His investigations focused upon the dimensions of capacity and treatment assumed by experts to be related to the formation of self-esteem, as well as the age

Many factors other than vision influence the development of the visually handicapped child. Few identifiable characteristics typify all visually handicapped children.

Factors that influence the development of self-esteem seem to be identical for all children, regardless of handicap.

Parents of children with high self-esteem are consistent in their relationships with their children and demonstrate an affectionate acceptance of them.

factors and areas of experience that seem to influence greatly that formation.

Dr. Coopersmith examined the lives of 271 children to identify the most influential factors that determine the growth of high self-esteem. He found that parents of children with high self-esteem demonstrated not only consistency in their relationships with their children but also affectionate acceptance of them.

The most general statement about the antecedents of self-esteem can be given in terms of three conditions: total or nearly total acceptance of the children by their parents; clearly defined and enforced limits; and the respect and latitude for individual action that exist within the defined limits. In effect, we may conclude that the parents of children with high self-esteem are concerned and attentive toward their children. They structure the worlds of their children along lines they believe to be proper and appropriate. They permit relatively great freedom within the structures they have established (Coopersmith, 1967).

Parents, upon the discovery that their child has a visual handicap, often experience feelings of shock, disappointment, and guilt. They wrestle with the questions "Why me? Why my child?" Dreams of sharing experiences with him are shattered; suddenly they and their child have been placed in two different worlds. These initial feelings are normal, but most parents accept the challenge and find that many experiences and activities can be shared. The acceptance of this challenge is essential to the healthy growth of the parent/child relationship. Then many parents find their focus changes from what cannot be to what can be and from what is not possible to what is possible. They explore games that have been adapted to the visually handicapped child, and they are often surprised to find how many games need no adaptation at all. They discover a wealth of activities that the whole family can enjoy together, such as roller skating, bicycling (using a tandem), camping, and backpacking. As more and more activities are added to the list, the family as a unit gains a sense of high self-esteem. How parents have dealt with crises in the past will probably determine the length of time they will require for each stage of adjustment and the degree of professional guidance they will need.

Some visually handicapped children seek perfection because they believe sighted persons are super beings who do not make mistakes.

Sometimes parents search out or meet by chance high-functioning visually handicapped teenagers or adults in the community. They can become powerful model figures for the family. It is important for parents to see them as individuals having innate capabilities and differing backgrounds of experience and training; an individual is not born high-functioning but becomes so because of natural capabilities and training. A myriad of life experiences and well-established vocational training program may be crucial in fostering a high level of functioning. A child's acquiring a broad experiential background will require ingenuity and creativity on the part of parents and teachers and on the part of the visually handicapped child herself.

To seek perfection is futile, yet some visually handicapped children persist in doing this because they believe sighted persons are super beings incapable of spilling food, bumping into things, or making naive statements. Parents can help the visually handicapped child realize that others make mistakes too. Verbalize such statements as "Sometimes I think I am the world's sloppiest cook; just look at the counter," or "I saw a lady in the store yesterday; she was careless and knocked a jar of strawberry jam onto the floor," or "What a mess! Your brother spilled pop all over his shirt." Gradually the child will see her own errors in proper perspective and will not be overly concerned when mistakes occur.

If pushed too hard into tactile exploration, the child will develop an aversion to these experiences.

The visually handicapped child must learn about his environment; he must accomplish this with a total lack, or greatly diminished amount, of visual input. The trick is to build upon his natural curiosity and make it possible for him to explore the environment tactually. One should, however, take care not to go beyond his natural curiosity and interest. In other words, he should not be forced into tactile exploration; if pushed too hard, he will surely develop an aversion to tactile experiences. Remember that the child's exploration of the environment is by no means limited to the tactile sense. Once he understands shapes, size, and textures he can gain vast amounts of knowledge about the world through verbal description. For example, a kidney-shaped swimming pool can easily be described to the child if he has experienced other kidney-shaped objects; if he does not have this basic knowledge of shape, the pool description will be very difficult indeed.

A visually handicapped child is frequently asked, "What's the matter with your eyes?" Questions that draw attention to a physical disability may have a negative effect upon self-esteem if appropriate training and modeling are not provided. The following steps may be taken to avoid this negative effect.

- The child should be provided with factual information concerning her visual loss. Explanations should be in a vocabulary appropriate to her age and understanding. Help her collect the questions that are asked most frequently, and periodically review the list to be certain she can easily answer all typical questions.
- Engage the child in dramatic play that demonstrates a typical situation. This allows him to rehearse his answer in a familiar setting and to become comfortable with his role in the dialogue. Reverse the roles so the child may elicit answers from the other player.
- Provide opportunities for the child to test her new answering skills in familiar settings.
- Assist the child with appropriate answers when she appears to be at a loss for words.
- Gradually expect the child to assume full responsibility for answering questions.

Contrary to common belief, most questions are born out of a natural curiosity rather than malice. It is vital that handicapped children know this and do not feel verbally abused about their physical disability. A typical question of a sighted first-grade child is, "Does it hurt?" First graders frequently bump knees, fall down, and understand pain; the question is therefore understandable. Encourage a discussion that focuses on such topics as: "What things hurt?" "What can you do well?" "What do you like about yourself?" This helps the handicapped child realize that she is not alone in having problems and that people need to help one another by sharing their strengths.

Well-defined limits provide the child with a basis for evaluating his present performance and for determining the growth he is making in behavior and attitude. They delineate areas of safety and danger, specify acceptable avenues through which to obtain goals, and enumerate the criteria that others use to judge success and failure. The handicapped child needs to learn that there is indeed a social reality that makes demands, provides rewards for accomplishments, and rejects those who do not demonstrate acceptable behavior.

Often parents and teachers have difficulty determining whether the limits they have established are appropriate. Even though visually handicapped children are more like than unlike normally sighted children, limits sometimes must be altered to accommodate special needs. Most standards for behavior and personal management for sighted children are also appropriate for visually handicapped children and should not be lowered. When an additional multi-handicapping condition is present, the standards may need to be adjusted to meet individual abilities.

A concentrated effort to discover the characteristic abilities and typical duties of certain age groups will yield invaluable information with which to establish meaningful limits. Sudden extreme exhaustion or outbursts of emotion are to be expected from three year olds. Giggling and nonsensical jokes are typical of nine and ten year olds. Feeling alone and self-conscious is characteristic of fourteen year olds. Taking the time to become acquainted with a number of children in a given age group helps interested adults view the growth and development of the visually handicapped child with more objectivity and a better perspective.

Questions that draw attention to a physical disability may have a negative effect upon self-esteem if the child is not trained to deal with them.

Even though visually handicapped children are more like than unlike sighted peers, the limits set for them must sometimes be altered to accomodate special needs.

Standards for behavior should be clearly specified and enforced in light of what is typical for the child's age group. When the adults in a child's life demonstrate that they firmly believe a skill may be mastered, the child will begin to convince herself. Constant encouragement and praise of work well done will help a child maintain the persistence required for eventual mastery. Many children need longer than average lengths of time when beginning to learn such new skills as buttoning shirts, making beds, or eating correctly. Allow the extra time, but do not reduce the limits of what is acceptable. As the skill becomes more automatic, the speed of completion will increase immensely if exciting activites are planned to be enjoyed after the task is done. When possible, the goal should be based upon what is typical of sighted peers.

Verbal and physical feedback are vital elements in maintaining motivation and persistence. A sensitive and quiet smile does not communicate adult approval to a child who does not have detail vision. "That's great! You worked much faster than you did yesterday," along with an occasional hug or squeeze, indicates to the visually handicapped child that you are pleased with his performance.

Consistent recognition of desired behavior will increase the frequency of the behavior and raise self-esteem. Pointing out to a child that she does something incorrectly (touched the food on her plate with her fingers) only indicates to her the unacceptable action. Without the avenue of vision she cannot observe others eating, and she may not have any idea what is expected. Commenting when a child does something correctly, "I like the quiet, straight way you are sitting," will provide a model of behavior that you would like to see maintained. The child experiences a sense of self-worth by knowing that she has pleased you. The self-esteem of the child rises as the comments about her actions become increasingly more positive. Many visually handicapped children have developed unacceptable postures and have not learned the social etiquette of turning toward the person speaking or being spoken to. Continuous negative comments about the failure to face someone or about poor posture generally yield little improvement in the behavior. A more fruitful approach is to tell the child honestly that it is socially unacceptable to stand with his back to someone when they are speaking. Quietly, calmly, and consistently position the child correctly before you begin speaking to him, so that you are facing him when you talk. If his posture begins to slump, stop talking and wait quietly until his head rises before you continue speaking. Hours and hours of practice must ensue to overcome long-established undesirable habits; so be patient. The frequent acknowledgment that he is doing something correctly will increase his feeling of well-being and worth.

Your recording established limits and then documenting progress as the child performs successfully within those limits will strengthen his awareness of his positive characteristics. Keep lists of all the skills that have been mastered. Everything should be included, from closing the door quietly to making a bed. Following are possible sample pages for such a book.

I CAN..	I CAN..
1	2
Wash the dishes	Tie my shoes
Dial the telephone	Dress myself
Vacuum the rugs	Sweep the sidewalk
Mow the lawn	Make my bed
Cut the meat	Put my toys away
Pack my lunch	Brush my teeth

It is easier for a child to accept his physical disability if he can point with pride to a long list of accomplishments. Children with high self-esteem believe they are good at many different things.

When adults demonstrate that they believe the child can master a skill, the child will begin to convince herself it can be done.

It is easier for a child to accept his disability if he can point with pride to a long list of accomplishments.

98

Visually handicapped children are sometimes astounded to discover that some things they do easily are difficult for siblings or peers. Allow a child to compare his list of achievements with someone else's list of achievements. It is an excellent way for him to discover that individuality of skills is a human characteristic to be expected of us all.

The following partial list of activities may help establish a positive repertoire of achievements for those children who have not yet experienced success.

Beginning Household Tasks
- Sweeping the sidewalk
- Washing yard furniture
- Emptying wastebaskets
- Folding towels
- Setting the table
- Bringing in the mail every day
- Making the bed
- Taking the silverware from the dishwasher and putting it away
- Washing the dishes
- Cleaning the sink and bathtub
- Changing light bulbs
- Collecting dirty towels from the bathroom
- Opening and closing windows
- Unlocking and locking the door with a key
- Straightening magazines in a pile or in a rack
- Changing the toilet paper

Beginning Cooking Skills
- Washing little tomatoes and taking off the stems
- Making frozen lemonade or juice
- Opening potato chips and filling a bowl
- Making toast
- Buttering toast
- Arranging presliced cheese on a plate
- Pouring breakfast food into a bowl
- Taking ice cubes out of the tray and refilling the tray
- Making instant pudding
- Baking cookies:
  Frozen prepared cookies—just bake
  Prepared cookie dough in the refrigerator of the store—cut and bake
  Cookie mix—prepare and bake
  Old fashioned put-together cookies
- Boiling hot dogs
- Rolling hot dog in one uncooked, prepared crescent roll; placing on cookie sheet and baking about the same time as directed on the roll package.

A number of investigators have reported that two combinations of attitudes occur frequently among parents of children with high self-esteem. High parental self-esteem is often associated with acceptance; consistent limit definitions are likely to be found accompanied by respect for individual expression (Gateson, 1944; Sears, 1957; Whiting, 1954). The general consensus among various authors appears to be that the child's identification with her parents is greatly increased if she has developed self-esteem. The high self-esteem is a reflection of her parents' acceptance. In essence, she is more likely to follow in the footsteps of her parents and willingly yield to their desires if they indicate approval more frequently than disapproval. This is not to suggest that parents should never criticize, correct, or punish the unacceptable behavior of children. The issue is one of maintaining balance. Nurturing high self-esteem requires that responsi-

99

ble adults recognize and praise observable progress whenever possible. The child will accept criticism and appropriate punishment without loss of self-esteem if she can offset her feelings of failure with the knowledge that there are many other things she can do very well.

Normally sighted children with high self-esteem frequently imitate the actions, dress, or attitudes of their parents. Following in mother's or father's footsteps is a typical dream for the future of five, six, and seven year olds. The young visually handicapped child sometimes realizes he will not be able to follow in the lifestyle established by his parents because of his lack of vision. It is important for parents to indicate to their child that they are not concerned about his handicap or the potential influence it may have on the future. He needs to know you love him *just the way he is.*

Sophisticated optical aids and electronic devices that may increase the independence of visually handicapped persons are now available. Only those individuals who become comfortable using the devices in public will function optimally. A child who needs elaborate aids should be encouraged to experiment with the equipment in different settings. Continued hard work will improve his skills, and words of encouragement as you and he recognize his improvement will enhance his self-esteem. Your encouragement serves as a stamp of approval and negates his need to be embarrassed about special equipment. Instill the philosophy that *what* a person does is more important than *how* he does it.

Meaningful leisure-time activities greatly enhance self-esteem. Many visually handicapped adults enjoy snow-skiing, water-skiing, bicycling, jogging, mountain climbing, and boating. The prerequisite skills, however, need to be started in the family setting when the child is young. Jungle gyms, tumbling classes, running, skipping, jumping, learning to fall down properly, and the joy of participating in group activities will build a foundation for a child's life-long enjoyment. Physical flexibility, directionality, and quick response to directions are mastered only after years of practice in typical children's games.

The child's self-esteem is greatly enhanced when she can bring personal meaning to the activities and events described to her by others. Only by twisting, turning, falling, and tumbling herself will she be able to fully appreciate and enjoy these activities when others verbally relate them to her. An armchair traveler experiences joy and sorrow with an author only if she can relate to the activities being described.

Even though physical fitness and movement exercises strengthen the body, they aren't always pleasurable. They are, however, prerequisite to more expressive activities, such as creative dance. When a child becomes aware of what his body is able to do with encouragement and practice, his self-esteem will soar. "Thus, dance, although it is a very useful means by which to enhance purposeful movement, . . . goes beyond that in offering a means by which to express as release the inner energy forces of life" (Duehl, 1979).

Developing a command of flexibililty, strength, and agility will bring about inner strength and a sense of warmth.

Activities should be geared to the interest level typical of your child's age. A 20 year old has learned to function appropriately by having functioned appropriately as a five, eight, and 12 year old. You may not approve of the hair styles or dress codes of modern teenagers, but if your child is to have an active social life, she needs to look the part. She will gain self-confidence as friends comment about her up-to-date apperance. The teenage years are not easy under the best of circumstances; the visually handicapped child has additional crises to face. Driving a car is a prime objective for most fifteen year olds. No amount of wishing will make it possible for the visually handicapped child, but he will face that disappointment more easily if you have a number of enjoyable activities for him after school or on weekends. Jogging, hiking, camping, and picnics at the beach help balance a threatened self-esteem.

References

Axelrod, S. 1959. *Effects of early blindness: performance of blind and sighted children on tactile and auditory tasks.* Research report No. 7, American Foundation for the Blind.

Clark, L., and Warren, D. 1978. Research notes, sensory awareness. *Journal of Visual Impairment and Blindness 72:191.*

Coopersmith, S. 1967. *Antecedents of self-esteem.* San Francisco: W. H. Freeman Co.

Duehl, A. 1979. The effects of creative dance movement on large muscle control and balance of congenitally blind children. *Journal of Visual Impairment and Blindness (April):60.*

Gateson, G. 1944. Cultural determinants of personality. In *Personality and the behavior disorders,* vol. 2, edited by I. J. McVickers Hunt. New York: Royal Press.

Rogow, S. 1975. Perceptual organization in blind children. In *New Outlook for the Blind.* New York: American Foundation for the Blind.

Scott, R. 1969. Socialization of blind children. In *Handbook of socialization theory and research,* edited by D. Goslin. New York: Rand McNally.

Sears, R. 1957. Identification of a form of behavioral development. In *The concept of development,* edited by I. D. B. Harris. Minneapolis: University of Minnesota Press.

Tillman, M., and Williams, H. 1968. The performance of blind and sighted children on the Wechsler Intelligence Scale for Children, study 2. *International Journal for Education of the Blind,* no. 16.

Witkin, H. A.; Birnbaum, J.; Lomonaco, S.; Lehr, S.; and Herman, J. 1938. Cognitive patterning in congenitally totally blind children. *Child Development,* no. 39.

Whiting, J. W. 1954. In *Discussions on child development II,* edited by J. M. Tanner and B. Inhelder. New York: International Universities Press.

Zweibelson, I., and Barg, C. F. 1967. Concept development in blind children. In *New Outlook for the Blind,* no. 61. pp. 218–222. New York: American Foundation for the Blind.

CHAPTER 12

Educating Visually Handicapped Students at the Secondary Level

Robert McMullen, J.D.
Tom Kellis, M.A.

DEVELOPING SKILLS SPECIFIC TO THE VISUALLY HANDICAPPED STUDENT IN SECONDARY PROGRAMS

In the past, the traditional role for the teacher of visually handicapped in secondary programs has been one of arranging the myriad of materials a secondary student uses in appropriate forms (braille, recordings, large print) and assisting where necessary to smooth the way for the student through the academic subjects. However, many teachers now realize that preparation in the academic subjects may not be the greatest need of their students. Having an adequate preparation is of little value if a person does not have the personal and social skills necessary to utilize this academic preparation. These skills may include living skills such as personal hygiene, using money, or telling time; communication skills such as writing letters or using a telephone; orientation and mobility skills necessary for travel; and social and recreational skills necessary for dealing with other people.

Visually handicapped students often do not acquire skills which other individuals pick up by observation. They also may be "protected" from having to do many things that are normally expected from most other children as they grow up. As a result, a very capable academic student may have serious deficiencies in handling certain skills expected of all people. In addition, the visually handicapped student may have become adept in avoiding situations which call for the use of these skills or in covering up their lack of skill in certain areas.

Teachers of the visually handicapped should be aware of the many skills that are needed for successful living by an individual and should be able to assess students either formally or informally in their use of these skills. If they find their students lacking in these skills, they should find ways for the students to acquire them. This might be done in several ways. The teacher may be able to find time to instruct the student in the skill necessary. The school district may be willing to hire a specialist to assist in teaching certain skills, such as those of orientation and mobility. If parents or family are made aware of the deficiencies of students and the importance of their learning a skill, they often will assist in the teaching of it. Sometimes it may be necessary for students to enroll in special programs that are offered for the purpose of teaching skills. These programs may be offered by different agencies after school, on weekends, or during the summer, and in some instances it may be necessary for students to enroll in a full-time program after the completion of their regular academic program.

Robert McMullen holds a J.D. degree from the University of Denver, an M.S. in education of the visually handicapped from San Francisco State University, and three California state teachers' credentials (general secondary, visually handicapped, and administration). He practiced law for four years in Denver. He has taught the visually handicapped for one year as an itinerant teacher in San Jose, California; six years as a high school resource teacher in San Leandro, California; and for four years at the California School for the Blind in Berkeley. He is now serving in his fifth year as assistant superintendent of the California School for the Blind.

Tom Kellis holds an M.A. in education of the visually handicapped from San Francisco State University. He has taught visually handicapped children in grades K through 12 as an itinerant and resource teacher in the Berkeley, California, public schools for 16 years.

The following list is offered as a guide to teachers who are seeking to determine what skills their students may have or may be lacking and for which skills further instruction is needed. The list is not complete and should be used as a stimulus to aid in determining other needs which the individual student should have acquired. Be aware that a teacher cannot rely on asking students or even parents whether the students can do something independently. Students may seek to cover their deficiencies or may not know enough to know whether they can do something correctly. Parents often think that their children are doing something independently when in fact they are adding just enough "extra" help, which their children may be unaware of, so that the children cannot really do the task independently. Wherever possible, teachers should observe students using a skill to see if they can really use it independently.

Techniques of Daily Living

1. Can the student handle all his or her personal grooming and hygiene needs, including bathing, toothbrushing, use of deodorant, care of hair, shaving, use of makeup, care of feminine hygiene needs?

2. Is the student knowledgeable about his or her bodily functions and their implications?

3. Does the student have appropriate eating skills and know the use of dining utensils?

4. Does the student have appropriate information concerning nutrition and balanced meals?

5. Can the student acquire, prepare and cook foods necessary for basic nutritional meals?

6. Can the student appropriately order and eat nutritional meals in restaurants?

7. Can the student secure appropriate housing for his or her needs?

8. Can the student properly operate household appliances for the maintenance of home and clothing (vacuum cleaner, washer, dryer, iron, stoves, small kitchen appliances, etc.)?

9. Can the student perform regular household duties (sweeping, cleaning, use of small tools for maintenance, etc.)?

10. Can the student acquire his or her own clothing and maintain it (do cleaning, mending, ironing, etc.)?

11. Does the student identify coins correctly, have a system for identifying bills, and use money appropriately in purchasing items from a variety of different stores?

12. Can the student obtain appropriate medical, dental and opthalmological assistance when required, including emergencies?

13. Is the student familiar with checking acounts, savings accounts, check-cashing, credit cards, loans, and so on, and the use and abuse of these items?

14. Is the student familiar with normal living expenses and the approximate cost of food, utilities, clothing, rent, and other necessities?

15. Can the student budget the money available to cover the necessary living expenses for the time necessary?

16. Is the student able to read braille watches, braille clocks, or other appropriate time devices and to follow his or her own time schedule for daily activities?

17. Is the student familiar with the various agencies that provide assistance and service for the handicapped, and does he know what types of services and assistance are available?

Communication Skills

1. Has the student acquired listening skills for a variety of purposes, such as acquiring information from a variety of sources (radio, TV, lectures, recorded material, etc.), orienting himself or herself in space, and engaging in recreation?

Parents often think their children are doing something by themselves when they are adding just enough "extra" help so that the children cannot really do the task independently.

2. Is the student able to carry on appropriate conversations for his or her age level in a variety of different situations?

3. Is the student able to formulate and ask clear, concise questions in an appropriate manner for the purpose of securing information, obtaining directions, and so on?

4. Can the student secure needed assistance or help from others in an appropriate and tactful manner?

5. Has the student developed skill in reading in appropriate mediums (braille, print, or recordings) for a variety of uses such as gaining information, doing academic work, engaging in recreation, and pursuing special interests (which might involve charts, graphs, maps, etc.)?

6. Has the student developed appropriate writing modes (braille, typewriting, handwriting, recording) for a variety of uses, such as letter writing, report writing, note-taking, message taking, labeling, signing a signature, and so forth?

7. Has the student been made aware of and learned the use of special equipment appropriate for his visual handicap and interests, such as braillewriters, slate and stylus, opticon, low vision aids, typewriter, closed-circuit TV, abacus, talking calculators, special measuring devices, Nemeth and Music braille codes, paperless braille machines, and so on?

8. Is the student proficient in the use of the different types of telephones (dial, push-button, coin-operated)?

9. Is the student proficient in operating basic communication devices, such as radios, cassette recorders, reel-to-reel recorders, talking book machines, and phonographs?

Orientation and Mobility Skills

1. Has the student become proficient in utilizing perceptual clues, such as sounds, wind currents, terrain, and odors, in determining the spatial relationships of objects around him or her?

2. Is the student skilled in techniques for obtaining and giving information, directions, and assistance which may be necessary in moving about in his or her environment?

3. Is the student familiar with the terminology related to orientation and mobility?

4. Is the student proficient in the special techniques for the modes of travel which are most appropriate for him or her (long cane, dog guide, utilization of residual vision, use of sighted guide)?

5. Can the student travel safely and independently by use of his or her primary mode of travel in his or her environment, including crossing streets at controlled and uncontrolled intersections and using public transportation?

6. Does the student have the skills necessary to travel safely and independently in unfamiliar areas and by various modes of transportation (plane, bus, taxi, etc.)?

7. Is the student familiar with the special provision for travel on trains, buses, taxis (in some locations), and so on, that are provided for the visually handicapped?

Personal, Social, and Recreational Skills

1. Does the student have an understanding and acceptance of his or her visual handicap, and is as well as the ability to cope maturely with the implications of this visual impairment and the problems that may arise because of it?

2. Does the student display appropriate behavior in a variety of different social situations or groups?

3. Has the student developed facial expressions, body posture, control of body movement, and elimination of distracting mannerisms which are appropriate for a variety of social situations?

4. Has the student developed appropriate manners in eating and other social situations?

5. Is the student aware of and does he or she dress appropriately for a variety of social situations?

6. Is the student aware of and sensitive to the feelings, attitudes, mores, and preferences of other people and of various groups?

7. Has the student developed a familiarity and competency in a variety of different social activities (games, arts, crafts, music, theatre, spectator sports, active sports, aesthetic appreciation, etc.)?

8. Is the student cognizant of the rights and responsibilities of citizenship, including voting, civic responsiblity, legal matters, and so forth?

Pre-Vocational Skills

1. Has the student developed a realistic self-concept, and what are his or her abilities, interests, and potential for development?

2. Has the student become familiar with the concepts of employment and the duties and responsiblities that are associated with work in our society?

3. Has the student explored a variety of different career areas and determined what types of careers might be available to him or her in relation to his or her abilities and interests?

4. Is the student familiar with preparation of job applications, resumes, and personal data sheets, and with interviewing techniques?

5. Is the student familiar with the language and concepts associated with, and the implications of, work (for example, unions, union dues, payroll taxes, Social Security taxes and benefits, health benefits, vacation policies, sick leave, etc.)?

6. Is the student knowledgeable about local, state and national resources that may be helpful in securing training, special equipment and materials, and so forth?

7. Has the student elected to take courses that might relate to possible appropriate vocational goals?

8. Has the student participated in a work experience or work training program leading to the development of appropriate vocational skills?

A CHECKLIST OF THE YEAR'S TASKS FOR THE RESOURCE OR ITINERANT TEACHER OF MAINSTREAMED SECONDARY VISUALLY HANDICAPPED STUDENTS

Before Classes Begin

A. Check materials (in resource room or in itinerant teacher's office).
1. Find out if needed textbooks have been ordered.
2. Determine which materials have arrived.
3. Check books, records, tapes, etc.—for defects or missing volumes or sections.
4. Inventory equipment to see that repairs have been completed.
5. Mail letters regarding materials ordered and not yet received.
6. Mail off materials requested by other schools.
7. Check progress of transcribers on materials requested.
8. Set up library.
9. Get files in order as much as possible at this point.
10. Clean up the room.

B. Plan for student instruction
1. Go over records of the new students, getting pertinent information preliminary to setting up their schedule.
2. Go over records of returning students to refresh memory.
3. Contact parents and get information regarding the following if not in records:
   a. Onset of visual problem, visual functioning level, visual acuity
   b. Relevant family information
   c. Previous schooling of child
   d. Location of friends
   e. Travel experiences
   f. Social activities and hobbies

Social skills include an awareness of and sensitivity to the feelings and attitudes of others.

Students should explore a variety of career areas to determine the careers that suit their abilities and interests.

g. Health and medications

h. Check equipment and materials in the home (e.g., braillewriter, tape recorder)

4. Set up a master schedule of all students' programs, complete with teachers' names, and check to see if you have the right books.

    a. Meet with the children and find out their level of visual functioning and other handicaps; consider mobility problems and motor ability; work out schedules according to the children's physical ability (e.g., type of courses they can take in the morning and afternoon)

    b. Work out schedules with classroom teachers so that they will match the itinerant teacher's schedule relative to time and transportation problems.

    c. Match the books and other materials that the teachers require with those that are already in the resource room.

5. Talk to previous teachers of new students when possible.

6. Talk to nurse about health problems of students.

7. Meet with teachers before school when possible, inviting counselor and/or principal.

8. If you have students in more than one school, make some tentative decision about amount of time to spend at each school or with each student.

9. Consult with the counselor in setting up individual programs for the children.

10. Distribute books to the classrooms or schools.

11. Locate the rooms and closet to be used in the itinerant program.

12. Show new students the school plant, introduce them to teachers who may be present, and teach them routes to new classrooms.

13. Arrange transportation and insurance, if this is your responsiblity, or check on arrangements.

14. Call parents about the child's program. Discuss such things as schedule and transportation.

15. Discuss the resource program—with the entire faculty in a faculty meeting, if it is a new program, or with the new teachers having visually handicapped students for the first time.

16. Discuss the itinerant program with the teachers involved in the program, plus someone from the administration such as a counselor or principal.

17. Inform students' teachers in a written memo about the following:

    a. The positive aspects of the students' abilities

    b. Reader services

    c. Transcription services

    d. Procedures for testing

    e. Students' mobility skills

    f. Difficulty in changing texts and obtaining materials

    g. Equipment available to students

    h. Addresses and phone numbers where you can be reached

    i. Ways in which students will complete assignments (e.g., braille, typescript, etc.)

Resource or itinerant teachers should work out their schedules with classroom teachers and parents to avoid time and transportation problems.

During the first week of school, invite the teachers to the resource room. Let them know how they can reach you if they have to.

First Week of School

A. On the first day, have program cards, equipment, paper, and so on waiting for the students in the office or resource room.

B. Make any final changes necessary in students' programs and be sure your schedule coincides with those of the students.

C. Check with teachers to see that each student has the proper books and materials for each class.

D. Invite the teachers to the resource room.

E. Remind them of your schedule and of ways to reach you.

106

F. Set up the reader program.

G. Instruct children in the use of equipment.

H. Check on students' attendance, punctuality, and orientation to classrooms.

Second Week of School

A. Check again for book changes.

B. See each teacher and discuss any new problems. Remind the teachers of procedures for getting tests and other materials transcribed.

C. Establish schedule for paid transcribers.

D. Locate additional volunteers.

E. As new problems arise, remember to keep other school personnel involved.

Throughout School Year

A. Maintain assessment records (standardized, criterion-referenced, checklists), ordering appropriate instruments in correct media (braille, large type, etc.).

B. Maintain contact with teachers to check on new materials planned for your students' classes.

C. Schedule a meeting with parents—individual or group. Invite parents for coffee, making the meeting as informal as possible. Do not make the parents apprehensive about coming. Let them know that you are interested in *their* children. Explain the following to the parents:
   1. Available after-school activities.
   2. Teacher's schedule so that parents can reach teacher.
   3. Special services available (transcriber, readers).
   4. Equipment available.
   5. General goals of program for the visually handicapped.

D. With other staff, as required, arrange mandated planning and review conferences (e.g., Public Law 94-142-mandated individualized education program planning [IEP] conference)

E. In addition to scheduled conferences, maintain continuing regular contact with parents and students, asking for their concerns regarding students' assigned programs and progress.

Invite parents for coffee and let them know you are interested in their children.

End of School Year

A. Determine needs for coming fall term and order. Successful textbook procurement usually demands these spring (late April or May) actions:
   1. Get list of books to be used in students' fall courses from teachers or department heads.
   2. Send request letters to sources of prepared transcriptions.
   3. Obtain print copies of books to be transcribed and put them in hands of transcribers with editing suggestions and deadlines.

B. Collect and inventory all materials and equipment. Note replacement and repair needs.

C. Return borrowed materials to sources.

D. Send out letters requesting return of material borrowed from you.

E. Evaluate resource room or itinerant work spaces and inform administration of needs.

Maintain regular contact with parents and students. Find out their concerns regarding the students' progress.

Mid-Year (in advance of program changes at new term or semester)

A. Check program changes for new semester or quarter.

B. Meet at new term with new teachers to explain program and describe students' abilities.

C. Order new books and materials.

D. Teach students routes to new classrooms and introduce them to their new teachers.

CHOOSING THE APPROPRIATE READING AND WRITING MODE FOR VISUALLY HANDICAPPED STUDENTS IN SECONDARY SCHOOLS

At their entrance to secondary school, students often find a large increase in demands from school, especially in the amount of independent homework and reading. At this time a careful choice of the appropriate reading and writing mode for the visually handicapped student can help meet these demands.

Casual reading rates for adults average between 100-400 words per minute (wpm). This is slightly above the normal rate of speech for English speakers (170-200 wpm). Most sighted secondary students have reached this range (170-200 wpm) by senior high school. Very low vision print readers using large print or magnification and braille readers are, on the average, considerably below this speed at this age. The differential between these rates continues as young people mature. At high school graduation (in the opinion of these writers), the average rate of a braille and very low vision large print reader is probably less than half the average rate of sighted peers in mainstream classes.

By high school graduation the average rate of a braille or very low vision large print reader is probably less than half the rate of sighted peers.

Given these averages, it would seem wise generally to advise visually handicapped students at the secondary level to use recorded speech for their reading. However, the choice of the best reading medium is not simply a function of reading rates. Other factors influence the desirability of one mode over the other:

1. The student's relative comprehension in each mode
2. The flexibility of format (book vs. tape or reader)
3. The higher efficiency and clarity of coding information in Nemeth braille, in raised-line graphics, or in print graphics over coding in recorded speech or literary braille
4. The student's need for practice in braille or print reading to maintain skills in expressive written language
5. The student's need for an expressive writing mode that allows easy proofreading, revision, editing, and precise orthography
6. The student's visual efficiency
7. The prognosis for the student's eye condition and visual fatigue factors.

Mathmatics and science materials are usually most effective when presented in Nemeth code for the braille user and in photographically or optically enlarged print for the low vision student. It is a very rare student who can handle the complexities of even elementary algebra without a written expressive medium such as braille or print. In literature courses, braille or print may often be preferable for particularly detailed student of poetry, of drama, and even of unfamiliar styles in prose. In social studies, if reading is done exclusively in recorded speech, the recording must present spelling and text format effectively and clearly. If not, at least a print or braille transcription of the basic vocabulary and proper names should be available.

It is the very rare student who can handle the complexities of even elementary algebra without a written expressive medium such as braille or print.

These considerations of best reading mode suggest that the individual solution may be a choice of more than one mode and that these modes be used differentially according to the greatest benefit for the student. At any point in a visually handicapped student's educational career, the complex of reading and writing modes may differ from those needed the term before or following. Generally the choices should be a function of close consultation between the itinerant or resource teacher, the student, and the classroom teacher. As a student's skills and needs change, change in choice of mode should immediately follow.

To illustrate this variable and changing complex, the matrix shown in Figure 12.1 shows a set of modes used by an adventitiously visually handicapped student in the 11th grade. Her braille reading speed was approximately 30 wpm; her CCTV reading rate was approximately 15 wpm. Using a broad felt-tip pen the student could write and read her own digits and math operation signs slowly but at a rate equal to Nemeth braille reading. She could easily comprehend live and recorded speech at about 150 wpm. She could write in grade II braille and

Figure 12.1 Sample matrix showing one visually handicapped student's choices of reading and writing media for different activities.

Name   **Grade:**   **11**

	Braille	Magnified Print (LP Optical Aids CCTV)	Recorded Speech	Live Reader	Type-writing	Optacon
Language Arts						
Reading fiction	R		R	R		R (in training)
Poetry & drama	R Ex			R	Ex	
Language exercises	R Ex				Ex	
Composition	Ex (1st draft)		Ex (1st draft)		Ex (final draft)	
Mathematics						
Textbook reading	R	R Ex				
Textbook exercises						
Computation		Ex				
Testing	R	R Ex				
Science						
Textbook reading	R			R		
Laboratory exercises	R Ex	Ex		R		
Testing	R Ex			R		
Social Studies						
Textbook & research	R			R		
Map work	R	R Ex				
Testing	R Ex	R (maps) Ex		R		
Essays	Ex (1st drafts)				Ex (final drafts)	
Living Skills						
Records (e.g., banking)		R Ex		R		
Labels	Ex	R Ex		R		
Recipes & directions	R recipes	R		R		

R = receptive language use (e.g., print, braille, Optacon, reading, listening)
Ex = expressive language use (e.g., handwriting, brailling, typing, tape recording, speech)

had basic typing skills. Where the student used a particular mode in a curriculum area, the fact is noted by an "R" for a receptive mode (i.e., reading or listening) and "Ex" for an expressive mode (i.e., writing in print, typing, braille, or recording on tape).

The entries in each cell are *not* equally weighed. For example, the entry in Recorded Speech/Composition is a notation of only a few instances in the year's experience, while the Braille/Composition entry is more typical of this student's use of mode for first drafts of composition assignments.

The individual chosen as an example here was using an unusually high variety of reading and writing media. This is the result of several factors. One is the fact that her vision loss was adventitious. Her remaining vision was sufficient for some functional uses aided by CCTV magnification. Her braille reading rates were still very much below speech speeds. The student was mainstreamed, and reading assignments could not have been met with braille and CCTV reading alone.

Though not typical, this example should make the point that choice of reading media is not a simplistic decision to have a student use one means of reading and writing. Especially at secondary level, this decision should be based on a careful observation of the interaction of the individual's levels of skills and the many variable needs generated by the individual's educational situation.

This matrix should lend itself to both assessment and planning functions. The column headings across the top should cover most media used by the visually handicapped at all age and developmental levels if, for the higher functioning low vision student, Regular Print is substituted for Braille and Handwriting is substituted for Optacon. The row headings in the left column are, of course, variable and should be changed to match the individualized program of each student.

CHAPTER 13

Art Experience Is Fundamental to Creative Thinking

Compiled by Sally S. Mangold, Ph.D.

It is possible to become a creative person without becoming a professional artist. Artists are of course creative people. There are also creative chefs, bricklayers, electricians, salespersons, parents, and teachers. An individual's "creativity" refers to his or her ideas, feelings, and ability to act upon things in the environment so that they are used in a unique way. Creative functioning results when students are given the opportunity to explore their environment, experiment with objects and media in their environment, and grow comfortable with their originality, even when it differs greatly from the functioning of those around them.

Creativity is a process of individual experience that enhances the self. It is an expression of one's uniqueness. To be creative is to be oneself.

Educators must be concerned with developing individuals who have original ideas and who welcome opportunities to put them into action. Parents and teachers must help students maintain an interest in new experiences. Students should never feel threatened by possible failure or fear that adults might be disappointed. The creative experience is a very personal one and should never be judged by superimposed standards.

Collect as many raw materials as possible without predetermining how they will be used. *Reduce the environment to a manageable size.* Shoeboxes full of items in the same category will allow the visually handicapped student to make comparisons independently of adult supervision. Boxes of all different kinds of string, all sizes and shapes of feathers, buttons of every description, styrofoam pieces, and scraps of textured paper are only a few ideas to get a collection started.

It is important to lead students into new experiences but to allow them to discover things for themselves. They must learn to perceive their environment in their own unique ways. The discovery of new smells, shapes, textures, and pliabilities adds excitement to the artistic process. Encourage discussion of possible qualities of objects and ways in which those qualities influence the way a person feels when engaging in a new experience. Appreciation takes time to verbalize. Allow ample time for students to collect their thoughts and answer in their own words when sharing their feelings about a new experience. Rushing them may force premature and shallow conclusions. Encourage your students to perceive, but not to judge—to enjoy the entire experience of a flower, not just to name it or to make a reproduction of it. Experiencing a flower might include determining these factors:

    the weight of the flower
    the softness of the petals
    the length of the petals
    how easily the petals break or fall
    whether or not the petals have veins
    whether or not all parts of the flower smell the same
    what it feels like to rub the petal on your cheek

Dr. Mangold is associate professor in Special Education at San Francisco State University.

Appreciation is extended to the many teachers who have contributed the descriptions of art activities found in this chapter. The ideas presented here have been collected over a number of years.

Reproducing an object that has been experienced should be a pleasurable aspect of the artistic expression. *The process is always more important than the product.*

Modern education recognizes that individuals learn and perform at different rates. The curriculum available to students allows for individual learning styles and permits a great deal of freedom for scheduling in order to promote maximum learning in each student. Numerous enrichment activities are provided that may be enjoyed by students when they finish the basic subjects of reading, writing and arithmetic.

Art activities, as they are called, may be in evidence in almost all classrooms. They provide an opportunity for students to express themselves with a variety of media. They are valid activities, no doubt, but this kind of activity seldom allows a student to experience life before reproducing it. Care should be taken to ensure the experience of the essence of life for all students as they grow toward maturity.

The activities described in this chapter will allow students to experiment with various media, but cannot be considered artistic experiences unless someone in the students' environment takes the time to help the students explore the components that make each experience unique.

The ideas presented here have been contributed by many teachers of visually handicapped students.

COLLAGES

Bean and Grain Collages
Materials
Beans of various sizes; grains of various sizes; contact paper; rubber cement; oak tag paper; flat dishes for beans and grains.
Procedure
Have students press the beans and grains onto the sticky side of the contact paper. Have them glue down the beans and grains with brushes in various places to create designs or patterns that they would like to feel. It will work best if they work on one section at a time, gluing down one area of beans and grains and then moving on to another. It they are using only contact paper, merely have them place objects in desired places on sticky side of contact paper. The contact paper can be mounted on tag board.

Mosaics
Materials
Different types of dry peas, beans, and pastas (spaghetti, elbow macaroni, twistees, small shells, bows, rigatonnis, popcorn, etc.); contact paper.
Procedure
Have students cut out contact paper in desired shape and size. Secure contact paper to boards in front of students (use pushpin boards or tape contact paper to desk.) Make sure that the sticky side of the contact paper is facing upward. Allow students to place materials on contact paper. Items can be placed, removed, and rearranged on the paper. To keep paper from losing its stickiness, the students can rest their free hands on previously glued shells to hold the paper in place instead of putting their hands directly on the paper. Some items (bows, twistees) do not stick well, and if the students want to take the project home, it might be necessary to secure those items with glue or paste. The result of this art project can be used as a wall hanging or as a doily.

SOFT MATERIALS PROJECTS

Soft Soap Sculptures
Materials
Large bowl; Ivory soap flakes; water in a pitcher; 1-cup measure; ½-cup measure; large spoon; wax paper; masking tape.

Reproducing an object that has been experienced should be a pleasurable aspect of the artistic expression.

Activities cannot be considered artistic experiences unless someone helps the student explore the components that make each experience unique.

112

Procedure

Tape wax paper square on table or desk. Have students pour 1 cup of soap flakes and ½ cup of water into a large bowl and stir the mixture with the spoon, adding more soap or water until stickiness is gone (this makes about a baseball-size glob). Place "glob" on wax paper and let students start sculpturing. The longer they let it set, the harder it gets. Once it gets hard, students can carve it with tools or smooth it by wetting their fingers.

Play Dough (enough for one student)
Materials

1-cup measure; 1-teaspoon measure; 1 pot; 1 plate; 1 container; 1 wooden spoon; 2 cups flour; 1 cup salt; 4 teaspoons cream of tartar; 2 cups water; 1 teaspoon oil; 15 drops of food coloring.

Procedure

Combine all ingredients in a pot. Stir for 2 minutes until all ingredients are blended (not too lumpy—test with hands). Cook over medium heat for 5 minutes. Stir occasionally; mixture will begin to get doughy and harder to stir. After 5 minutes remove the mixture from the heat. Transfer to a plate. Mixture will be quite warm to the touch. Cool 15 minutes. Play Dough is ready to use or place in containers.

Decorative Ornaments
Materials

Bowl; spoon; cookie sheet; foil; cookie cutters; 2 cups flour; 1 cup salt; 1 cup water; anything to make interesting indentations with.

Procedure

Mix together ingredients. Add more flour or water, as needed. The dough should be dry enough not to stick to fingers, but wet enough to stick to itself. Knead the dough 5–10 minutes. If color is desired, split dough into as many sections as you want to color, and knead food color into each section. Bake dough at 250° F. for about 1½ hours for ¼ inch thickness. Create anything you want or need for a particular art lesson.

MOBILE AND WIND CHIMES

Ceramic Wind Chimes
Materials

Ceramic clay; nylon thread or fishing line; wooden dowels or tree limbs or driftwood (about 1 foot long); yarn; rolling pin; knives and anything else that will make a mark or leave an impression in clay.

Procedure

Have the students make medallions of various shapes from ceramic clay—circles, squares, rectangles, free-forms, blobs. These shapes can be made in several ways:

1. Students can place a large piece of clay between two ¼ inch sticks and roll the clay into a large pancake using the rolling pin. (The sticks assure an even thickness.) The students can then cut shapes out of the pancake with a knife or pointed object or can use cookie cutters.

2. Students can make a piece of clay into a pancake with the palms of their hands and then cut out the forms.

3. Students can take small pieces of clay (ones that will fit in the palms of their hands) and make free-form shapes by pinching and pulling the clay.

The medallions should be no more than ¼ in. thick so that they will ring after firing. The shapes can be decorated with lines or shapes drawn and pressed into the clay or with added pieces of clay. Make holes in the tops of the medallions with a straw or a nail for strings to pass through. Medallions must be laid out to dry and then fired in a kiln. Drying takes about a week. (If the school doesn't have a kiln, ceramic shops will fire them for a small fee.) After the medallions are dry, they can be glazed before they are put in the kiln. Glazing cuts down on the noise they will make as wind chimes. The students should tie nylon fishing line or thread through the holes in the medallions and then tie the medallions onto the dowels (or limbs or driftwood) about ½ in. apart (depending on the size of the medallion). Leave the strings about 12 in. long. The students should use their own judgment for the arrangements they want. Have them tie pieces of yarn to each end of their twigs so the wind chimes can be hung.

Mobile Balloons
Materials
Balloons; flour; water; string; spoon; bowl; pin.
Procedure
The students are to blow up balloons and knot the ends. (They may need help in knotting the ends.) Give students mixing bowls, flour, and water. Have the students mix flour and water until the mixture is a consistent paste. (Using flour and water instead of glue tends to work better than glue because it keeps the string stiff after it dries.) Each piece of string should be dipped in the paste. The students should cover the balloons with the pieces of dipped string until there is a fine network of string covering the entire surface of each balloon. Hang the balloons up to dry. When the balloons are dry, the students should pop them. They will then have a string mobile.

Mobiles
Materials
Square pieces of construction paper; scissors; rubber bands.
Procedure
Students should fold squares of paper diagonally three times and cut them from the folded edges, first from one side and then from the other, to within ¼ in. of the opposite edge. They should then carefully unfold the shapes and stretch them out. The shapes should be hung with rubber bands by knotting one end of each band so it doesn't slip through the smallest end of the shape.

PROJECTS THAT CAN BE USED WHEN FINISHED

Cookie Magnets
Materials
Flour; salt; water; magnets; forks; pens.
Procedures
Make the desired amount of dough by mixing 2 parts flour to 1 part salt and adding water to make a desired consistency. Have the students shape out cookies with hands and put the cookies on the foil paper. Then have them dip forks in flour and press them onto the cookies to make them look like peanut butter cookies. To make cookies look like chocolate chip cookies, they can dab the tops with a brown-colored pen. The students should press magnets into the bottom of each cookie. Bake the cookies in the oven for 20 minutes at 350° F. When the cookies are cool, spray them all over with silicone spray.

Tambourines
Materials
Sturdy paper plates; pinto beans (elbow macaroni, or small rocks); staplers; several 1 in. wide and 15 in. long strips of brightly colored fabric; several 4 in. circles of different-textured fabric; rubber cement; trays to hold all of the items.
Procedure
Have students select a paper plate and three or four long strips of colored fabric. Let them staple one end of each fabric strip to the edge of the paper plate and place one to two handfuls of beans on this paper plate. They should then take another paper plate and place it on top of the first plate so that the two form a container for the beans inside. Have the students staple the two paper plates together

and staple around the edge of the plate. The staples should be about 1 in. apart all the way around the circumference of the plate. Finally, the students should select two or more of the fabric circles and glue the fabric circles to each side of their tambourines.

Salt and Flour Bead Necklaces
Materials
Water; salt; flour; powdered alum; mixing bowl; toothpicks; food colorings or dry tempera for coloring mixture; egg cartons; string or elastic or wire for stringing beads; shellac or gloss paint.
Procedure
Every student should mix 1 cup of salt, 1 cup of flour, and 1 tablespoon of alum, and then add water until the mixture is the consistency of putty. Students should be careful not to use too much water; they can add coloring if desired, and should use hands to mix. They should then pinch off lumps of the mixture and shape them into beads. Different shapes can be made by rolling or pressing flat. A hole should be punched through the center of each bead with a toothpick. The toothpicks should be left in the beads and stuck into overturned egg cartons for drying. (The toothpicks should be turned occasionally to prevent them from sticking to the beads.) When beads are dry, the students should either spray the entire carton with beads on it with the shellac or should brush on gloss. Tell them to use caution! When beads are dry, the students should string them. Wire works well, as the stiffness makes the stringing easier.

Sock Octopus
Materials
Several pairs of socks; push pins; flat pieces of styrofoam; pieces of 6-inch-long braided yarn.
Procedure
Have each student roll a pair of socks into a ball by stuffing one sock inside the other. This is the body of the octopus. The body should be placed on styrofoam board with push pins, and braided yarn strips should be placed around body for the legs.

Junk Necklaces
Materials
Shoestrings; aluminium foil; straws; macaroni or spaghetti rings.
Procedure
Give each student a shoestring and a small section of aluminium foil. Ask the students to tear the aluminium foil into small pieces. Have them pick up one piece, poke the end of the shoestring through the foil, and then wad the ball while on the string. Give the students macaroni or spaghetti rings and straw sections so that they may add to their necklaces.

Decorated Boxes
Materials
Boxes with attached lids (pin container, cigar boxes, file boxes); scraps of material, paper, and suede to cover lids; different small objects to decorate lids (seashells, dried flowers, buttons).
Procedure
Have each student select a box, covering, and small objects. Students should be encouraged to exercise their individuality and should go for the textures and shapes which please them. They should put some glue on the lids of the boxes, making sure that all the edges as well as the center get enough glue. They should then place the scraps of material or paper on top of the lids, covering them completely and leaving about an inch of material overlapping on all sides of each box. Let the glue dry overnight. Following the outer edge of the box lids, the students should then trim the surplus material or paper off with the scissors. To

glue the objects to the boxes, they should dip them gently into the dish of glue and then place them on top of the lids. Let the lids dry overnight.

Pipe Cleaner Art

Materials

Pipe cleaners.

Procedure

Pipe cleaners can be purchase inexpensively and are available in a variety of widths, colors and lengths. They are soft to the touch and are wonderful for twisting into designs of various sorts. Each student should be given a generous amount of pipe cleaners and encouraged to explore them thoroughly. Allow the students to design things, using their imaginations. Fun is almost guaranteed, and the twisting and bending is excellent for finger dexterity and coordination. For variations, you may suggest jewelry, geometric shapes, and so forth, and give the students real pieces of such items to feel and then to copy. Pipe cleaners can also be glued onto paper or woven through holes punched into paper. There are a variety of activities that are suitable for using pipe cleaners; all they take is imagination.

Herbal Sachets

Materials

Square pieces of cloth 8 × 8 in. (lightweight cottons work the best); various herbs—lavender, rose petals, mints, jasmine, thyme, rosemary, camomile; deep bowls for each herb; 8–12 in. lengths of ribbon.

Procedure

Place herbs separately in bowls in a line on the work table. Help the students to locate, pick up, and smell each herb. Give the students pieces of the cloth so they can feel the edges (the cloth may have been pinked using pinking shears). Place the cloths on a mat so they won't slip. Allow the students to select the herbs of their choice, placing about a tablespoon of each herb in the center of the cloth. (It may be necessary to help the students locate the center of the cloth.) Repeat until each cloth has about two handfuls of herbs in it. The students can actually pick up the cloths with their hands to measure. Hand the students the contents of the cloth. Help them draw up the edges, gathering them up in their hands. Hold each cloth and allow each student to tie a ribbon around it and into a bow.

Vase and Paper Flowers

Materials

Coke bottles; masking tape; shoe polish; organized tray with pins; florist tape; pipe cleaners; squares of tissue paper.

Procedure

Have the students cover the coke bottles with ½ in. torn strips of masking tape. Students should keep applying strips until bottles feel covered. They should then rub shoe polish as evenly as possible over the taped bottles until they are coated, let them dry, and spray them with varnish. To make flowers, have the students examine a previously completed paper flower. They should then fold squares of paper into fourths and cut them into circles. They should stack the circles on top of each other, poke a pin through center of each set of circles and pull tissue up around the top of the pin. Finally, they should hold the pin against a pipe cleaner and wrap florist's tape around the pin, the pipe cleaner, and the base of tissue paper petals.

Spice Ropes

Materials

Yarn; scissors (preferably pinking shears); cotton balls; whole cloves; clove extract; cotton material (print or solid but so that it goes with the yarn); rubber bands; small curtain rings; other spices if desired.

116

Procedure

The students should measure 9 strands of yarn 30–36 in. long, thread all 9 through a curtain ring, and position the ring in the middle of the strands. They should then fasten the ring on something solid and braid the yarn. From material, they should cut three circles 4–5 in. in diameter. They should then place three whole cloves in the middle of the wrong side of one circle, place a drop of clove extract on one cotton ball and put the cotton ball on top of the cloves. The edges of the circle shuld then be gathered around the cotton ball and secured with a rubber band. This process should be repeated with the other two circles. Finally, the students should position the three spice balls evenly along braided yarn and tie them on with a piece of yarn, making a bow.

Sweet Pete's or Pomander Balls
Materials

Oranges or lemons, with soft skins if possible; toothpicks; whole cloves; ribbon or yarn; thumb tacks or straight pins.

Procedure

Pour cloves into a bowl. Provide each student with a lemon or orange. If the finished project will be hung, then have each student pick out ribbon or yarn, make the ends of the ribbon meet at the top of the lemon or orange, and stick a pin or tack through both pieces of ribbon to make the hanger secure. Then the students can stick the whole cloves, pointed end first, in the skins of the oranges to form a face or design. If skins are too tough, toothpicks may be used to stab the skins first, and then the cloves may be inserted. For best results, students should leave a very small amount of space between cloves, or they may pop out.

CHRISTMAS ART PROJECTS

Snowman Collages
Materials

Construction paper; pencils; a tracing wheel; cotton; glue.

Procedure

The first part of this project involves preparation by the teacher. The teacher draws three circles on a sheet of construction paper. Each of the last two circles is drawn on top of the one before it and each is progressively larger (the top circle is the smallest). Then each circle is traced over with a tracing wheel (the kind used in sewing). In order to make a raised-line image on the underside of the paper, poke a pair of scissors through the paper following the patterns of the circle. Each student is given a dish of Elmer's glue and about 35 cotton balls to work with. The students dip each cotton ball in the glue. With one hand they place the cotton within the area of the circles. The other hand locates the raised area of the paper. The dipped ball is then pressed inside one of the circles. A dampened cloth can be placed adjacent to the glue dish, which may be used to keep hands clean.

Christmas Tree Wreath
Materials

Evergreen tree branches (about 2 feet long); a bowlful of raw cranberries; popped popcorn; large sewing needles; sewing thread; ribbon (preferably green, red, or white); scissors.

Procedure

Give each student 3 tree branches, 60–70 cranberries, 60–70 pieces of popcorn, 1 sewing needle, 6 pieces of thread (1½ feet long), 1 piece of thread (4 yards long), 1 piece of ribbon (5 feet long), and scissors. The students should thread the needles with thread, knot the ends together, and string cranberries and popcorn alternately onto the needles and thread. These should then be put aside until later. The students should twist the ends of two of their branches together, then twist the free end of one of these to an end of the third branch, and then twist the last two ends together. String should be wrapped and tied around the twisted ends of the joined areas. The result should look like a big "donut" shape. Each student should then take a string of popcorn and cranberries and tie one end to his or her branch wreath. When the string is secured, the student should wrap the string over and under and around the branches until they have covered their entire wreaths and have run out of string. Each should then secure the other end of the string to the branches, take the ribbon and make a bow with it, and attach the ribbon to the wreath with string wherever he or she would like the top of the wreath to be.

Pine Cone People
Materials
Various sizes of pine cones, walnuts, acorns, or styrofoam balls; yarn felt stick'em dots; macaroni; felt or material for clothes; pipe cleaners; glue.
Procedure
Have the students choose pine cones and attach heads to them by using smaller pine cones. They should cut out the material in the shapes of clothing they would want the "persons" to wear. They should then glue the clothes onto the pine cones, decorate the faces, and put hair on the heads, arms, and legs, using pipe cleaners.

A Cotton Ball Christmas Tree
Materials
Styrofoam shaped cones; large packets of cotton balls; packets of assorted sequins; straight pins.
Procedure
Make sure the supplies are in accessible areas. Have each student place a sequin on a pin and a cotton ball following the sequin, insert the pin into a styrofoam cone, and continue this process until the whole cone is covered.

Aural Reading

Rose-Marie Swallow, Ed.D.
Aikin Conner, Ed.D.

CHAPTER 14

INTRODUCTION

In order to gain information, human beings have always listened to either the sounds in their environment or to the vocalizations of others. Humans have traditionally transmitted knowledge through spoken language. Children have learned by listening to their elders. It was not until after the development of the printing press that visual reading became a more important means for recording information. With the advent of public education, society deemed it necessary and desirable for its children to be literate. But, unfortunately, not all persons have been able to learn effectively to read conventional print for a variety of reasons, visual impairment being one. Some have reading deficiencies in either print or braille codes; some read visually or tactually at a very slow rate; some may tire quite quickly from visual fatigue when reading. For these and other reasons, an alternate mode of reading is necessary.

One group needing adaptations of reading material is the visually handicapped, including both blind and partially seeing students. Whether it is necessary to transcribe conventional print into large type for visual reading or braille for tactual reading, or whether it is necessary to record onto discs or tapes for aural reading, visually handicapped children, in general, have required adaptations or modifications of the original reading material. Also, they have needed immediate access to a variety of learning materials. If none of the reading media is available—visual, tactual, or aural—another person is often present to read the desired passage to the child.

Of relevance, then, to the education of the visually handicapped is the child's ability to process auditory information. Most of the cognitive processes required in listening to someone read a book are the same needed in listening to a talking book or tape. In which ways do these skills differ from those required to comprehend visual or tactual reading materials? The format and the channel of communication are different, but the cognitive skills which contribute to understanding what was read remain the same. The ability of the child to listen, speak, read, and/or write has its basis in the child's ability to handle his or her particular language code (a term that, in this chapter, specifically refers to English).

How, then, do these language art skills relate to each other? In the process of verbal development, the child listens before speaking and reads before writing. Both listening and reading are *decoding* skills, while speaking and writing are *encoding* skills. It is relatively easier to decode than to encode. Expressing ideas is harder than understanding the message. A person may understand a principle through listening but find it difficult to explain that same principle to another person. Also, it is less difficult to read about a subject than to write about what has been read. Encoding requires more cognitive organization.

Let's look into a learning center where three visually handicapped children

Dr. Swallow is professor of Special Education at California State University at Los Angeles, California.

Dr. Conner is director of the Aural Medial Center, California Depository, a resource center for handicapped students in Sacramento, California.

are sitting around a table reading a social studies assignment. One student has a large type book, another student has a braille book, and the third student is listening to a recorded tape. Is each "reading" the social studies lesson? By definition, what constitutes the reading process? What is involved if a child is to read?

If "reading" is defined as the meaningful interpretation of verbal symbols, then all three students are reading if they understand the stated message. But, if "reading" is a visual symbol system superimposed upon a previously acquired language system, then neither the braille reader nor the recorded tape user is reading. For our purposes, the term *reading* relates to the meaningful understanding of a verbal message in which there is no interaction between the originator of that message and the decoder of the message. For the purposes of this chapter, then, aural reading (often called "auding") is defined as the process of hearing, listening, recognizing, and interpreting previously recorded language, that is, tapes and records.

No child should be asked to listen to a cassette tape and be expected fully to understand what he or she has heard without some prior instruction in auding skills. The interdependent factors constituting auditory-linguistic processing begin at birth and require approximately a decade of development. Auditory perception and linguistic competence are both developmental and learned aspects of auding. Therefore, it should be quite apparent to the teacher of any visually handicapped child that, from the very onset of both infant stimulation and preschool programs, special attention and training are required for the development of auding skills.

Can these skills be taught effectively? Not only can listening and auding be taught, but, as learning takes place, there is definite improvement in the other language skill areas as well. An interactional effect exists between listening and speaking, reading and writing. But in spite of the educational significance of listening and auding skills, their development is often slighted by teachers of visually impaired students.

Although lip service is frequently paid to the use of the auditory channel, not all visually impaired children receive consistent, systematic instruction in listening and auding skills. Most visually handicapped children in the elementary and intermediate grades are not being adequately prepared if they are not receiving instruction in listening and auding. Most of our children require more than large type or braille modifications of their learning materials. Many require and benefit from channel substitution—decoding the content of an education via another channel. If a child is a poor or slow visual or tactual reader, the teacher should not keep him or her at that low level of functioning for all educational content. Rather, the teacher should switch to another, more effective channel, thus keeping the child exposed to all, or most, of the curriculum content during the educational process. Insufficient exposure to subject matter content seriously impedes learning during the educational process.

Adequate auditory perception and proper linguistic development facilitate all learning. Since it behooves the teacher to tailor a program to the unique needs of blind and partially seeing students, knowledge of the development of auditory-linguistic skills is essential. Most children, however, do not develop functional listening and auding skills by themselves and will require consistent and systematic training.

THE DEVELOPMENT OF AUDITORY-LINGUISTIC PROCESSING
The following abilities and suggested activities are viewed as helpful in the development of auditory-linguistic processing skills. Three levels of listening have been defined: analysis of auditory stimuli, sequencing of aural data, and comprehension of symbolic representation. The listener must be able to attend, perceive, and analyze auditory stimuli; be able to sequence the temporal units and develop the patterns of language; and be able to comprehend the language sym-

No child should be expected to understand fully what he has heard on a cassette tape without prior instruction in auding skills.

If a child is a poor visual or tactual reader, the teacher should switch to a more effective learning channel so that she will be exposed to most or all of the curriculum content. Insufficient exposure to subject matter seriously impedes learning.

bols through both increased vocabulary development and the corresponding comprehension of words and ideas in their verbal context. This understanding will be related to the experiential and cognitive development of the particular visually handicapped child.

Analysis of Auditory Stimuli

This level relates to the child's perceptual awareness of sound. Auditory stimuli are all the environmental sounds significant to the visually handicapped child's experience. The listener must become aware of sounds, contrast sounds, locate the direction of sounds, and associate sounds with objects.

Auditory Attending. Children must become auditorially sensitive to environmental sounds about them. Sounds like cars, bells, animals, or indoor and outdoor sounds can be attended to and identified. These sounds may be recorded—transportation sounds, musical instruments, animal sounds. Ask the children to identify the source. Teacher-made sounds (for example, the sounds of a light switch, a pair of scissors, or a stapler) or sound shakers (filled with stones, beans, salt, sand, rice) are fun to use with children.

Sound Localization. Relationships of direction, distance, and space can be developed by asking the child to identify the place from which a sound emanated. Teachers find the portable goal locator from the American Printing House for the Blind (APH) helpful, although ringing, shaking, or clicking sound makers are just as useful. Blind children in particular need to recognize the direction of sound, the distance that sound is away from them, and sound-source relationships in space.

Auditory Focus-Field. The child's ability to sustain auditory attention and to shift intentionally from one auditory stimulus to another is required for auditory focus-field. The child can focus on the significant auditory stimulus and mask out irrelevant information. Training children to attend auditorially to significant sounds in their environment and not be distracted by field noise is the real educational goal. For some learners who are easily distracted by field sounds during study times, earphones and headsets may be beneficial for listening to recorded material.

Auditory Discrimination. This is the ability to differentiate sounds. For the visually handicapped child, mobility sounds are differentiated and identified. Mobility sounds such as footsteps, traffic noises, and movement patterns are involved in training. Auditory discrimination of environmental sounds leads to the ability to perceive and recognize the phonemes of language. The order for presenting language sound discrimination tasks is this: first, consonant sounds; then vowel sounds; then initial sounds in words; and, finally, ending sounds in words. Rhyming words games, nursery rhymes, and riddle rhymes are enjoyable activities for students. Make up riddles, such as "it rhymes with book and you hang your coat on it."

Sequencing of Aural Data

This skill in processing aural stimuli relates to the temporal order in which events occur. The ability to sequence auditory and linguistic stimuli and the ability to retain and recall their orderings are equally important. Any difficulty with the sequencing of auditory-linguistic events seriously affects a person's ability to operate effectively in every day circumstances. What happens when a person cannot remember the sequence of directions to somewhere or the proper steps in making something? Confusion!

Ordering does not only relate to the pattern of sounds or the sequence of words, but also to the meaning of the message. Syntax relates to word order (e.g., "eat the bear" or "bear the eats"). This example clearly illustrates how word order carries the meaning of the phrase or sentence. Any interference in the ability to sequence aurally interrupts the decoding process.

Cue systems within language have been identified on both the integrative and

A child who lacks auditory memory (the ability to recall the order of what he has heard) is unable to order words, directions, or ideas.

cognitive basis. The typical child learning to read his or her native language internalizes these cue systems so that he or she is responding without conscious awareness. The cue systems include the automatic patterning of auditory stimuli (i.e., discrimination, sequencing, blending, and closure), and the automatic patterning of linguistic stimuli (i.e., morphological development and syntactical control). Interestingly, it is at the automatic level of auditory-linguistic skills that children with learning problems often display processing deficits. A child with a disability in visual, tactual, or aural reading shows evidence of dysfunctioning in the integrative level of both the auditory and linguistic cue systems.

Sound Blending. The proper blending of sounds in words is an important sequencing skill that is easily learned by children when presented in a methodologically correct order. For these tasks, children are presented with words, syllables, and sounds to blend into meaningful wholes. Many compounded words need to be presented before going into more difficult forms of sound blending. The child learns visually and auditorially to blend words such as "birdhouse," "baseball," "mailbox," and "toothbrush." Next, two-syllable words are presented, such as "candle," "sucker," and "apple." Short words, longer words, and then auditorially similar words are finally introduced. This is one skill which is easily learned when presented correctly.

Auditory Memory. The process by which the visually handicapped child recalls the order of what he has heard is called "auditory memory." It aids him or her in repeating lists, retelling stories, or following directions. A child lacking in this ability is unable to order words, directions, or ideas (e.g., the alphabet or numbering system, the days of the week, the seasons, or the months of the year). The child may mispronounce words or may not remember directions.

Activities include clapping to simple rhythms, using buzzer boards, repeating rhythm patterns, coloring work sheets from taped directions or setting up pegboards from taped instructions, repeating a simple series of words or directions, acting out a series of commands, or playing games like "Simon Says" or the "Telephone Game." It is extremely important not to play these games on an elimination basis because the child who most needs the activity is always the one to lose first! Many handicapped children develop superior auditory memory abilities, but others do not. However, all should receive training in this area.

Auditory Closure. The ability to fill in missing segments or parts of words or sentences to form meaningful wholes is referred to as "auditory closure." Often parts of words may not be heard, or a section of a message may be missing. The listening automatically completes the whole in order to understand and gain meaning. Auditory closure is an important listening skill for visually handicapped children. When listening to a recorded tape, the student cannot watch the lips of the speaker for visual cueing. When a sighted child is being helped to overcome an auditory closure deficiency, he or she is instructed to watch the speaker's lips. Many students do this naturally as an aid to getting all the words and ideas from a lecturer or speaker. But for the low vision or blind child, this technique is not useful. Learning tasks and activities where the child is presented a partial auditory stimulus which he must translate into meaningful wholes—for example, (t)elevision and eleva(tor). Some teachers may restructure the fun, as in this example: "It goes up and down, and people ride in it in tall buildings; it is called an eleva(tor)."

Language Usage. Language usage is the student's ability to handle standard English (both its syntax and its grammatical structures); it is the student's ability to respond in a correct grammatical form. Because of the highly redundant nature of any language, standard or nonstandard patterns become automatic within the system. To the extent that these patterns are automatic, the student responds to standard or nonstandard English sentences as sounding "right" or "wrong." Students with problems in language usage use only short, simple sentence structures and show little variety in their language. They incorrectly

Games that teach auditory skills should not be played on an elimination basis because the child who most needs the activity is always the one to lose first.

use possessives and pronouns; they do not use plurals or past tense correctly; they often confuse prepositions.

Encourage the correct imitation of phrases or sentence patterns. Request the child to rephrase a sentence or to ask the question in another way. Provide records to memorize or participation in choral reading or speaking, but provide direct repetition and instruction in proper syntax.

It has been noted that the child's deeply internalized knowledge of the systems of sound and grammar in his or her own English dialect sets up expectations which strongly influence the child's perceptions and, in fact, the ability to perceive. By the time the child is seven years of age, most grammatical errors in language (e.g., use of double negatives) are commonplace to the child's cultural environment; therefore, around this time definite instruction in grammar should be commenced. The constant use and many redundancies of language lead to highly overlearned habits for handling the pattern or syntax of language without conscious awareness. Since automatic habits eliminate the need for conscious attention to the form of the information processed, this allows the child to concentrate on the content or cognitive aspects of the message.

Comprehension of Symbolic Representation

This skill is the child's ability to comprehend spoken language and to understand representational thought. At about seven years of age, language becomes increasingly symbolic, language patterns are established, and phonology is mastered by most girls and some boys. By eight years of age, auditory and linguistic developments have occurred. The child is now ready for further development of the capacity for operational thought.

This is a very significant point in the development of cognition. It is also a time when a breakdown or slowdown in the development of many of the language arts skills may occur. From this point on, linguistic functioning becomes more complex and adult-like. The relationship among the language arts (listening, speaking, reading, and writing) continues to increase. Apparently, growth in one area of language ability reinforces growth in other areas. The most significant factor in language ability is the increased relationship of language and thought. This is probably the best time to start a visually handicapped child in a structured listening skills (aural reading) program. His or her language and thought have both become more logical. Particular attention should be directed to the child's vocabulary development, to the child's ability to relate concepts presented orally, and to the child's listening comprehension (auding skills).

Auditory Reception. The ability to derive meaning from verbally presented material requires auditory reception. Most often this skill is represented by vocabulary development. Children with auditory reception problems do not correctly answer questions about stories which have been read to them; they have problems learning abstract words but not words with visual or tactual representations; they do not laugh at funny stories or do not get the joke; they do not really like verbal games or participation in "Show and Tell"; they are not generally interested in listening to conversations and have difficulty in understanding recorded tapes or talking books.

All children benefit from systematic instruction in a listening skills program. But build the student's receptive vocabulary beforehand by using natural experiences whenever possible. Give short directions and use lots of props and pictures when appropriate. Have children talk about the objects they are handling, their properties and functions, and describe what they are doing with these objects. Be concrete; provide direct experiences; use pantomine or act out the activity. In addition, provide synonym and antonym experiences, both orally and with paper-pencil tasks.

Auditory Association. Auditory association is the ability to relate words in a meaningful way. Students without this skill will give foolish and inappropriate answers to questions; they do not like riddles or guessing games; they do not know simple opposites; they cannot make simple associations orally; and they do not ask "why" or "how" questions because they show no interest in cause-and-effect or means-to-an-end relationships.

These particular children require work on similes, classification, and conservation tasks. Train the child's ability to find and verbalize common characteristics in objects, events, and stories. Talk about functions, changes, and means. Identify incongruities in stories. Work on meanings, differentiate between fact and opinion, make inferences, and draw conclusions.

Auditory Comprehension. Activities involving auditory comprehension are the precursors to a systematic listening skills program. The child can now carry on a conversation, listen to a story, and discuss what he or she has heard. The teacher may be using APH's *Listen and Think* series or other such commercially prepared cassette tapes which develop listening and thinking skills. But, basically, the teacher should capitalize on all natural situations within the classroom which lend themselves to the development of listening and comprehension skills. Develop insight into problems and logical solutions to situations. Have the students tell what happened in current events, predict outcomes, and announce future actions. This develops comprehension of current events and prediction of future events based upon factual logic.

At this level, reasoning skills affect comprehension skills. The ability of a child to analyze, synthesize, form analogies, draw conclusions, and predict outcomes all relate to his or her ability to comprehend auditorially. As one might expect, intensive and direct instruction in listening skills also improves reading comprehension abilities. But the student's future in aural reading depends upon the teacher's ability to design and direct appropriate learning activities for the aural comprehension of tapes and talking books. Educators cannot assume that students will automatically read well aurally, any more than they will read large print or braille without well-planned instruction. Any reading skill must be taught, whether it uses the visual, tactual, or aural sense.

TYPES OF LISTENING SKILLS USED IN AURAL READING

In analyzing the skills needed for aural reading, it is difficult to differentiate individual skills so that each may be isolated to determine its own structure of development. In fact, one of the criticisms the authors have of many commercially produced listening skills programs is that they fail to make such distinctions, thereby offering no help to the teacher (or learner) in developing collateral practice materials. When responses to items for either assessment or practice require a complex of two or more different skills, it is virtually impossible to analyze the learner's errors so that additional practice or instruction in the deficient skill can be arranged.

For this reason, we have focused on what seem to be four well-differentiated, relatively independent skills: listening for details, listening for sequence, listening for word meaning, and listening for the main idea.

We do not suggest that students, in fact, apply these skills one at a time as they read or listen to an aural presentation. We do, however, believe that to help students develop an overall ability to receive information through the auditory channel efficiently and effectively, teachers must plan learning and practice activities in each of these skills individually.

Listening for Details

For people who read aurally, the difficulty of rereading and scanning in review to retrieve a missed detail is far greater than it is for visual readers. It is easy to see, then, that the more details the aural reader can retain on first reading, the more efficiently he or she can study. Since aural reading is inherently slower than visual reading (speech is, typically, 175-200 words per minute [wpm], while "silent" visual reading speed is typically 300 wpm and much higher), it does behoove the aural reader to be efficient!

Capitalize on all natural situations within the classroom that lend themselves to the development of listening and comprehension skills.

The student's future in aural reading depends upon the teacher's ability to design and direct appropriate learning activities.

In the present context, details may be thought of as facts. A person's name is a detail, as is eye or hair color. The date of a battle is a detail; so is its location. To the student, exams may seem to be made up of details!

Listening for Sequence

The need to recall, accurately, a sequence or order is easily seen by considering even the simplest two-step directions. If the direction "Turn left one block, then right for three blocks" is recalled as "Turn right for three blocks and left for one," a person is going to wind up in the wrong place.

More subtle, but equally important in using the auditory channel for learning, is the ability to recall the sequence of events or parts of a story. Plot motivation could become murky, indeed, if the sequence of events is mistakenly recalled.

In developing practice exercises or assessment of this skill, the teacher must be very careful not to use natural sequences of events, since the student will be able to respond correctly simply from experience or previous learning—not necessarily from having recalled such sequences from the aural presentation.

Listening for Word Meaning

Vocabulary is not built by studying a dictionary, but by learning to derive the meaning of unfamiliar words from their context. In fact, even when teachers introduce new words with their definitions, it is not until the student can successfully "use" the word in a sentence (i.e., construct an appropriate context for it) that learning is considered accomplished. In aural reading, homonyms and "sound-alikes" pose frequent problems, just as multiple meanings for one word cause difficulty in visual vocabulary-building. A person must, after all, realize that he or she has heard a new word!

Listening for the Main Idea

Words do, presumably, communicate ideas or concepts. Obviously, then, grasping the communicational purpose of what is read is as important to the aural reader as it is to the visual or tactual reader. In conveying an idea through words, the author may employ two basic approaches: an explicit statement, such as a topic sentence, or an implicit idea which emerges from the context of statements. In either case, the aural reader must have the skill to sift through the statements presented and frame the main idea in his or her own mind before communication is successful.

The aural reader must have the skill to sift through the statements presented and frame the main idea in her own mind.

THE PRACTICE-INSTRUCTION-ASSESSMENT SPIRAL

One way of regarding the art of teaching is to consider it as inducing and expediting learning. The old adage that "You can lead a horse to water, but you can't make him drink," almost seems to have been aimed at teachers, for its implication is that, ultimately, the *student* does the learning, and all the *teacher* can do is make information available.

In this respect, aural reading skills are no different from any other skills. They are acquired by practicing, extending, assimilating by practicing, extending, and so on. The teacher must provide opportunities for purposeful practice and assistance in extending the skill. But, in order to do this successfully, the teacher must know on what level the student can function with regard to that skill, as well as how to help him or her broaden that skill. Periodic assessment, then, is crucial.

The flow of activities involved in developing aural reading skills (or any others) may be conceived as a spiral involving assessment, practice, and instruction, as in Figure 14.1, with the Instruction phase raising the level each time it is passed through.

The teacher must do the following:
1. Assess the student's level of functioning.
2. Provide opportunities for practice at the student's current level of functioning —any skill must be practiced.

In order to provide opportunities for the student to practice and extend his skills, the teacher must know on what level he can function. Periodic assessment is crucial.

Figure 14.1

3. Provide practice at a slightly higher level, using prompting devices to assure successful practice.
4. Gradually remove prompts.
5. Assess skill at higher level when success seems probable.
6. Repeat steps 2–5, beginning at the new level.

Practice

A key activity in the development of aural reading skills is practice. Practice in using or applying skills should be encouraged by the teacher whenever listening or aural reading assignments are made. But it is important that special practice sessions in which the teacher is involved be arranged as well. With relatively little additional preparation, the teacher can make an aural presentation, stopping periodically to be sure the student or class is applying those skills already developed by asking appropriate questions.

The presentation should consist of materials the students would normally read, such as social studies or literature. It is not good practice to divorce listening practice from the subject matter curriculum by setting aside time and using special (and usually irrelevant) material. Students are *learning to listen* so they can *learn by listening*.

Instruction

Skills are best extended when the teacher helps the student acquire or develop new skills. Such help may include both preparation and prompting. As the student successfully practices, such teacher help should be slowly faded out.

Preparation. Preparing the student by focusing attention on those aspects of the presentation on which questions will be asked is a good way to lead the student to enhance his or her skills. For example, "Be sure you notice what days of the week are mentioned." Or "Don't forget to make a mental note of the order of events leading up to the Boston Tea Party."

Prompting. A second way of leading the student to a successful response is to offer built-in prompts. In a multiple-choice item, the correct choice may be the only really sensible one. Or the correct choice may be the one which was *not* mentioned in the presentation.

126

Assessment

In most circumstances, assessment should be relatively frequent, informal, and successful. Teachers should always be willing to trust their own judgments. Did Susie seem to have "lucked out" on that answer? Did Mark seem able to do even more? The teacher who has practiced with the student will soon be able to judge through informal assessment whether the student actually has the skill at a given level. Remember that assessment of aural reading skills is always an assessment made with reference to a criterion; it is not a reflection of how well the student does when compared to other students.

AN AURAL READING PROGRAM

In the aural reading program suggested below, the principle of spiral development is also used. Objectives become more and more difficult as the student progresses. As each new level of skill is reached, the length of the aural presentation again becomes short and the response mode is easier.

Note that three main elements in the program vary from the more simple to the more difficult: presentation, type of response, and response specification.

Presentation

It is important to realize that small children will probably not be able to attend to and recall a lengthy aural presentation. For this reason, the aural reading program outlined below begins with aural presentations of only one or two sentences. If the program is to be used with high school students, it should be adapted to fit expectations of longer attention spans.

Type of Response

Two types of responses are called for in the aural reading program: recognition and restatement.

Recognition. A recognition response requires only that the respondent recognize having heard a specific item. Clearly this is the simplest type of response. Here is one example: "Which of these boys was mentioned in the story: Bob, Stephen, or Andy?"

Restatement. The restatement of something contained in the aural presentation is a more difficult type of response, since it requires an actual recall, as in this example: "What was the name of the boy in the story?"

Response Specification

Another element that the teacher should vary when the aural reading program is used with high school students is the specifcation of the response. Note that in the aural reading program below, the specification for the first response is to recognize *one* detail. As the student progresses, the specification increases to *three* details.

Using the Aural Reading Program

Note that in the aural reading program given, the four skill areas are developed separately, with some skills not starting at the same time as others. Although students should be expected, in time, to apply all four skills to the same aural presentation, the practice–instruction–assessment spiral must be applied by the teacher to each separate skill.

No specified or recommended time period can be given, since students will move through the spiral at their own individual paces. In fact, a student is likely to move at different paces with regard to the development of each skill. He or she may well be able to function at Level 5 of the Main Idea skill while still at Level 3 of the Details skill. Expect and prepare for individual differences.

OBJECTIVES FOR AN AURAL READING PROGRAM

Level 1

Details

1.1   Recognizes one detail from one- or two-sentence statements.

Assessment should be relatively frequent, informal, and successful. Teachers should be willing to trust their own judgments.

Assessment of aural reading skills is made with reference to a criterion; it is not a question of how the student compares with other students.

1.2   Recognizes two details from one- or two-sentence statements.

1.3   Recognizes three details from one- or two-sentence statements.

Sequence

Skills begin at Level 4.

Word Meaning

Skills begin at Level 4.

Main Idea

Skills begin at Level 4.

Level 2

Details

2.1   Restates one detail from one- or two-sentence statements.

2.2   Restates two details from one- or two-sentence statements.

2.3   Restates three details from one- or two-sentence statements.

Sequence

Skills begin at Level 4.

Word Meaning

Skills begin at Level 4.

Main Idea

Skills begin at Level 4.

Level 3

Details

3.1   Recognizes one detail from short paragraph.

3.2   Recognizes two details from short paragraph.

3.3   Recognizes three details from short paragraph.

Sequence

Skills begin at Level 4.

Word Meaning

Skills begin at Level 4.

Main Idea

Skills begin at Level 4.

Level 4

Details

4.1   Restates one detail from short paragraph.

4.2   Restates two details from short paragraph.

4.3   Restates three details from short paragraph.

Sequence

4.1   Recognizes from a list of choices which event or object was last in a sequence or list given in a short paragraph.

4.2   Recognizes from a list of choices which event or object was first in a sequence or list given in a short paragraph.

4.3   Recognizes from a list of choices which unrelated events or objects were first and last in a sequenced or list given in a short paragraph.

4.4   Recognizes from a list of choices the order of three unrelated events or objects in a sequence or list given in a short paragraph.

Word Meaning

4.1   Identifies from a group of four similar-sounding words an unfamiliar word defined by context in a paragraph.

4.2   Recalls an unfamiliar word defined by context in a paragraph when given its synonym.

Main Idea

4.1   Recognizes from three choices the explicitly stated main idea or a short paragraph.

4.2   Restates with good accuracy the explicitly stated main idea of a short paragraph.

Level 5

Details

5.1 Recognizes one detail from long paragraph.

5.2 Recognizes two details from long paragraph.

5.3 Recognizes three details from long paragraph.

Sequence

5.1 Restates last object or event in a list or sequence given in a short paragraph.

5.2 Restates first object or event in a list or sequence given in a short paragraph.

5.3 Restates first and last unrelated events or objects in a sequence or list given in a short paragraph.

5.4 Restates the order of three unrelated events or objects in a sequence or list given in a short paragraph.

Word Meaning

5.1 Identifies from a group of three phrases the one related to an unfamiliar word defined by context in a paragraph.

5.2 Recalls a phrase related to an unfamiliar word defined by context in a paragraph when given the word.

Main Idea

5.1 Chooses from three titles the one which best expresses the implied main idea of a short paragraph.

5.2 Chooses from three statements the one which best expresses the implied main idea of a short paragraph.

Level 6

Details

6.1 Restates one detail from long paragraph.

6.2 Restates two details from long paragraph.

6.3 Restates three details from long paragraph.

Sequence

6.1 Recognizes from a list of choices which object or event was last in a list or sequence given in a long paragraph.

6.2 Recognizes from a list of choices which object or event was first in a list or sequence given in a long paragraph.

6.3 Recognizes from a list of choices which object or unrelated events were first and last in a list or sequence given in a long paragraph.

6.4 Recognizes from a list of choices the order of three unrelated events or objects in a sequence or list given in a long paragraph.

Word Meaning

6.1 Chooses correct definition from a group of four of an unfamiliar word defined by context in a paragraph.

6.2 Gives a short definition or synonym for an unfamiliar word defined by context in a paragraph when given the word.

Main Idea

6.1 Gives an appropriate title to express the main idea of a short paragraph.

6.2 Gives a statement expressing the implied main idea of a short paragraph.

Level 7

Sequence

7.1 Restates the last event or object in a sequence or list given in a long paragraph.

7.2 Restates the first event or object in a sequence or list given in a long paragraph.

7.3 Restates the first and last unrelated events or objects in a sequence or list given in a long paragraph.

7.4 Restates the order of three unrelated events or objects in a sequence or list given in a long paragraph.

Main Idea

7.1 Gives an appropriate title to express the main idea of a long paragraph or story.

7.2 Gives a statement expressing the implied main idea of a long paragraph or story.

USING RECORDED MATERIALS

The visual reader reads print, either regular or large type; the braille reader reads braille; the aural reader reads recorded text. The recorded text may use open-reel tapes, cassette tapes, or discs, but it is recorded verbatim, with the addition by the recordist of verbal descriptions of illustrative material and occasional spelling of names, foreign words, and the like. A recorded text is *not* a dramatization of the book.

Ordinarily the recorded book begins with the title, author, publisher, copyright date, and any other such pertinent information. Sometimes the table of contents will include not only the page number of a chapter or section, but the track number where it may be found, as well. The text, then, is recorded word for word, with each page number announced and the identification of the track number and book given at the beginning and ending of each recorded track. (Each tape or cassette may have one to four tracks recorded on the surface of the tape, each track representing one pass of the tape across the recording or playback head. Normally, tracks of a textbook recording are numbered consecutively, no matter how many are recorded per cassette or reel tape.)

Duplication Modes

Before ordering duplications of tape-recorded books, the teacher must know the kind of equipment they will be played back on and the characteristics of that equipment. There are three types of equipment currently used in listening to recordings of textbooks: the open-reel tape recorder/player, the cassette tape recorder/player, and the disc player.

Open-Reel Tape Recorder/Player

This machine was the first type of tape playback device available, and many libraries have old recorded books on open reels (as opposed to cassettes) that can only be played on such machines. These recordings may be two tracks per reel or four tracks per reel and are usually played at a speed of 3¾ inches per second (ips), with some at 1⅞ ips and others at 7½ ips speeds. The size of the reel may be anywhere from two or three inches to seven inches in diameter. The length of each track may vary, but the most common lengths are 600 feet (at 3¾ ips, 30 mins. playing time), 900 feet (45 mins. playing time), or 1200 feet (1 hour playing time). Ordinarily, playback and recording capabilities are the same; that is, if it will record at 1⅞ ips, it will play at that speed.

Cassette Recorder/Player

By far the most commonly used recorded media are cassette tapes, usually referred to simply as "cassettes." Virtually all cassette recorders/players record and play two tracks at 1⅞ ips; however, some have been modified especially for playback of recorded textbooks. These machines will play four tracks at $^{15}/_{16}$ ips, as well as the standard two tracks at 1⅞ ips. This capability is very important, since it reduces the cost of tape recorded material by approximately 75%.

There are currently two major sources for modified cassette players—American Printing House for the Blind (APH) and National Library Services for the Blind and Physically Handicapped, Library of Congress (NLS). The cassette player from APH can be purchased with Federal Quota allotment or directly, as

A text is recorded verbatim, with the addition of descriptions of illustrative material and occasional spelling of names.

A recorded text is not a dramatization of the book.

from any other vendor. This machine now records and plays back four tracks, although earlier models would record only two tracks but play four tracks. All models have a built-in variable speed control to allow the aural reader to speed up the tape so that less time is required to listen to the tape (see also "Compressed Speech," below). All models also have been adapted to permit "tone indexing" (see explanation, below).

One very troublesome problem for the aural reader is that of finding a specific page or chapter.

The NLS cassette player is a playback-only unit; no recording is possible. Like the APH machine, it will play four tracks at $^{15}/_{16}$ ips or two tracks at $1^{7}/_{8}$ ips. All NLS materials, as well as those from Recording for the Blind, Inc. (see "Resources for Acquisition" below), are on four tracks at $^{15}/_{16}$ ips. Some models of the NLS machines have variable speed control built in; some require a separate accessory unit. The NLS machine also is modified to permit tone indexing. All NLS equipment is available on long-term loan to individuals who qualify, that is, those who are blind or physically handicapped and unable to read inkprint books. (For a complete description of NLS services and requirements, see item in "Resources for Acquisition." Under certain circumstances, schools may also borrow equipment.)

A third source for modified cassette recorders/players is Science Products for the Blind, a company that specializes in aids, appliances, and equipment for the blind or visually handicapped. Several models of cassette recorders/players are available, with somewhat different characteristics. All are for purchase only.

Disc Player (Phonograph)

Talking books, available from NLS and APH, are recorded on special discs to be played at very slow speeds of 8, 16, and 33 revolutions per minute. Talking book players are made to take rough treatment without damage and, like the cassette players, are available from NLS on long-term loan to qualified individuals or schools. They may also be acquired from APH through the Federal Quota Program or direct purchase. Many periodicals and nontextbooks are recorded on discs to be played on these machines.

Tape Indexing Systems

One very troublesome problem the aural reader has is that of finding a specific page, chapter, or section of a recorded book. Since class assignments usually contain directions to read, for example, "pages 13 through 24 of the textbook," the problem of finding a specific page on the tape or cassette is one frequently encountered by the student.

Two solutions to this problem are voice indexing and tone indexing.

Two solutions to this problem are voice indexing and tone indexing.

Voice Indexing. There is a technique of recording which permits the recording of key words, such as chapter titles or page numbers, at fast-forward speed, so that those words are discernible only when the player is in the fast-forward mode. This technique is called "voice indexing" or, less commonly, TAFF (titles at fast-forward). Voice indexing may be on the *same* track as the text, or on the *adjacent* track, but always is comprehensible only at fast-forward so that the reader may scan the tape quickly to find his or her place.

Tone Indexing. By far the most frequently used system of indexing tape recorded books is called "tone indexing." This system, like voice indexing, requires listening at fast-forward. A low-frequency tone is recorded (at the time the book is being recorded) when each new page is begun. This tone is accompanied, at regular playback speed, by the announcement of the page number. Chapters are usually identified by two tones. The low-frequency tone becomes a clear "beep" when played at fast-forward. To locate a specific page, then, the reader counts beeps from some known point until he or she reaches the desired number. For example, the reader puts the cassette player in fast-forward until a beep is heard. The machine is then stopped and the page number identified by listening in playback mode. Putting the machine back in fast-forward, the reader then counts beeps until the right number is reached. Tone indexing can be used in the rewind mode, as well.

Note: All recorded indexing systems require players that have been modified so that the tape remains in contact with the playback head at all times. Tape players (whether cassette or open reel) are designed with "tape lifters" which move the tape *away* from the playback head except in playback mode. These lifters must be removed or rendered inoperable for indexing systems to be used. The need for indexing cannot be exaggerated. To use a tape without having an index system is like trying to use a textbook without page numbers!

Compressed Speech

Because speech rates are substantially slower than visual reading rates, aural readers must spend much more time with reading assignments than their sighted peers. In order to increase the speed of the recorded presentation, many playback units have a speed control built in.

Normally, when a recording is speeded up, the voice pitch becomes higher and higher, finally resembling the chatter of chipmunks. Although some blind people, with years of practice, learn to listen to and understand recordings at up to double the original speed, most find it difficult or impossible. New equipment has been developed, however, which permits the aural message to be speeded up without distorting the voice pitch. This results in "compressed speech."

Early processes for compressing speech required rerecording a tape at a preselected rate of compression, usually 25%-50%. In recent years electronic circuitry has been developed which allows the reader to control the rate of presentation of any recording without producing voice distortion. Cassette players are available with such circuits built in, or an accessory module may be acquired from APH. The accessory will operate, however, only if the equipment to which it is attached is provided with a speed control device.

Research has indicate that comprehension actually increases with an increase in speed of the aural presentation—up to a point. For most students, this point is at about 300 words per minute, above which comprehension drops rapidly.

RESOURCES FOR ACQUISITION

Occasionally, a publisher issues a recorded version of a printed textbook, but more often, the teachers of the visually handicapped need to acquire recorded materials for their aural reading students from other sources. The most important of those sources are discussed below.

Textbooks on Tape

Except for a few talking books from APH, virtually all recorded textbooks are available only on tape—most often, cassette tape.

Recording for the Blind, Inc. The most important national resource for acquiring tape-recorded textbooks is Recording for the Blind, Inc. (RFB), a non-profit, nongovernment agency. The RFB headquarters are in New York City, but there are also 27 studios scattered throughout the United States (see below).

All books are recorded by volunteers who are carefully screened and trained to read textbooks. Many books are recorded by experts in the specific subject matter covered, and occasionally a book may be read by its author. Although RFB records textbooks at all levels, most of its very large library consists of high school and college textbooks.

Beginning in January 1980, RFB now supplies only four-track cassette duplicates to be played at $^{15}/_{16}$ ips. All cassettes are available on loan for a period of up to a year.

According to the 1979/80 RFB Catalog, "Anyone whose visual, physical or perceptual handicap prevents him or her from reading normal printed material is eligible to become an RFB borrower. Services of RFB are provided exclusively on an individual borrower basis. . . . For applicants with learning disabilitiles, the application must define in detail the exact nature of the disability, how it prevents the applicant from reading normal printed material and be medically certified."

Because speech is slower than visual reading, aural readers spend much more time with reading assignments than their sighted peers.

For most students, reading comprehension actually increases with an increase in speed of the aural presentation—up to the speed of 300 words per minute.

The RFB headquarters address is Recording for the Blind, Inc., 215 East 58th Street, New York, NY 10022; Tel. 212/751-0860.

Regional studios of RFB are located in these states and cities:

Arizona:

Phoenix	602/273-7084	Orland Park	312/349-9356
Sun City	602/977-6020	Champaign	217/333-4610
California:		Naperville	312/420-0722
Los Angeles	213/664-5525	*Kentucky:*	
Claremont	714/624-4156	Louisville	502/895-9068
Palo Alto	415/493-3717		502/588-5856
Santa Barbara	805/687-6393	Anchorage	502/245-5811
Colorado:		*Massachusetts:*	
Denver	303/388-6594	Lenox	413/637-0889
Connecticut:		Williamstown	413/458-3641
New Haven	203/865-5038	*Michigan:*	
District of Columbia:		Detroit	313/833-0048
Washington	202/244-8990	Bloomfield Hills	313/642-4561
Florida:		*New Jersey:*	
Coral Gables	305/666-0552	Princeton	609/921-6534
Georgia:		*Tennessee:*	
Athens	404/549-1313	Oak Ridge	615/482-3496
Illinois:		*Texas:*	
Chicago	312/939-4162	Austin	512/477-9390
	312/288-7077	*Virginia:*	
Winnetka	312/446-3338	Charlottesville	804/293-4797

American Printing House for the Blind. Many talking books, usually not textbooks, are available from APH. Another important contribution APH makes in this area is the production of the *Central Catalog of Volunteer and Commercially Produced Materials for Visually Handicapped Children.* This catalog lists not only recordings, but braille and large type transcriptions produced commercially and by volunteer groups throughout the nation. Inquiries should be directed either to APH, 1839 Frankfort Ave., Louisville, KY 40206 (502/895-2405), or to the agency in the state that is responsible for the Federal Quota Program.

Other Public and Private Agencies. In many states, an agency of the state department of education is charged with the responsibility for providing recorded material (as well as material in braille or large type) for handicapped students. Such agencies usually rely on local volunteer recordists or recording groups to produce materials, but frequently are able to acquire such materials from other states as well. In addition, there may be other public and nonpublic agencies who can help in acquiring recorded materials. (See *Volunteers Who Produce Books*, Washington, D.C.: National Library Service, 1978.)

Fiction or Nonfiction (Nontextbook)

Most of the sources listed above provide only those books needed by students for classes, although some may be fiction or best-seller nonfiction. The NLS, however, provides most of the "leisure" reading material available in recorded form.

National Library Service. The National Library Service for the Blind and Physically Handicapped of the Library of Congress was formerly known as the Division for the Blind and Physically Handicapped and is located in Washington, D.C. The address is National Library Services, Library of Congress, 1291 Taylor Street, NW, Washington, DC 20542; Tel. 800/424-8567.

There are regional branch libraries of the NLS located in virtually every state with two branches in some states. Some branches serve more than one state.

Eligibility for NLS services may be certified by a physician, an eye specialist (e.g., an optometrist), or school personnel for blind or visually handicapped students; a learning disability must be verified by a physician as arising from a physical condition, such as a neurological impairment.

Under certain circumstances, schools may qualify to serve their visually and physically handicapped students as a local depository for the NLS. If so, NLS will provide equipment to be used on site. Direct inquiry should be made to the state or regional branch library of the NLS, whose address is available at any public library.

American Printing House for the Blind. The most important source of information about non-textbook recordings by volunteer groups is the APH *Central Catalog* (see above). In addition to this catalog, APH produces many talking books appropriate to all ages.

HOW TO HAVE MATERIALS RECORDED

Most recorded material is produced by volunteer, school, or state personnel, usually for the cost of recording materials (e.g., tapes and cassettes) only. But before requesting that a book be recorded, the teacher should make every effort to see if a recording is already available. The following procedure has been adapted, with permission, from "How to Have Materials Transcribed" in *Access for the Visually Handicapped Student (to Special Materials, Equipment, and Services)*, California Transcribers and Educators of the Visually Handicapped, 1980.

1. Have complete bibliographic information: author (or editor)—first and last names; publisher; edition (if any); copyright date (most recent date given in book *you* will use—there may be earlier or later copyrights).
2. Search catalogs available to you.
3. If material is textbook, contact the appropriate state agency, APH, and/or RFB; if material is nontextbook, contact NLS, as well.

If the recorded book is not available, follow the procedures given below.

4. Make recording arrangements
   a. Locate volunteer recording organization in *Volunteers Who Produce Books* or *Directory of Agencies Serving the Visually Handicapped*, American Foundation for the Blind, 1978.
   b. Provide print copy (some may require two).
   c. Discuss business arrangements, such as cost to you (normally cost of materials only), time needed, arrangements for delivery (partial or complete), type of duplication (see "Using Recorded Materials," above), etc.
   d. When material arrives, let transcribers know and thank them for their help.

Note: You should allow as much time as possible for transcribers to complete the material before it is needed. Try to stay a semester ahead. If you are unable to provide sufficient time, consider asking recordist to start the book at a point where the student will be in a few weeks and use a live reader until then.

FINAL WORD ABOUT AURAL READING

Aural reading skills are vital to the visually handicapped student, but a cautionary word should be added. *Every* person must acquire good communication skills in order to be truly literate. People whose vision will allow them to read large type need to develop skills in both writing and visual reading.

If the student lacks enough vision to read large type, he or she *must* develop braille and typing skills to be literate. Important though aural skills are, teachers of the visually handicapped must not neglect the teaching of good visual or tactual skills as well.

If students lack enough vision to read large type, they must develop braille and typing skills to be literate.

Important as aural skills are, teachers must not neglect the teaching of good visual or tactual skills.

Bibliography

Alber, M. *Listening: A curriculum guide for teachers of visually impaired students.* Springfield, Ill.: Illinois Office of Education, 1974.

Bannatyne, A. *Language reading and learning disabilities.* Springfield, Ill.: Charles C Thomas, 1971.

Berko, J. The child's learning of English morphology. *Word,* 1958, *14,* 150-177.

Brown, J. The management of listening ability. *School and Society,* 1950, *71,* 69-71.

Bush, W., and Giles, M. *Aids to psycholinguistics.* Columbus, O.: Charles E. Merrill, 1969.

Canfield, G. Lessons on listening? *Elementary School Journal,* 1961, *61,* 147-151.

Chalfant, J., and Scheffelin, M. *Central processing dysfunction in children* (United States Department of Health, Education, and Welfare, NINDS Monograph #9). Washington, D.C.: U.S. Government Printing Office, 1969.

Daugherty, K. Listening skills: A review of the literature. *The New Outlook for the Blind, 68,* 1974.

'Foulke, E. Non-visual communication: Reading for listening. *Education of the visually handicapped,* 1969 and 1970.

Hanninen, K. *Teaching the visually handicapped,* (2nd ed.). Detroit: Blindness Publications, 1979.

Hartlage, L. Differences in listening comprehension of the blind and the sighted. *International Journal for the Education of the Blind,* 1963, *13.*

Johnson, I. *Developing the listening skills.* Palo Alto, Calif.: Peek Publications, 1974.

Lerner, J. *Children with learning disabilities.* Boston, Mass.: Houghton Mifflin Co., 1971.

Masland, M., and Case, L. Limitation of auditory memory in delayed language development. *British Journal of Disorders of Communication,* 1968, *3,* 139-142,

Miller, G. *Language and communication.* New York: Grune & Stratton, 1954.

Nolan, C., and Morris, J. Learning by blind students through active and passive listening. *Exceptional Children,* 1969, *36,* 173-181.

Piaget, J. *Play, dreams and imitation in childhood.* New York: W. W. Norton & Co., 1962.

Wepman, J. Auditory discrimination, speech and reading. *Elementary School Journal,* 1960, *60,* 325-333.

Wepman, J. The perceptual basis for learning. In Frierson, E. and Barbe, W. *Educating children with learning disabilities.* New York: Appleton-Century-Crofts, 1967.

Wepman, J. Auditory perception and imperception. In Cruickshank, W., and Hallahan, D. (Eds.). *Perceptual and learning disabilities in children* (Vol. 2). Syracuse, N.Y.: Syracuse University press, 1975.

Wilt, M. Teaching of listening and why. In Anderson, V., et al. (Eds.), *Readings in the language arts.* New York: Macmillan, 1964.

Zigmond, N., and Cicci, R. *Auditory learning.* San Rafael, Calif.: Dimensions Publishing Co., 1968.

<table>
<tr><td>CHAPTER 15</td></tr>
</table>

A Special Education Introduction for Normally Sighted Students

Wendy Scheffers, M.Ed.

It is a common observation that the placement of a visually impaired student into a regular classroom can cause many problems for the visually impaired student, the classroom teacher, and the other students. Many of these problems could be avoided or minimized if the classroom teacher and students had received some previous education about blindness and low vision. The unit described in this chapter was designed in 1976 with that purpose in mind. Judging by the responses to the questionnaire included in this chapter and by the students' enthusiasm, the unit was considered highly successful. This unit can be adapted for use at any age and for any depth of study. Twenty lesson plans (plus additional ideas) are presented here; however, as such a lengthy unit will be impractical in many situations, the assumption is that teachers will take into account the reason for the lessons and will select the appropriate number of lessons and subject matter. One word of caution: These lessons should be presented or closely supervised by someone knowledgeable in the area of the visually impaired.

OBJECTIVES OF ENTIRE UNIT
1. The students will have knowledge of how blind and low vision people make adaptations to live in a sighted world (braille, large print, magnifiers, monoculars, dog guide, cane, development of other senses, etc.).
2. The students will understand the difference between sympathy and understanding and will know which way blind and low vision people would want to be treated.
3. The students will know how the eye functions, what causes people to go blind, and how to take care of their eyes.
4. The students will have greater appreciation of their own sight and other senses.

LESSON 1
Materials
Questionnaire (see Figure 15.1); blindfolds (one per child); any short story book with illustrations; construction paper for folders.
Procedure
Without any previous discussion, administer questionnaire as a pretest. Then blindfold entire class. Explain that you are going to read a story out loud and will be doing things that will bother them. Have them think about what you should be doing differently, knowing that you have "blind" students in the classroom.

Write the title of the book and the author's name on the board without saying them. Read the story and show pictures without describing them.

Lead a discussion about what frustrated the class. Possible questions:

What could I have done or said differently so that you would have understood more?

So if you meet a blind person, what things would you be sure to do? (Elicit: Verbalize and describe things a lot more—don't just point or write).

Ms. Scheffers was a graduate student at San Francisco State University at the time of the 1976 project described in this chapter. She is currently a mobility specialist and teacher of the visually impaired for Marin County Schools in California.

Figure 15.1. The Questionnaire.

Name _____

	Yes	No
I know a blind person.	____	____
I have seen a blind person.	____	____
Blind people need to be taken care of by other sighted people.	____	____
Blind people like to be taken care of by other sighted people.	____	____
Blind people are born with better ears than sighted people.	____	____
Blind people can go sailing, horseback riding, skiing, bike riding, and so forth.	____	____
Blind people can take care of themselves.	____	____
Blind people have developed their other senses to be better than those of sighted people.	____	____
Blind people have different ways of getting around by themselves.	____	____
People either are blind or they can see perfectly.	____	____
I feel that I know a lot about blind people.	____	____
I've sometimes wondered what it might be like to be blind.	____	____
I would like to know more about blind people.	____	____

Suppose some blind students were to come to
_____ school next year.

	Yes	No
Do you think they should be in a special classroom?	____	____
Do you think they should have their own separate recess from the rest of school?	____	____
Do you think they should be in a regular classroom?	____	____
Would you try to be friends with them?	____	____
Would you feel uncomfortable or unsure about how to be friends with them?	____	____
Should they be graded more easily than the sighted students?	____	____

If you were walking with a blind person who had a dog guide, how would you get the blind person and the dog to understand where you want them to go?

Circle one: I would tell the dog which way to go.
                    I would tell the blind person which way to turn.
                    I would take hold of the dog's collar and lead them.

What is braille?

_____
_____
_____

If you see a blind person with a cane getting ready to cross a very busy intersection, what would you do?

_____
_____
_____

Pass out construction paper and have the students make folders for the worksheets to come. Tell them that they will be studying about blind and low vision people.

LESSON 2
Materials
Films—*Kevin* or *Ricky's Great Adventure* (both films show a blind boy outdoors, describing and experiencing things by touch, smell, or sound).
Procedure
Instruct class to watch the film and look for things that are the same between them and the boy in the film, and the things that are different.

Show film, and then discuss the similarities (the boy likes to do the same things we all like to do) and the differences (we describe things visually while blind people describe things through their other senses). Possible questions:

How would you describe where the boy was?

How did he describe it?

What things does he like or want to do?

As this may be the first time some of the students have seen a blind person, questions may come up about the blind child's eyes looking different from normal eyes.

If the student has never seen a blind person, questions may come up about the way the blind child's eyes look.

LESSON 3
Materials
Blindfolds.
Procedure
Divide the class into pairs, one blindfold per pair. Go outside onto the playground. Instruct the students to have the "blind" student walk without help. The partner is there only to keep the "blind" student from getting hurt.

After each student has had the experience, return to the classroom and lead discussion about how frightening and uncertain it is to move with no help at all.

Ask the students how they think blind people get around, and then briefly discuss the three ways: sighted guide, cane, and dog guide.

LESSON 4
Materials
Blindfolds; film—*What Do You Do When You Meet a Blind Person?*
Procedure
Demonstrate the sighted guide technique (blind person holds sighted person's arm just above the elbow and walks slightly behind the sighted person). Discuss when and how to offer assistance to a blind person.

Divide the class as in Lesson 3. Have partners go outside and try the sighted guide technique.

Sighted students can learn about blindness by going blindfolded to lunch and recess.

Introduce and begin "lunch program." Each day, send a different student blindfolded to lunch and recess with a sighted guide. In this way, the students will get firsthand experience of how blind people are treated and how they would have to figure out their own adaptations and situations.

For the older grades (junior high and up), show the film. Lead discussion about the common errors people make in their first contact with a blind person: offering assistance inappropriately, walking too slowly as a sighted guide, talking to the blind person as if he or she were also deaf, talking to the blind person through a third person, and so forth.

LESSON 5
Materials
Long cane; pamphlets with photographs of Laser Cane and the Sonicguide; film—*The Guide Dog Story.*

138

Procedure

Show cane and demonstrate how it is used to allow a blind person to move independently. Show pictures of electronic mobility aids. Show film, and discuss what the guide dog does and does not do. Discuss the pros and cons of each mobility method. Which one is easiest to learn as a newly blinded person? Which one allows the blind person to live and move independently?

If there is enough time and interest, a short route with a few obstacles could be set up in the classroom. The students could try using the cane while blindfolded.

Demonstrate how a cane allows a visually impaired person to travel independently.

LESSON 6

Materials

"Low vision" glasses (using inexpensive sunglasses, make two to three pairs to simulate each of these four types of vision loss).

1. To simulate tunnel vision caused by retinitis pigmentosa, tape entire lens leaving a hold in the center. Tape paper or cardboard on the sides of the glasses to block peripheral vision.

2. To simulate cone or macular degeneration which causes a central field loss, place tape in the center of each lens.

3. To simulate scotomas (blind spots) or floaters, place small pieces of tape throughout the lens.

4. To simulate cataracts, tape gauze over the lenses.

5. To simulate poor visual acuity: a. smear a thin coat of glue (e.g. Elmer's) on lenses and allow to dry; b. purchase inexpensive +3 magnifier reading glasses at a drug store.

Film—*Not Without Sight*

Procedure

Lead a discussion on the following points:

1. Many people have something wrong with their vision.

2. Most of these people can correct the problem with glasses or contacts—do any of the students wear glasses or know anyone that does?

3. Some people who are *not* blind have problems with their vision that cannot be corrected; these people are called partially sighted or low vision. They can see, but they cannot see as well as most people.

For older grades (junior high and up), show *Not Without Sight*. Follow up the film by passing around "low vision" glasses. Make it clear that, even though the vision is poor, it allows for a lot more freedom, especially in mobility. Depending upon amount of vision the low vision person may or may not need mobility aids and techniques described in Lessons 4 and 5. Reading and other small-sized tasks become difficult. Discuss how lighting affects a low vision person. Give examples: a person with tunnel vision will be blind in the dark; a person with cataracts will see better in dim light or with the sun or light behind him.

For younger grades, share the glasses and discuss the fact that even though the vision is poor, the person is not blind.

Make glasses that simulate low vision and pass them around the class.

LESSON 7

Materials

Braille book; slate and stylus; at least one brailler (five or more if possible); large print book; magnifier; monocular; bold-line paper; Worksheet 1 (see Figure 15.2); and braille alphabet card for each child.

Procedure

Ask the students if they know how blind people read or write things down for themselves (braille) and for sighted people (typewriter). Discuss talking books, optacon, and use of tape recorders. Show a braille book, a slate and stylus, and a brailler. Draw a braille cell and a brailler keyboard on the board (see Figure 15.3).

Figure 15.2. Worksheet 1.

The Braille Alphabet

This is a Braille cell. It is made up of six dots.

```
1    4
2    5
3    6
```

The Braille alphabet is made up of different combinations of the six dots in the cell. Fill in the empty spaces below.

a = dot 1

b = dots 1, 2

c = dots 1, 4

d = dots 1, 4, 5

e = dots _____

f = dots _____

g = dots _____

h = dots _____

i = dots _____

j = dots _____

k = dots _____

l = dots _____

m = dots _____

n = dots _____

o = dots _____

p = dots _____

q = dots _____

r = dots _____

s = dots _____

t = dots _____

u = dots _____

v = dots _____

w = dots _____

x = dots _____

y = dots _____

z = dots _____

? = dots _____

_____ = dots _____

_____ = dots _____

put this in front of a letter to make it a capital = dots _____

Figure 15.3.
At left: a braille cell.
At right: a brailler keyboard.

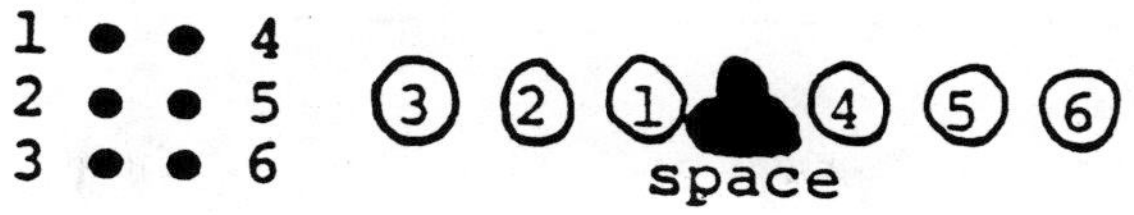

```
1 ● ● 4
2 ● ● 5
3 ● ● 6
```

③ ② ① 🖤 ④ ⑤ ⑥
space

Ask how the writing method works, explaining how to write the different letters (e.g., letter b = dots 1 and 2, so press keys 1 and 2 at the same time). Hand out two worksheets: Worksheet 1 and AFB alphabet card. After figuring out the alphabet on Worksheet 1, the children will "decode" what the braille says on the bottom of the AFB card.

If you have access to five or more braillers, while the students work on the worksheet, work with five students at a time with the braillers, showing them how they work. Have the brailler keys marked as shown above, and have the students write the alphabet on the braillers.

Ask the students if they know how low vision people might read print. Discuss the need for holding the book up close to the eyes, for good lighting, and for either large print or a magnifier. Show the class a large print book and a magnifier used with a small print book. Show the class bold-line paper and talk about how normal paper would be difficult for the low vision person to use.

Ask the class how a low vision person might be able to read the blackboard. Make it clear either that the person would have to walk up to the board and that the class would have to be understanding about this, or that the person could use a monocular. Pass a monocular around and let the students look through it.

LESSON 8
Materials
Film or book—*Hailstones and Halibut Bones* (both describe color using all the senses and emotions).
Procedure
Ask the students how they might describe color to a blind person. Make it clear that no description will ever really explain it—that blind people who have never seen colors do not really know what color is. Show the film as an example of ways in which color might be described.

Discuss the ways in which color is explained in the film; how color tastes and smells, how it feels to the touch, which objects are what color. Assign a creative writing assignment: each child is to choose and describe a color.

LESSONS 9, 10, and 11 (Three Learning Centers)
The students are divided into three groups. Each day each group goes to a different learning center. Ask the students what happens to people's other senses when they go blind. Make it clear that they become stronger and more acute (that blind people are not born with better senses). Tell the students that they are going to have a chance to see how good their senses are and how much their senses can tell them.

Taste and Smell Center
Materials
Eight containers with different smells (I used peanut butter, coffee, cinnamon, garlic, lemon, pepper, dish soap, and vanilla); 10 containers with different tastes (I used carrot, orange, potato, apple, lemon, chocolate, Coke, 7-up, orange drink, and potato chips); Worksheet 2 (see Figure 15.4).
Procedure
If the room has teacher aides, blindfold the students and have the aides give the tastes and smells and record the students' answers on Worksheet 2. Otherwise, have the students work in pairs.

Sound Center
Materials
Cassette tape recorder and tape with 11 sounds (I used sounds from a record:

Figure 15.4. Worksheet 2.

Name _____

Only The Nose Knows

Blind persons will use their noses sometimes to tell them where they are and what's happening. How good is your nose?

PART I

Get a partner. Put on a blindfold, and, using only your sense of smell, try to identify the objects in each container. Have your partner write your answers below:

1. _____
2. _____
3. _____
4. _____
5. _____
6. _____
7. _____
8. _____

PART 2

1. Using only your sense of smell, how would you know you were in a laundromat? What smells would be there?

2. By smell alone, how would you know you were in a gas station? What smells would be there?

3. If you walked into a kitchen and smelled a sweet smell, what might be happening? (What do you think might be cooking?)

Taste

Can you identify what something is by tasting it? Let's see! Get a partner. Then blindfold yourself. Have your partner give you the different things to taste, and have him write down what you think you've tasted. Have your partner write your answers below.

1. _____
2. _____
3. _____
4. _____
5. _____
6. _____
7. _____
8. _____
9. _____
10. _____

Figure 15.5. Worksheet 3.

Name _____

How Is Your Hearing?

Blind persons must use their ears to tell them where they are and what's happening. Let's see how good your ears are.

PART 1

Here is a group of everyday sounds. Listen to the sounds just once and try to identify each one. Good luck!

Write your answers below:

1. _____
2. _____
3. _____
4. _____
5. _____
6. _____
7. _____
8. _____
9. _____
10. _____
11. _____

PART 2

1. Go sit quietly in a corner of the room. Time yourself for three minutes.

    How many voices do you hear? _____

    How many are girls' voices? _____

    How many are boys' voices? _____

2. Go to another corner. Time yourself for three minutes.
    What sounds do you hear *besides* voices? List them.

3. Go outside. Close your eyes and sit quietly for a minute or two. Then, list all the sounds you heard.

4. Go to the office. List all the sounds you hear there. Are they different from sounds in our room or sounds outside? _____

5. Had you ever realized that there are so many sounds in our environment? _____

6. Were the sounds outdoors different from the sounds indoors? _____

7. Name a sound you heard outside that you didn't hear inside.

PART 3

1. Different places have different sounds.
What sounds might you hear in a grocery store?

2. What sounds would you probably hear in a restaurant?

3. What sounds might you hear in a zoo?

doorbell, door opening and closing, dog barking, car horn, telephone, cat meowing, timer, knocking, seagulls, wind, and police siren); Worksheet 3 (see Figure 15.5).

Procedure

Have the entire group listen to the tape together, and then do the worksheet on their own.

Touch Center

Materials

10 bags with different objects (I used pencil, sock, stone, orange, scotch tape, spoon, leaf, ring, cup, rubber band); braille clock or clock without glass front;

Figure 15.6. Worksheet 4.

Name _____

Are You In Touch?

PART 1

Blind persons must use their sense of touch to tell what objects are. How good is your sense of touch?

Inside each bag is a different object. Put your hand into each bag and feel the object. No peeking! Write down what you think is in each bag.

1. _____
2. _____
3. _____
4. _____
5. _____
6. _____
7. _____
8. _____
9. _____
10. _____

PART 2

1. Get the book called *Which is Longest?*. Close your eyes and turn to page 1. Feel the three objects and find the longest one. Open your eyes. Were you right? _____ Close your eyes again and do the same thing for all six pages.
   How many times were you right? _____
2. Get the book called *Which is Biggest?*. Close your eyes and turn to page 1. Feel the three objects and find the biggest one. Open your eyes. Were you right? _____ Close your eyes again and do the same thing for all six pages.
   How many times were you right? _____
3. Get the book called *Which is Smooth?*. Close your eyes and turn to page 1. Feel the two objects and find the smoothest one. Open your eyes. Were you right? _____ Close your eyes again and do the same thing for all six pages.
   How many times were you right? _____

PART 3

1. Blind people tell time with a braille watch. Let's see how well you can tell time by touch. Sit down in front of the clock with the 6 closest to you. Close your eyes. Move the hands until you think they say 3:00. Open your eyes. Were you right? _____ Try it one more time, and set the clock for 4:45. Were you right? _____
2. Now close your eyes and have another person set the clock.
   What time did you think it was? _____ What time was it set at? _____

Name _____

Your Eyes

1. Get a partner and look at and around each other's eyes. Write down everything that you see in your partner's eyes. Also write down what you think each part's function is —what does it do?
   (You should be able to list at least five parts.)

2. Get a partner. Have your partner close his or her eyes tight for the count of 30. Have him or her open his or her eyes and watch closely.
   What happens to the size of the pupil? _____
   What part of your eye changes the size of the pupil? _____
   Why do you think the pupil changes size? _____

3. Hold this page in front of you at a comfortable reading distance. Can you make this page, close up, and the blackboard, far away, clear at the same time? _____
   What part in the inside of your eye do you think is working? _____

4. Move your eyes to the left, to the right, up, and down.
   What part of your eye is working to do that? _____

5. Each of us has a blind spot in each eye. Hold this page as far from you as you can. Close your left eye. Look straight at the X with your right eye. You'll see the dot out of the corner of your eye. Slowly move the page towards you. Suddenly you will stop seeing the dot out of the corner of your eye. You will see the dot as you move the page closer.

   X
   •

---

books—*Which is Longest? Which is Biggest?* and *Which is Smooth?*; Worksheet 4 (see Figure 15.6).

Procedure

Each student will complete worksheet.

LESSON 12

Materials

Worksheet 5 (see Figure 15.7).

Procedure

Tell students that they have been learning about blind people and that the next few lessons will be spent learning about how eyes work and what makes people blind or causes low vision.

Divide the students into pairs and have them complete the worksheet. Discuss the answers when the students are done. Parts of the eye that they can see and the function of the parts are as follows:

Iris—eye color, opens and closes pupil.

Eyelashes and eyebrows—keep dust and rain from falling into eye.

Eyelids—close to keep out light and to protect eye.

Sclera (white part)—tough covering of eye, protects eyeball.

Cornea (clear part at the front of the eye; it can be seen from the side)—lets in light, starts focusing light.

Tear layer—keeps eyes warm and clean.

Pupil—window of eye, lets in correct amount of light;

Number 3 on the worksheet is impossible as the lens inside eye can only focus for one distance at a time; number 4 will make the students think about the muscles that move their eyes; number 5: the iris changes the pupil size according to the light available.

Ask the students what sympathy is and what understanding is. Discuss the difference between the two.

LESSON 13

Materials

Film or filmstrip about the parts of the eye and how the eye works; eye model, Worksheets 6 and 7 (see Figures 15.8 and 15.9).

Procedure

Show film or filmstrip. Discuss how the eye works. (Three important parts—eye, optic nerve, and brain. Light comes through pupil, and after being focused on retina as an upside down image by the cornea and lens, the image is sent through the optic nerve to the brain, which turns it right side up.) Using an eye model to help show the parts of the eye, have the students complete Worksheets 6 and 7.

LESSON 14

Materials

Worksheet 8 (see Figure 15.10).

Procedure

Make it clear that eye problems range from minor problems such as near-sightedness and far-sightedness, to legal blindness, to total blindness. Complete the worksheet together, explaining each eye disorder more thoroughly. Discuss the care of the eye. (Three main rules—work in good light, keep sharp objects away from eye, and get enough sleep).

LESSON 15

Materials

Blindfold; paper bags; construction paper; glue.

Procedure

Divide the students into pairs with one student under the blindfold and the other student acting as sighted guide. Have the students go outdoors and collect things that are nice or interesting to touch.

When all students have been "blind" and have a small bag of objects, have them take a tactile collage by gluing their findings on paper.

LESSON 16

Materials

Blindfolds; beepball.

Procedure

Ask the students which sports they think blind people can participate in. Discuss how they can do almost anything (e.g., sailing, skiing, bicycling, horseback riding, baseball, etc.), and explain what adaptations have to be made (usually a sighted guide). Explain how baseball has been adapted to beepball, in which the ball beeps and the bases beep at a different pitch.

Show the students a beepball. Seat them in a circle with blindfolds on. Have them pass the ball around the circle, locating the ball by sound only. Have each student try rolling the ball to another student, using the second student's voice as direction. Play any number of simple games. For example, have students sit in a large circle with space between each student. Divide them into two teams. Object is to roll the ball past students of the other team. Team gets one point each time they succeed. Turn off the ball and try it—this makes it much harder.

LESSON 17

Materials

None.

Procedure

Make it clear that they've been studying a lot about the differences between blind and sighted people, but that what is most important is that we are all people. Ask the students what sympathy is, and what understanding is. Discuss the difference between the two. Ask them which they would want if they were blind.

Figure 15.8. Worksheet 6.

Name _____

Parts of the Eye

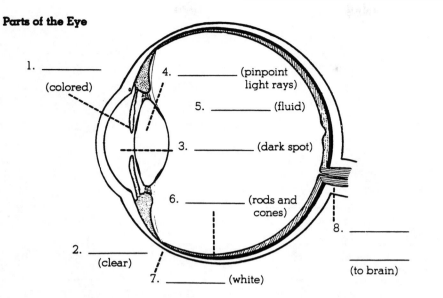

1. _____
   (colored)

4. _____ (pinpoint light rays)

5. _____ (fluid)

3. _____ (dark spot)

6. _____ (rods and cones)

8. _____

2. _____
   (clear)

7. _____ (white)

(to brain)

Fill in the above spaces with the following words:

optic nerve	iris	lens
cornea	sclera	pupil
vitreous	retina	

Figure 15.9. Worksheet 7.

Name _____

How Does My Eye Work?

Circle the correct answer(s) in each sentence.

1. Light travels in a (straight, curved) line.

2. Light travels through the (pupil, iris), through the (sclera, lens) and lands on the (cornea, retina).

3. The (cornea, retina) is sensitive to light and registers a (right side up, upside down) image.

4. The image is sent to the brain through the (optic nerve, vitreous), where the image is turned (right side up, upside down).

5. It takes the brain (one-millionth of a second, one minute) to do this.

Figure 15.10. Worksheet 8.

Name _____

Draw a line to the correct description.

Eye Problems

1. Nearsighted

The lens or the cornea is slightly bumpy, so the light is focused incorrectly. This can be corrected by glasses.

2. Farsighted

The person cannot see things close up. The eye is too short, so the image falls behind the retina. This can be corrected by glasses.

3. Astigmatism

The person cannot see things far away. The eye is too long, so the image doesn't reach the retina. This can be corrected by glasses.

4. Crossed Eyes (Strabismus)

The cones in the eye are not good, so the person may not be able to see some colors or all colors. This cannot be corrected.

5. Color Blindness

One eye has weak muscles. This can be corrected by an operation, or by putting a patch over the good eye so the bad eye has to work. If not corrected soon enough, the bad eye can become useless.

6. Night Blindness

With age, a person's lens does not adjust as well as it used to. This can be corrected by bifocal glasses.

7. Old Sight

Cornea turns white, so that the person cannot see through it. One can get a cornea transplant; this is the *only* kind of eye transplant. After the operation, this person can see perfectly again.

8. Scarred or Punctured Cornea

The rods in the eye are bad, so the person cannot see at night. This cannot be corrected.

9. Damaged or Undeveloped Optic Nerve

Even if the eye is okay, without this the person cannot see. This cannot be corrected.

10. Cataracts

The fluid in the eye does not drain properly, so the pressure builds up in the eye. The pressure will slowly destroy the retina. However, there are eyedrops to control the pressure.

11. Glaucoma

As the result of an eye injury usually, the retina comes loose from the eye. This can be corrected by burning the retina back on to the eye with a laser beam.

12. Detached Retina

The lens turns white, so the person must have an operation, and have the lens removed. The person will then wear very thick glasses or will have a lens implanted in the eye. He will also have reading glasses.

Once the *optic nerve*, or the *retina, or the seeing part of the brain* is destroyed, these three things can never be repaired, and the person will always be blind.

List the three main eye care rules:

1. _____

2. _____

3. _____

LESSON 18
Materials
Writing paper.
Procedure
Discuss some of the experiences the students had on the "day" each of them spent under the blindfold. Have them write a short story, "If I Were Blind . . .", in which they describe their experiences of how they liked to be treated that day, how they would like to be treated if they were blind, how they were able to get around during the day, and how they would like to get around if they were blind.

Have students write a story, "If I Were Blind," in which they describe how they get around and how they would like to be treated by others.

LESSONS 19 and 20
If you know a blind person who can visit with the class, this is obviously a valuable culminating lesson. Lesson 19 should be spent talking about what the students would like to ask the blind person. Lesson 20 would be spent talking with the blind person. Here are a few things you might ask the blind person to do: write with a brailler and with a slate and stylus; read some braille; show his or her braille watch; talk about mobility methods they use; explain what's wrong with their eyes and what they "see."

Give questionnaire as post-test (see Figure 15.2) and compare the answers to those given on the pretest.

ADDITIONAL LESSON IDEAS

Have eye test in room and have students test their own eyes.
Have a tactile show and tell time with the students blindfolded.
Have each student do a different task around the room blindfolded.
Cut out pictures from magazines that show the five senses and what they do, make a collage.
Have the students do clay sculpture while blindfolded.
Read *Sound of Sunshine, Sound of Rain*, by Florence Parry Heide, out loud to the class.
Dissect cow eyes.
Have the students write a braille letter to a blind person.
Developmental Learning Materials (DLM) developed a kit in 1977 called "Accepting Individual Differences." It has a unit on each handicapping area; the one on visual impairment is good.
Play a game to show how you can recognize people by their voices: Have one student stand at the front of the room with their back to the class. Have another student say something. The first student must guess who is speaking.

Play a game in which students must guess who is speaking by voice alone.

RESOURCE LIST

Films
Ricky's Great Adventure (11 minutes, 1968)
Released by Atlantis Productions
1252 La Granado Drive
Thousand Oaks, CA 91260

Kevin (16 minutes, 1968)
Released by Churchill Films
662 North Robertson Boulevard
Los Angeles, CA 90069

Hailstones and Halibut Bones Part 1 (6 minutes), Part 2 (8 minutes) (1968)
Released by John Grace
Sterling Educational Films
207 Calle Serena
San Clemente, CA 92672

The Guide Dog Story
Free of charge from: Guide Dogs for the Blind, Inc.
P.O. Box 1200
San Rafael, CA 94902

Not Without Sight and *What Do You Do When You Meet a Blind Person?*
American Foundation for the Blind
15 West 16th Street
New York, NY 10011
(Check for availability through a regional AFB office, a university with a special education program, or an agency for the blind.)

Books

Sound of Sunshine, Sound of Rain—Florence Heide
Hailstones and Halibut Bones—Mary O'Neill
Which is Biggest?, Which is Longest?, and *Which is Smooth?*
Free of charge from: Oakmont Visually Handicapped Workshop
Oakmont Adult Community
6637 Oakmont Drive
Santa Rosa, CA 95405

Pamphlets

Sonicguide
Available from Telesensory Systems, Inc.
1889 Page Mill Road
Palo Alto, CA 94304

The Bionic C-5 Laser Can Project
Available from Bionic Instruments, Inc.
221 Rock Hill Road
Bala Cynwyd, PA 19004

Braille Alphabet and Numerals
Available from American Foundation for the Blind
15 West 16th Street
New York, NY 10011

Kits

Accepting Individual Differences
Available from Developmental Learning Materials
7440 Matchez Avenue
Niles, IL 60648

References

Scheffers, W. S. Sighted children learn about blindness. *Journal of Visual Impairment and Blindness*, 1977, **71**, 6, 258-261.

Selected Reading

Adapt Press, Inc. *Special Education Bookcase.* Adapt Press, 1209 W. Bailey, Sioux Falls, S.D. 57104.

Provides information on diagnostic and remediation programs.

American Foundation for the Blind (AFB). *Products for People with Vision Problems.* AFB, Customer Service Division, 15 West 16th Street, New York, N.Y. 10011.

Free catalog of aids and appliances.

American Printing House for the Blind (APH). *Commercially Available Recorded Instructional Materials for the Development of Communication Skills.* February 1972. APH, 1839 Frankfort Avenue, Louisville, Kentucky 40206.

American Printing House for the Blind. *Educational Aids for Visually Handicapped.* September 1971. APH, 1839 Frankfort Avenue, Louisville, Kentucky 40206.

American Printing House for the Blind. *General Catalog of Talking Books.* APH, P.O. Box 6085, Louisville, Kentucky 40206.

A catalog of talking book textbooks and supplementary reading.

Bush, Catharine. *Language Remediation and Expansion: 100 Skill-Building Reference Lists.* Communication Skill Builders, Inc., 3130 N. Dodge Blvd., P.O. Box 42050, Tucson, Arizona 85733.

A source book for the remediation of language learning problems, language skill development, and expansion and enrichment of language.

Calovini, Gloria. *Mainstreaming the Visually Impaired Child.* State Board of Education, Illinois Office of Education, Springfield, Illinois 62777.

A publication for regular classroom teachers.

Champion, Ann & Hamilton, Virginia. *Beginning Discovery: Learning Center for Ideas for Early Childhood.* Discovery Learning, P.O. Box 1114, Burlingame, California 94010.

Calvin, Mary Paris. *Instructor's Big Basic Book.* The Instructor Publications, Inc., Dansville, New York 44307.

Contains classroom dittos in the areas of reading, basic language skills, applied language, social studies, math, and science.

H & H Enterprises. *1981 Catalog Books, Training Materials, Films for Teachers, Parents, and Students.* Box 1070, Lawrence, Kansas 66044.

Hall, Marilyn, & Hall, Vance. *How to Use Planned Ignoring (Extinction).* H & H Enterprizes, Box 1070, Lawrence, Kansas 66044.

Halliday, Carol. *The Visually Impaired Child: Growth, Learning, Development—Infancy to School Age.* APH, 1839 Frankfort Avenue, Louisville, Kentucky 40206.

Development sequences of the visually impaired child's growth, including school readiness and the problems of the multiply handicapped child.

Hamilton, Virginia & Fischer, Charlotte. *Discover New Ways: Alternatives for Learning.* Hillsborough School District, Hillsborough, California.

Discusses the value of and how to set up learning centers, and how to present new tasks and games.

Hamilton, Virginia & Fischer, Charlotte. *Planning Discovery.* Discovery Learning, P.O. Box 1114, Burlingame, California 94010.

A guide to help teachers plan for discovery experiences and individualized learning in the classroom.

Jensen, V. & Haller, D. *What's That?* Children's Book Music Center, 2500 Santa Monica Blvd., Santa Monica, California 90404.

A book for blind children, who can follow the pictures with their fingers as they listen to the story.

Library of Congress. *Talking Book Topics* and *Braille Book Review: Sports.* Division for the Blind and Physically Handicapped, Library of Congress, Washington, D.C. 20542.

A selected list of books from the two periodicals, including sports such as baseball, basketball, football, golf, and tennis. (Includes a record.)

Library of Congress. *Braille Book Review,* September-October 1979, Vol. 48, No. 5. Library of Congress Catalog Card Number: 1SSN-0006-873x 53-31800. Library of Congress, Washington, D.C. 20542.

Description of braille books in adult nonfiction, adult fiction, children's fiction, children's nonfiction, and braille magazine categories.

Lorton, Mary Baratta. *Workjobs: Activity-Centered Learning for Early Childhood Education.* Addison-Wesley Publishing Co., SandHill Road, Menlo Park, California.

Learning tasks for preschoolers in the form of manipulative activities built around a single concept.

Mack, Nancy. *Tracy.* Children's Book Music Center, 2500 Santa Monica Blvd., Santa Monica, California 90404.

A large-print book with photographs about a multiply handicapped child.

McLeod, Pierce. *Readiness for Learning: A Program for Visual and Auditory Perceptual-Motor Training.* California State Series, California State Dept. of Education, Sacramento, California.

New York Lighthouse. *Low Vision Service Catalogue of Optical Aids.* The New York Association for the Blind, 111 East 59th Street, New York, N.Y. 10022.

Nousanen, Diane. *A Guide to Library Resources for Teachers of the Visually Impaired.* NAPVI, Inc., 2011 Hardy Circle, Austin, Texas 78757.

Nousanen, Diane & Robinson, Lee, W. *Take Charge!* National Association for Parents of the Visually Impaired, Inc., 2011 Hardy Circle, Austin, Texas 78757.

A guide to resources for parents of the visually impaired.

Olson, Myrna R., & Mangold, Sally S. *Guidelines and Games for Teaching Efficient Braille Reading.* American Foundation for the Blind, 15 West 16th St., New York, N.Y. 10011.

Panyan, Marion. *How to Use Shaping.* H & H Enterprises, Inc., Box 1070, Lawrence, Kansas 66044.

Parker, Sue. *Four Math Scratch ' Sniff Gameboards.* (Additional and Subtraction Facts 11-20, Primary Series). Creative Teaching Press, Inc., Huntington Beach, CA 1978.

Includes gameboards, cards, and "Scratch 'n Sniff" labels.

Penguin Books. *Smells: Things to do With Them.* Penguin Books, 625 Madison Avenue, New York, N.Y. 10022.

For children.

Perkins School for the Blind. *Salesmanship Curriculum, Typewriting Curriculum, Physical Education Curriculum, Communications and Personal Management Curriculum, Office Practice Curriculum, Reading Curriculum, Transcription Curriculum, Basic Mathematics Curriculum Guide,* and *Sex Education and Family Life Curriculum.* Perkins School for the Blind, Watertown, Massachusetts 02172, Attn: Charles C. Woodcock, Director.

Petersen, Palle. *Sally Can't See.* The John Day Company, New York, N.Y.

Teaches the nonhandicapped child how the blind child experiences things and the adaptations she makes.

Sanders, Richard M. *How to Plot Data.* A manual for students, researchers, and teachers of the behavioral sciences.

Schirmer, G. M. *Performance Objectives for Preschool Children.* Adapt Press, 808 West Ave., N., Sioux Falls, South Dakota.

Science for the Blind Products. *Print-a-Log: Aids and Materials for the Visually Impaired.* SFB Products, Box 385, Wayne, PA 19087.
    A catalog of products.

Simmons, Judith I. A Manual of Speech and Language Development Activities for Visually Impaired, Multi-Handicapped Children. Boston Center for Blind Children, 147 South Huntington Avenue, Boston, MA 02130.

Sykes, K., Watson, G. & Menze, R., *Creative Arts and Crafts for Children with Visual Handicaps.* Instructional Materials Reference Center, American Printing House for the Blind, 1839 Frankfort Ave., Louisville, Kentucky 40206.

Telephone Pioneers of America. *Fishburne Alphabet for the Non-Braille Blind.* J. J. Sabin Chapter, Telephone Pioneers of America, 2700 Watt Ave., Sacramento, CA 95821.